ESCAPE FROM FREEDOM

BOOKS BY

ERICH FROMM

ESCAPE FROM FREEDOM

MAN FOR HIMSELF

PSYCHOANALYSIS AND RELIGION

THE FORGOTTEN LANGUAGE

THE ART OF LOVING

SIGMUND FREUD'S MISSION

THE SANE SOCIETY

Escape
from Freedom

BY

ERICH FROMM

RINEHART & COMPANY, INC.

New York   Toronto

First Printing, July 1941
Second Printing, March 1942
Third Printing, January 1943
Fourth Printing, December 1943
Fifth Printing, January 1945
Sixth Printing, November 1945
Seventh Printing, June 1946
Eighth Printing, May 1947
Ninth Printing, May 1948
Tenth Printing, October 1949
Eleventh Printing, October 1950
Twelfth Printing, January 1952
Thirteenth Printing, February 1953
Fourteenth Printing, December 1954
Fifteenth Printing, December 1955
Sixteenth Printing, January 1957
Seventeenth Printing, August 1957
Eighteenth Printing, May 1958
Nineteenth Printing, March 1959
Twentieth Printing, January 1960

If I am not for myself, who will be for me?
If I am for myself only, what am I?
If not now—when?

Talmudic Saying
Mishnah, Abot

Neither heavenly nor earthly, neither mortal nor immortal have we created thee, so that thou mightest be free according to thy own will and honor, to be thy own creator and builder. To thee alone we gave growth and development depending on thy own free will. Thou bearest in thee the germs of a universal life.

Pico della Mirandola
Oratio de Hominis Dignitate

Nothing then is unchangeable but the inherent and inalienable rights of man.

Thomas Jefferson

FOREWORD

THIS book is part of a broad study concerning the character structure of modern man and the problems of the interaction between psychological and sociological factors which I have been working on for several years and completion of which would have taken considerably longer. Present political developments and the dangers which they imply for the greatest achievements of modern culture—individuality and uniqueness of personality—made me decide to interrupt the work on the larger study and concentrate on one aspect of it which is crucial for the cultural and social crisis of our day: the meaning of freedom for modern man. My task in this book would be easier could I refer the reader to the completed study of the character structure of man in our culture, since the meaning of freedom can be fully understood only on the basis of an analysis of the whole character structure of modern man. As it is, I have had to refer frequently to certain concepts and conclusions without elaborating on them as fully as I would have done with more scope. In regard to other problems of great importance, I have often been able to mention them only in passing and sometimes not at all. But I feel that the psychologist should offer what he has to contribute to the understanding of the present crisis without delay, even though he must sacrifice the desideratum of completeness.

Pointing out the significance of psychological considerations in relation to the present scene does not imply, in my opinion, an overestimation of psychology. The basic entity of the social process is the individual, his desires and fears, his passions and reason, his propensities for good and for evil. To understand the dynamics of the social process we must understand the dynamics of the psychological processes operating within the individual, just as to understand the individual we must see him in the context of the culture which molds him. It is the thesis of this book that modern man, freed from the bonds of pre-individualistic society, which simultaneously gave him security and limited him, has not gained freedom in the positive sense of the realization of his individual self; that is, the expression of his intellectual, emotional and sensuous potentialities. Freedom, though it has brought him independence and rationality, has made him isolated and, thereby, anxious and powerless. This isolation is unbearable and the alternatives he is confronted with are either to escape from the burden of this freedom into new dependencies and submission, or to advance to the full realization of positive freedom which is based upon the uniqueness and individuality of man. Although this book is a diagnosis rather than a prognosis—an analysis rather than a solution—its results have a bearing on our course of action. For, the understanding of the reasons for the totalitarian flight from freedom is a premise for any action which aims at the victory over the totalitarian forces.

I forego the pleasure it would be to thank all those friends, colleagues and students to whom I am indebted for their stimulation and constructive criticisms of my own thinking. The reader will see in the footnotes reference to the authors to whom I feel most indebted for the ideas expressed in this book. However, I wish to acknowledge specifically my gratitude to those who have contributed directly to the completion of this volume. In the first place, I wish to thank Miss Elizabeth Brown, who both by her suggestions and her criticisms has been of invaluable help in the organization of this volume. Furthermore, my thanks are due to Mr. T. Woodhouse for his great help in editing the manuscript and to Dr. A. Seidemann for his help in the philosophical problems touched upon in this book.

I wish to thank the following publishers for the privilege of using extensive passages from their publications: Board of Christian Education, Philadelphia, excerpts from *Institutes of the Christian Religion,* by John Calvin, translated by John Allen; the Columbia Studies in History, Economics, and Public Law (Columbia University Press), New York, excerpts from *Social Reform and the Reformation,* by Jacob S. Schapiro; Wm. B. Eerdmans Publishing Co., Grand Rapids, Mich., excerpts from *The Bondage of the Will,* by Martin Luther, translated by Henry Cole; Harcourt, Brace and Company, New York, excerpts from *Religion and the Rise of Capitalism,* by R. H. Tawney; Houghton Mifflin Company, Boston, excerpts from *Mein Kampf,* by Adolf Hitler; the Macmillan Company, New York, excerpts from *The Civilization of the Renaissance in Italy,* by Jacob Burkhardt.

E. F.

CONTENTS

CONTENTS

ESCAPE FROM FREEDOM

CHAPTER I

Freedom—a Psychological Problem?

MODERN European and American history is centered around the effort to gain freedom from the political, economic, and spiritual shackles that have bound men. The battles for freedom were fought by the oppressed, those who wanted new liberties, against those who had privileges to defend. While a class was fighting for its own liberation from domination, it believed itself to be fighting for human freedom as such and thus was able to appeal to an ideal, to the longing for freedom rooted in all who are oppressed. In the long and virtually continuous battle for freedom, however, classes that were fighting against oppression at one stage sided with the enemies of freedom when victory was won and new privileges were to be defended.

Despite many reverses, freedom has won battles. Many died in those battles in the conviction that to die in the struggle against oppression was better than to live without freedom. Such a death was the utmost assertion of their individuality. History seemed to be proving that it was possible for man to govern himself, to make decisions for himself, and to think and feel as he saw fit. The full expression of man's potentialities seemed to be the goal toward which social development was rapidly approaching. The principles of economic liberalism, political democracy,

3

religious autonomy, and individualism in personal life, gave expression to the longing for freedom, and at the same time seemed to bring mankind nearer to its realization. One tie after another was severed. Man had overthrown the domination of nature and made himself her master; he had overthrown the domination of the Church and the domination of the absolutist state. The *abolition of external domination* seemed to be not only a necessary but also a sufficient condition to attain the cherished goal: freedom of the individual.

The World War was regarded by many as the final struggle and its conclusion the ultimate victory for freedom. Existing democracies appeared strengthened, and new ones replaced old monarchies. But only a few years elapsed before new systems emerged which denied everything that men believed they had won in centuries of struggle. For the essence of these new systems, which effectively took command of man's entire social and personal life, was the submission of all but a handful of men to an authority over which they had no control.

At first many found comfort in the thought that the victory of the authoritarian system was due to the madness of a few individuals and that their madness would lead to their downfall in due time. Others smugly believed that the Italian people, or the Germans, were lacking in a sufficiently long period of training in democracy, and that therefore one could wait complacently until they had reached the political maturity of the Western democracies. Another common illusion, perhaps the most dangerous of all, was that men like Hitler had gained power over the vast apparatus of the state through nothing but cunning and trickery, that they and their satellites ruled merely by sheer force; that the whole population was only the will-less object of betrayal and terror.

In the years that have elapsed since, the fallacy of these arguments has become apparent. We have been compelled to recognize that millions in Germany were as eager to surrender their freedom as their fathers were to fight for it; that instead of wanting freedom, they sought for ways of escape from it; that other millions were indifferent and did not believe the defense of freedom to be worth fighting and dying for. We also recognize that the crisis of democracy is not a peculiarly Italian or German problem, but one confronting every modern state. Nor does it matter which symbols the enemies of human freedom choose: freedom is not less endangered if attacked in the name of anti-Fascism or in that of outright Fascism.[1] This truth has been so forcefully formulated by John Dewey that I express the thought in his words: "The serious threat to our democracy," he says, "is not the existence of foreign totalitarian states. It is the existence within our own personal attitudes and within our own institutions of conditions which have given a victory to external authority, discipline, uniformity and dependence upon The Leader in foreign countries. The battlefield is also accordingly here—within ourselves and our institutions."[2]

If we want to fight Fascism we must understand it. Wishful thinking will not help us. And reciting optimistic

---

[1] I use the term Fascism or authoritarianism to denote a dictatorial system of the type of the German or Italian one. If I mean the German system in particular, I shall call it Nazism.

[2] John Dewey, *Freedom and Culture*, G. P. Putnam's Sons, New York, 1939.

formulae will prove to be as inadequate and useless as the ritual of an Indian rain dance.

In addition to the problem of the economic and social conditions which have given rise to Fascism, there is a human problem which needs to be understood. It is the purpose of this book to analyze those dynamic factors in the character structure of modern man, which made him want to give up freedom in Fascist countries and which so widely prevail in millions of our own people.

These are the outstanding questions that arise when we look at the human aspect of freedom, the longing for submission, and the lust for power: What is freedom as a human experience? Is the desire for freedom something inherent in human nature? Is it an identical experience regardless of what kind of culture a person lives in, or is it something different according to the degree of individualism reached in a particular society? Is freedom only the absence of external pressure or is it also the presence of something—and if so, of what? What are the social and economic factors in society that make for the striving for freedom? Can freedom become a burden, too heavy for man to bear, something he tries to escape from? Why then is it that freedom is for many a cherished goal and for others a threat?

Is there not also, perhaps, besides an innate desire for freedom, an instinctive wish for submission? If there is not, how can we account for the attraction which submission to a leader has for so many today? Is submission always to an overt authority, or is there also submission to internalized authorities, such as duty or conscience, to inner compulsions or to anonymous authorities like public opinion?

Is there a hidden satisfaction in submitting, and what is its essence?

What is it that creates in men an insatiable lust for power? Is it the strength of their vital energy—or is it a fundamental weakness and inability to experience life spontaneously and lovingly? What are the psychological conditions that make for the strength of these strivings? What are the social conditions upon which such psychological conditions in turn are based?

Analysis of the human aspect of freedom and of authoritarianism forces us to consider a general problem, namely, that of the role which psychological factors play as active forces in the social process; and this eventually leads to the problem of the interaction of psychological, economic, and ideological factors in the social process. Any attempt to understand the attraction which Fascism exercises upon great nations compels us to recognize the role of psychological factors. For we are dealing here with a political system which, essentially, does not appeal to rational forces of self-interest, but which arouses and mobilizes diabolical forces in man which we had believed to be nonexistent, or at least to have died out long ago. The familiar picture of man in the last centuries was one of a rational being whose actions were determined by his self-interest and the ability to act according to it. Even writers like Hobbes, who recognized lust for power and hostility as driving forces in man, explained the existence of these forces as a logical result of self-interest: since men are equal and thus have the same wish for happiness, and since there is not enough wealth to satisfy them all to the same extent, they necessarily fight against each other and want power to secure the future enjoyment of what they have at present. But Hobbes's picture became outmoded. The more the middle class succeeded in breaking down the power of the former political or religious rulers, the more men succeeded in mastering nature, and the more millions of individuals became economically independent, the more did one come to believe in a rational world and in man as an essentially rational being. The dark and diabolical forces of man's nature were relegated to the Middle Ages and to still earlier periods of history, and they were explained by lack of knowledge or by the cunning schemes of deceitful kings and priests.

One looked back upon these periods as one might at a volcano which for a long time has ceased to be a menace. One felt secure and confident that the achievements of modern democracy had wiped out all sinister forces; the world looked bright and safe like the well-lit streets of a modern city. Wars were supposed to be the last relics of older times and one needed just one more war to end war; economic crises were supposed to be accidents, even though these accidents continued to happen with a certain regularity.

When Fascism came into power, most people were unprepared, both theoretically and practically. They were unable to believe that man could exhibit such propensities for evil, such lust for power, such disregard for the rights of the weak, or such yearning for submission. Only a few had been aware of the rumbling of the volcano preceding the outbreak. Nietzsche had disturbed the complacent optimism of the nineteenth century; so had Marx in a different way. Another warning had come somewhat later from

Freud. To be sure, he and most of his disciples had only a very naïve notion of what goes on in society, and most of his applications of psychology to social problems were misleading constructions; yet, by devoting his interest to the phenomena of individual emotional and mental disturbances, he led us to the top of the volcano and made us look into the boiling crater.

Freud went further than anybody before him in directing attention to the observation and analysis of the irrational and unconscious forces which determine parts of human behavior. He and his followers in modern psychology not only uncovered the irrational and unconscious sector of man's nature, the existence of which had been neglected by modern rationalism; he also showed that these irrational phenomena followed certain laws and therefore could be understood rationally. He taught us to understand the language of dreams and somatic symptoms as well as the irrationalities in human behavior. He discovered that these irrationalities as well as the whole character structure of an individual were reactions to the influences exercised by the outside world and particularly by those occurring in early childhood.

But Freud was so imbued with the spirit of his culture that he could not go beyond certain limits which were set by it. These very limits became limitations for his understanding even of the sick individual; they handicapped his understanding of the normal individual and of the irrational phenomena operating in social life.

Since this book stresses the role of psychological factors in the whole of the social process and since this analysis is based on some of the fundamental discoveries of Freud—

particularly those concerning the operation of unconscious forces in man's character and their dependence on external influences—I think it will be helpful to the reader to know from the outset some of the general principles of our approach, and also the main differences between this approach and the classical Freudian concepts.[3]

Freud accepted the traditional belief in a basic dichotomy between man and society, as well as the traditional doctrine of the evilness of human nature. Man, to him, is fundamentally antisocial. Society must domesticate him, must allow some direct satisfaction of biological—and hence, ineradicable—drives; but for the most part society must refine and adroitly check man's basic impulses. In consequence of this suppression of natural impulses by society something miraculous happens: the suppressed drives turn into strivings that are culturally valuable and thus become the human basis for culture. Freud chose the word sublimation for this strange transformation from suppression into civilized behavior. If the amount of suppression is greater than the capacity for sublimation, individuals become neurotic and it is necessary to allow the lessening of suppression. Generally, however, there is a reverse relation between satisfaction of man's drives and culture: the more suppression, the more culture (and the more danger of neurotic disturbances). The relation of the individual

[3] A psychoanalytic approach which, though based on the fundamental achievements of Freud's theory, yet differs from Freud in many important aspects is to be found in Karen Horney's New Ways in Psychoanalysis, W. W. Norton & Company, New York, 1939, and in Harry Stack Sullivan's Conceptions of Modern Psychiatry—The First William Alanson White Memorial Lectures, Psychiatry, 1940, Vol. 3, No. 1. Although the two authors differ in many respects, the viewpoint offered here has much in common with the views of both.

to society in Freud's theory is essentially a static one: the individual remains virtually the same and becomes changed only in so far as society exercises greater pressure on his natural drives (and thus enforces more sublimation) or allows more satisfaction (and thus sacrifices culture).

Like the so-called basic instincts of man which earlier psychologists accepted, Freud's conception of human nature was essentially a reflection of the most important drives to be seen in modern man. For Freud, the individual of his culture represented "man," and those passions and anxieties that are characteristic for man in modern society were looked upon as eternal forces rooted in the biological constitution of man.

While we could give many illustrations of this point (as, for instance, the social basis for the hostility prevalent today in modern man, the Oedipus complex, the so-called castration complex in women), I want only to give one more illustration which is particularly important because it concerns the whole concept of man as a social being. Freud always considers the individual in his relations to others. These relations as Freud sees them, however, are similar to the economic relations to others which are characteristic of the individual in capitalist society. Each person works for himself, individualistically, at his own risk, and not primarily in co-operation with others. But he is not a Robinson Crusoe; he needs others, as customers, as employees, or as employers. He must buy and sell, give and take. The market, whether it is the commodity or the labor market, regulates these relations. Thus the individual, primarily alone and self-sufficient, enters into economic relations with others as means to one end:

to sell and to buy. Freud's concept of human relations is essentially the same: the individual appears fully equipped with biologically given drives, which need to be satisfied. In order to satisfy them, the individual enters into relations with other "objects." Other individuals thus are always a means to one's end, the satisfaction of strivings which in themselves originate in the individual before he enters into contact with others. The field of human relations in Freud's sense is similar to the market—it is an exchange of satisfaction of biologically given needs, in which the relationship to the other individual is always a means to an end but never an end in itself.

Contrary to Freud's viewpoint, the analysis offered in this book is based on the assumption that the key problem of psychology is that of the specific kind of relatedness of the individual towards the world and not that of the satisfaction or frustration of this or that instinctual need per se; furthermore, on the assumption that the relationship between man and society is not a static one. It is not as if we had on the one hand an individual equipped by nature with certain drives and on the other, society as something apart from him, either satisfying or frustrating these innate propensities. Although there are certain needs, such as hunger, thirst, sex, which are common to man, those drives which make for the *differences* in men's characters, like love and hatred, the lust for power and the yearning for submission, the enjoyment of sensuous pleasure and the fear of it, are all products of the social process. The most beautiful as well as the most ugly inclinations of man are not part of a fixed and biologically given human nature, but result from the social process which creates man. In other words, society has not only a suppressing function—although it has that too—but it has also a creative function. Man's nature, his passions, and anxieties are a cultural product; as a matter of fact, man himself is the most important creation and achievement of the continuous human effort, the record of which we call history.

It is the very task of social psychology to understand this process of man's creation in history. Why do certain definite changes of man's character take place from one historical epoch to another? Why is the spirit of the Renaissance different from that of the Middle Ages? Why is the character structure of man in monopolistic capitalism different from that in the nineteenth century? Social psychology has to explain why new abilities and new passions, bad or good, come into existence. Thus we find, for instance, that from the Renaissance up until our day men have been filled with a burning ambition for fame, while this striving which today seems so natural was little present in man of the medieval society.[4] In the same period men developed a sense for the beauty of nature which they did not possess before.[5] Again, in the Northern European countries, from the sixteenth century on, man developed an obsessional craving to work which had been lacking in a free man before that period.

But man is not only made by history—history is made by man. The solution of this seeming contradiction constitutes the field of social psychology.[6] Its task is to show not

[4] Cf. Jacob Burckhardt, The Civilization of the Renaissance in Italy, The Macmillan Company, New York, 1921. p. 139 ff.

[5] op. cit., p. 299 ff.

[6] Cf. the contributions of the sociologists J. Dollard and H. D. Lasswell, of the anthropologists R. Benedict, J. Hallowell, R. Linton, M. Mead, E. Sapir and A. Kardiner's application of psychoanalytic concepts to anthropology.

only how passions, desires, anxieties change and develop as
a *result* of the social process, but also how man's energies
thus shaped into specific forms in their turn become *productive forces,* molding the social process. Thus, for instance, the craving for fame and success and the drive to
work are forces without which modern capitalism could
not have developed; without these and a number of other
human forces man would have lacked the impetus to act
according to the social and economic requirements of the
modern commercial and industrial system.

It follows from what we have said that the viewpoint
presented in this book differs from Freud's inasmuch as it
emphatically disagrees with his interpretation of history as
the result of psychological forces that in themselves are not
socially conditioned. It disagrees as emphatically with
those theories which neglect the role of the human factor
as one of the dynamic elements in the social process. This
criticism is directed not only against sociological theories
which explicitly wish to eliminate psychological problems
from sociology (like those of Durkheim and his school),
but also against those theories that are more or less tinged
with behavioristic psychology. Common to all these theories is the assumption that human nature has no dynamism of its own and that psychological changes are to be
understood in terms of the development of new "habits"
as an adaptation to new cultural patterns. These theories,
though speaking of the psychological factor, at the same
time reduce it to a shadow of cultural patterns. Only a
dynamic psychology, the foundations of which have been
laid by Freud, can get further than paying lip service to
the human factor. Though there is no fixed human nature,

we cannot regard human nature as being infinitely malleable and able to adapt itself to any kind of conditions without developing a psychological dynamism of its own. Human nature, though being the product of historical evolution, has certain inherent mechanisms and laws, to discover which is the task of psychology.

At this point it seems necessary for the full understanding of what has been said so far and also of what follows to discuss the notion of *adaptation*. This discussion offers at the same time an illustration of what we mean by psychological mechanisms and laws.

It seems useful to differentiate between "static" and "dynamic" adaptation. By static adaptation we mean such an adaptation to patterns as leaves the whole character structure unchanged and implies only the adoption of a new habit. An example of this kind of adaptation is the change from the Chinese habit of eating to the Western habit of using fork and knife. A Chinese coming to America will adapt himself to this new pattern, but this adaptation in itself has little effect on his personality; it does not arouse new drives or character traits.

By dynamic adaptation we refer to the kind of adaptation that occurs, for example, when a boy submits to the commands of his strict and threatening father—being too much afraid of him to do otherwise—and becomes a "good" boy. While he adapts himself to the necessities of the situation, something happens in him. He may develop an intense hostility against his father, which he represses, since it would be too dangerous to express it or even to be aware of it. This repressed hostility, however, though not manifest, is a dynamic factor in his character structure. It may create new anxiety and thus lead to still deeper submission; it may set up a vague defiance, directed against no one in particular but rather toward life in general. While here, too, as in the first case, an individual adapts himself to certain external circumstances, this kind of adaptation creates something new in him, arouses new drives and new anxieties. Every neurosis is an example of this dynamic adaptation; it is essentially an adaptation to such external conditions (particularly those of early childhood) as are in themselves irrational and, generally speaking, unfavorable to the growth and development of the child. Similarly, such socio-psychological phenomena as are comparable to neurotic phenomena (why they should not be called neurotic will be discussed later), like the presence of strong destructive or sadistic impulses in social groups, offer an example of dynamic adaptation to social conditions that are irrational and harmful to the development of men.

Besides the question of what *kind* of adaptation occurs, other questions need to be answered: What is it that forces man to adapt himself to almost any conceivable condition of life, and what are the limits of his adaptability?

In answering these questions the first phenomenon we have to discuss is the fact that there are certain sectors in man's nature that are more flexible and adaptable than others. Those strivings and character traits by which men differ from each other show a great amount of elasticity and malleability: love, destructiveness, sadism, the tendency to submit, the lust for power, detachment, the desire for self-aggrandizement, the passion for thrift, the enjoyment of sensual pleasure, and the fear of sensuality. These and many other strivings and fears to be found in man develop as a reaction to certain life conditions. They are not particularly flexible, for once they have become part of a person's character, they do not easily disappear or change into some other drive. But they are flexible in the sense that individuals, particularly in their childhood, develop the one or other need according to the whole mode of life they find themselves in. None of these needs is fixed and rigid as if it were an innate part of human nature which develops and has to be satisfied under all circumstances.

In contrast to those needs, there are others which are an indispensable part of human nature and imperatively need satisfaction, namely, those needs that are rooted in the physiological organization of man, like hunger, thirst, the need for sleep, and so on. For each of those needs there exists a certain threshold beyond which lack of satisfaction is unbearable, and when this threshold is transcended the tendency to satisfy the need assumes the quality of an all-powerful striving. All these physiologically conditioned needs can be summarized in the notion of a need for self-preservation. This need for self-preservation is that part of human nature which needs satisfaction under all circumstances and therefore forms the primary motive of human behavior.

To put this in a simple formula: man must eat, drink, sleep, protect himself against enemies, and so forth. In order to do all this he must work and produce. "Work," however, is nothing general or abstract. Work is always concrete work, that is, a specific kind of work in a specific kind of economic system. A person may work as a slave in a feudal system, as a peasant in an Indian pueblo, as an independent businessman in capitalistic society, as a sales-girl in a modern department store, as a worker on the end-less belt of a big factory. These different kinds of work re-quire entirely different personality traits and make for different kinds of relatedness to others. When man is born, the stage is set for him. He has to eat and drink, and there-fore he has to work; and this means he has to work under the particular conditions and in the ways that are deter-mined for him by the kind of society into which he is born. Both factors, his need to live and the social system, in principle are unalterable by him as an individual, and they are the factors which determine the development of those other traits that show greater plasticity.

Thus the mode of life, as it is determined for the indi-vidual by the peculiarity of an economic system, becomes the primary factor in determining his whole character structure, because the imperative need for self-preservation forces him to accept the conditions under which he has to live. This does not mean that he cannot try, together with others, to effect certain economic and political changes; but primarily his personality is molded by the particular mode of life, as he has already been confronted with it as a child through the medium of the family, which repre-sents all the features that are typical of a particular society or class.[7]

---

[7] I should like to warn against one confusion which is frequently experi-enced in regard to this problem. The economic structure of a society in determining the mode of life of the individual operates as condition for per-sonality development. These economic conditions are entirely different from subjective economic motives, such as the desire for material wealth which was looked upon by many writers, from the Renaissance on up to certain Marxist authors who failed to understand Marx's basic concepts, as the domi-nant motive of human behavior. As a matter of fact, the all-absorbing wish

The physiologically conditioned needs are not the only imperative part of man's nature. There is another part just as compelling, one which is not rooted in bodily processes but in the very essence of the human mode and practice of life: the need to be related to the world outside onself, the need to avoid aloneness. To feel completely alone and isolated leads to mental disintegration just as physical starvation leads to death. This relatedness to others is not identical with physical contact. An individual may be alone in a physical sense for many years and yet he may be related to ideas, values, or at least social patterns that give him a feeling of communion and "belonging." On the other hand, he may live among people and yet be overcome with an utter feeling of isolation, the outcome of which, if it transcends a certain limit, is the state of insanity which schizophrenic disturbances represent. This lack of relatedness to values, symbols, patterns, we may call moral aloneness and state that moral aloneness is as intolerable as the physical aloneness, or rather that physical aloneness becomes unbearable only if it implies also moral aloneness. The spiritual relatedness to the world can assume many forms; the monk in his cell who believes in God and the political prisoner kept in isolation who feels one with his fellow fighters are not alone morally. Neither is the English gentleman who wears his dinner jacket in the most exotic surroundings nor the petty bourgeois who, though being deeply isolated from his fellow men, feels one with his na-

---

for material wealth is a need peculiar only to certain cultures, and different economic conditions can create personality traits which abhor material wealth or are indifferent to it. I have discussed this problem in detail in "Ueber Methode und Aufgabe einer analytischen Sozialpsychologie," *Zeitschrift für Sozialforschung*, Hirschfeld, Leipzig, 1932, Vol. I, p. 28 ff.

tion or its symbols. The kind of relatedness to the world may be noble or trivial, but even being related to the basest kind of pattern is immensely preferable to being alone. Religion and nationalism, as well as any custom and any belief however absurd and degrading, if it only connects the individual with others, are refuges from what man most dreads: isolation.

The compelling need to avoid moral isolation has been described most forcefully by Balzac in this passage from *The Inventor's Suffering*:

"But learn one thing, impress it upon your mind which is still so malleable: man has a horror for aloneness. And of all kinds of aloneness, moral aloneness is the most terrible. The first hermits lived with God, they inhabited the world which is most populated, the world of the spirits. The first thought of man, be he a leper or a prisoner, a sinner or an invalid, is: to have a companion of his fate. In order to satisfy this drive which is life itself, he applies all his strength, all his power, the energy of his whole life. Would Satan have found companions without this overpowering craving? On this theme one could write a whole epic, which would be the prologue to *Paradise Lost* because *Paradise Lost* is nothing but the apology of rebellion."

Any attempt to answer the question why the fear of isolation is so powerful in man would lead us far away from the main road we are following in this book. However, in order not to give the reader the impression that the need to feel one with others has some mysterious quality, I should like to indicate in what direction I think the answer lies.

One important element is the fact that men cannot live

without some sort of co-operation with others. In any conceivable kind of culture man needs to co-operate with others if he wants to survive, whether for the purpose of defending himself against enemies or dangers of nature, or in order that he may be able to work and produce. Even Robinson Crusoe was accompanied by his man Friday; without him he would probably not only have become insane but would actually have died. Each person experiences this need for the help of others very drastically as a child. On account of the factual inability of the human child to take care of itself with regard to all-important functions, communication with others is a matter of life and death for the child. The possibility of being left alone is necessarily the most serious threat to the child's whole existence.

There is another element, however, which makes the need to "belong" so compelling: the fact of subjective self-consciousness, of the faculty of thinking by which man is aware of himself as an individual entity, different from nature and other people. Although the degree of this awareness varies, as will be pointed out in the next chapter, its existence confronts man with a problem which is essentially human: by being aware of himself as distinct from nature and other people, by being aware—even very dimly —of death, sickness, aging, he necessarily feels his insignificance and smallness in comparison with the universe and all others who are not "he." Unless he belonged somewhere, unless his life had some meaning and direction, he would feel like a particle of dust and be overcome by his individual insignificance. He would not be able to relate himself to any system which would give meaning and direction to his life, he would be filled with doubt, and this doubt eventually would paralyze his ability to act—that is, to live.

Before we proceed, it may be helpful to sum up what has been pointed out with regard to our general approach to the problems of social psychology. Human nature is neither a biologically fixed and innate sum total of drives nor is it a lifeless shadow of cultural patterns to which it adapts itself smoothly; it is the product of human evolution, but it also has certain inherent mechanisms and laws. There are certain factors in man's nature which are fixed and unchangeable: the necessity to satisfy the physiologically conditioned drives and the necessity to avoid isolation and moral aloneness. We have seen that the individual has to accept the mode of life rooted in the system of production and distribution peculiar for any given society. In the process of dynamic adaptation to culture, a number of powerful drives develop which motivate the actions and feelings of the individual. The individual may or may not be conscious of these drives, but in any case they are forceful and demand satisfaction once they have developed. They become powerful forces which in their turn become effective in molding the social process. How economic, psychological, and ideological factors interact and what further general conclusion concerning this interaction one can make will be discussed later in the course of our analysis of the Reformation and of Fascism.[8] This discussion will always be centered around the main theme of this book: that man, the more he gains freedom in the sense of emerging from the original oneness with man and nature and the more

[8] In an appendix I shall discuss in more detail the general aspects of the interrelation between psychological and socio-economic forces.

he becomes an "individual," has no choice but to unite him-self with the world in the spontaneity of love and produc-tive work or else to seek a kind of security by such ties with the world as destroy his freedom and the integrity of his individual self.[9]

[9] After completion of this manuscript a study on the different aspects of freedom was presented in *Freedom, Its Meaning*, planned and edited by R. N. Anschen, Harcourt, Brace & Co., New York, 1940. I should like to refer here especially to the papers by H. Bergson, J. Dewey, R. M. McIver, K. Riezler, P. Tillich. Also cf. Carl Steuermann, *Der Mensch auf der Flucht*, S. Fischer, Berlin, 1932.

CHAPTER II

The Emergence of the Individual and the Ambiguity of Freedom

BEFORE we come to our main topic—the question of what freedom means to modern man, and why and how he tries to escape from it—we must first discuss a concept which may seem to be somewhat removed from actuality. It is, however, a premise necessary for the understanding of the analysis of freedom in modern society. I mean the concept that freedom characterizes human existence as such, and furthermore that its meaning changes according to the degree of man's awareness and conception of himself as an independent and separate being.

The social history of man started with his emerging from a state of oneness with the natural world to an awareness of himself as an entity separate from surrounding nature and men. Yet this awareness remained very dim over long periods of history. The individual continued to be closely tied to the natural and social world from which he emerged; while being partly aware of himself as a separate entity, he felt also part of the world around him. The growing process of the emergence of the individual from his original ties, a process which we may call "individuation," seems to have reached its peak in modern history in the centuries between the Reformation and the present.

In the life history of an individual we find the same process. A child is born when it is no longer one with its mother and becomes a biological entity separate from her. Yet, while this biological separation is the beginning of individual human existence, the child remains functionally one with its mother for a considerable period.

To the degree to which the individual, figuratively speaking, has not yet completely severed the umbilical cord which fastens him to the outside world, he lacks freedom; but these ties give him security and a feeling of belonging and of being rooted somewhere. I wish to call these ties that exist before the process of individuation has resulted in the complete emergence of an individual "primary ties." They are organic in the sense that they are a part of normal human development; they imply a lack of individuality, but they also give security and orientation to the individual. They are the ties that connect the child with its mother, the member of a primitive community with his clan and nature, or the medieval man with the Church and his social caste. Once the stage of complete individuation is reached and the individual is free from these primary ties, he is confronted with a new task: to orient and root himself in the world and to find security in other ways than those which were characteristic of his preindividualistic existence. Freedom then has a different meaning from the one it had before this stage of evolution is reached. It is necessary to stop here and to clarify these concepts by discussing them more concretely in connection with individual and social development.

The comparatively sudden change from foetal into human existence and the cutting off of the umbilical cord mark the independence of the infant from the mother's body. But this independence is only real in the crude sense of the separation of the two bodies. In a functional sense, the infant remains part of the mother. It is fed, carried, and taken care of in every vital respect by the mother. Slowly the child comes to regard the mother and other objects as entities apart from itself. One factor in this process is the neurological and the general physical development of the child, its ability to grasp objects—physically and mentally— and to master them. Through its own activity it experiences a world outside of itself. The process of individuation is furthered by that of education. This process entails a number of frustrations and prohibitions, which change the role of the mother into that of a person with different aims which conflict with the child's wishes, and often into that of a hostile and dangerous person.[1] This antagonism, which is one part of the educational process though by no means the whole, is an important factor in sharpening the distinction between the "I" and the "thou."

A few months elapse after birth before the child even recognizes another person as such and is able to react with a smile, and it is years before the child ceases to confuse itself with the universe.[2] Until then it shows the particular kind of egocentricity typical of children, an egocentricity which does not exclude tenderness for and interest in others, since "others" are not yet definitely experienced as really separate from itself. For the same reason the child's

---

[1] It should be noted here that instinctual frustration per se does not arouse hostility. It is the thwarting of expansiveness, the breaking of the child's attempt to assert himself, the hostility radiating from parents—in short, the atmosphere of suppression—which create in the child the feeling of powerlessness and the hostility springing from it.

[2] Jean Piaget, The Moral Judgment of the Child, Harcourt, Brace & Co., New York, 1932. p. 407. Cf. H. S. Sullivan, op. cit., p. 10 ff.

leaning on authority in these first years has also a different
meaning from the leaning on authority later on. The parents, or whoever the authority may be, are not yet regarded
as being a fundamentally separate entity; they are part of
the child's universe, and this universe is still part of the
child; submission to them, therefore, has a different quality
from the kind of submission that exists once two individuals have become really separate.

A remarkably keen description of a ten-year-old child's
sudden awareness of its own individuality is given by R.
Hughes in A High Wind in Jamaica:

"And then an event did occur, to Emily, of considerable
importance. She suddenly realised who she was. There is
little reason that one can see why it should not have happened to her five years earlier, or even five years later; and
none, why it should have come that particular afternoon.
She had been playing house in a nook right in the bows,
behind the windlass (on which she had hung a devil's-claw
as a door knocker) ; and tiring of it was walking rather aim-
lessly aft, thinking vaguely about some bees and a fairy
queen, when it suddenly flashed into her mind that she
was she. She stopped dead, and began looking over all of
her person which came within the range of her eyes. She
could not see much, except a fore-shortened view of the
front of her frock, and her hands when she lifted them for
inspection; but it was enough for her to form a rough idea
of the little body she suddenly realised to be hers.

"She began to laugh, rather mockingly. 'Well!' she
thought, in effect: 'Fancy you, of all people, going and getting caught like this!—You can't get out of it now, not for
a very long time: you'll have to go through with being a

child, and growing up, and getting old, before you'll be quit of this mad prank!'

"Determined to avoid any interruption of this highly important occasion, she began to climb the ratlines, on her way to her favorite perch at the masthead. Each time she moved an arm or a leg in this simple action, however, it struck her with fresh amazement to find them obeying her so readily. Memory told her, of course, that they had always done so before: but before, she had never realised how surprising this was. Once settled on her perch, she began examining the skin of her hands with the utmost care: for it was hers. She slipped a shoulder out of the top of her frock; and having peeped in to make sure she really was continuous under her clothes, she shrugged it up to touch her cheek. The contact of her face and the warm bare hollow of her shoulder gave her a comfortable thrill, as if it was the caress of some kind friend. But whether her feeling came to her through her cheek or her shoulder, which was the caresser and which the caressed, that no analysis could tell her.

"Once fully convinced of this astonishing fact, that she was now Emily Bas-Thornton (why she inserted the 'now' she did not know, for she certainly imagined no transmigrational nonsense of having been anyone else before), she began seriously to reckon its implications."

The more the child grows and to the extent to which primary ties are cut off, the more it develops a quest for freedom and independence. But the fate of this quest can only be fully understood if we realize the dialectic quality in this process of growing individuation.

This process has two aspects: one is that the child grows

stronger physically, emotionally, and mentally. In each of these spheres intensity and activity grow. At the same time, these spheres become more and more integrated. An organized structure guided by the individual's will and reason develops. If we call this organized and integrated whole of the personality the self, we can also say that the *one side of the growing process of individuation is the growth of self-strength.* The limits of the growth of individuation and the self are set, partly by individual conditions, but essentially by social conditions. For although the differences between individuals in this respect appear to be great, every society is characterized by a certain level of individuation beyond which the normal individual cannot go.

The other aspect of the process of individuation is *growing aloneness.* The primary ties offer security and basic unity with the world outside of oneself. To the extent to which the child emerges from that world it becomes aware of being alone, of being an entity separate from all others. This separation from a world, which in comparison with one's own individual existence is overwhelmingly strong and powerful, and often threatening and dangerous, creates a feeling of powerlessness and anxiety. As long as one was an integral part of that world, unaware of the possibilities and responsibilities of individual action, one did not need to be afraid of it. When one has become an individual, one stands alone and faces the world in all its perilous and overpowering aspects.

Impulses arise to give up one's individuality, to overcome the feeling of aloneness and powerlessness by completely submerging onself in the world outside. These impulses, however, and the new ties arising from them, are not identical with the primary ties which have been cut off in the process of growth itself. Just as a child can never return to the mother's womb physically, so it can never reverse, psychically, the process of individuation. Attempts to do so necessarily assume the character of submission, in which the basic contradiction between the authority and the child who submits to it is never eliminated. Consciously the child may feel secure and satisfied, but unconsciously it realizes that the price it pays is giving up strength and the integrity of its self. Thus the result of submission is the very opposite of what it was to be: submission increases the child's insecurity and at the same time creates hostility and rebelliousness, which is the more frightening since it is directed against the very persons on whom the child has remained—or become—dependent.

However, submission is not the only way of avoiding aloneness and anxiety. The other way, the only one which is productive and does not end in an insoluble conflict, is that of *spontaneous relationship to man and nature*, a relationship that connects the individual with the world without eliminating his individuality. This kind of relationship —the foremost expressions of which are love and productive work—are rooted in the integration and strength of the total personality and are therefore subject to the very limits that exist for the growth of the self.

The problem of submission and of spontaneous activity as two possible results of growing individuation will be discussed later on in great detail; here I only wish to point to the general principle, the dialectic process which results from growing individuation and from growing freedom of the individual. The child becomes more free to develop and express its own individual self unhampered by those ties which were limiting it. But the child also becomes more free from a world which gave it security and reassurance. The process of individuation is one of growing strength and integration of its individual personality, but it is at the same time a process in which the original identity with others is lost and in which the child becomes more separate from them. This growing separation may result in an isolation that has the quality of desolation and creates intense anxiety and insecurity; it may result in a new kind of closeness and a solidarity with others if the child has been able to develop the inner strength and productivity which are the premise of this new kind of relatedness to the world.

If every step in the direction of separation and individuation were matched by corresponding growth of the self, the development of the child would be harmonious. This does not occur, however. While the process of individuation takes place automatically, the growth of the self is hampered for a number of individual and social reasons. The lag between these two trends results in an unbearable feeling of isolation and powerlessness, and this in its turn leads to psychic mechanisms, which later on are described as mechanisms of escape.

Phylogenetically, too, the history of man can be characterized as a process of growing individuation and growing freedom. Man emerges from the prehuman stage by the first steps in the direction of becoming free from coercive instincts. If we understand by instinct a specific action pattern which is determined by inherited neurological structures, a clear-cut trend can be observed in the animal kingdom.[3] The lower an animal is in the scale of development, the more are its adaptation to nature and all its activities controlled by instinctive and reflex action mechanisms. The famous social organizations of some insects are created entirely by instincts. On the other hand, the higher an animal is in the scale of development, the more flexibility of action pattern and the less completeness of structural adjustment do we find at birth. This development reaches its peak with man. He is the most helpless of all animals at birth. His adaptation to nature is based essentially on the process of learning, not on instinctual determination. "Instinct ... is a diminishing if not a disappearing category in higher animal forms, especially in the human."[4]

Human existence begins when the lack of fixation of action by instincts exceeds a certain point; when the adaptation to nature loses its coercive character; when the way to act is no longer fixed by hereditarily given mechanisms. In other words, *human existence and freedom are from the beginning inseparable.* Freedom is here used not in its positive sense of "freedom to" but in its negative sense of "freedom from," namely freedom from instinctual determination of his actions.

Freedom in the sense just discussed is an ambiguous gift. Man is born without the equipment for appropriate action which the animal possesses;[5] he is dependent on his parents

---

[3] This concept of instinct should not be confused with one which speaks of instinct as a physiologically conditioned urge (such as hunger, thirst, and so on), the satisfaction of which occurs in ways which in themselves are not fixed and hereditarily determined.

[4] L. Bernard, *Instinct*, Holt & Co., New York, 1924. p. 509.

[5] Cf. Ralph Linton, *The Study of Man*, D. Appleton-Century Company, New York, 1936. Chapter IV.

for a longer time than any animal, and his reactions to his surroundings are less quick and less effective than the automatically regulated instinctive actions are. He goes through all the dangers and fears which this lack of instinctive equipment implies. Yet this very helplessness of man is the basis from which human development springs; *man's biological weakness is the condition of human culture.*

From the beginning of his existence man is confronted with the choice between different courses of action. In the animal there is an uninterrupted chain of reactions starting with a stimulus, like hunger, and ending with a more or less strictly determined course of action, which does away with the tension created by the stimulus. In man that chain is interrupted. The stimulus is there but the kind of satisfaction is "open," that is, he must choose between different courses of action. Instead of a predetermined instinctive action, man has to weigh possible courses of action in his mind; he starts to think. He changes his role toward nature from that of purely passive adaptation to an active one: he produces. He invents tools and, while thus mastering nature, he separates himself from it more and more. He becomes dimly aware of himself—or rather of his group—as not being identical with nature. It dawns upon him that his is a tragic fate: to be part of nature, and yet to transcend it. He becomes aware of death as his ultimate fate even if he tries to deny it in manifold phantasies.

One particularly telling representation of the fundamental relation between man and freedom is offered in the biblical myth of man's expulsion from paradise.

The myth identifies the beginning of human history with an act of choice, but it puts all emphasis on the sin-

fulness of this first act of freedom and the suffering resulting from it. Man and woman live in the Garden of Eden
in complete harmony with each other and with nature.
There is peace and no necessity to work; there is no choice,
no freedom, no thinking either. Man is forbidden to eat
from the tree of knowledge of good and evil. He acts
against God's command, he breaks through the state of
harmony with nature of which he is a part without transcending it. From the standpoint of the Church which
represented authority, this is essentially sin. From the
standpoint of man, however, this is the beginning of human freedom. Acting against God's orders means freeing
himself from coercion, emerging from the unconscious existence of prehuman life to the level of man. Acting against
the command of authority, committing a sin, is in its positive human aspect the first act of freedom, that is, the first
human act. In the myth the sin in its formal aspect is the
acting against God's command; in its material aspect it is
the eating of the tree of knowledge. The act of disobedi-
ence as an act of freedom is the beginning of reason. The
myth speaks of other consequences of the first act of freedom. The original harmony between man and nature is
broken. God proclaims war between man and woman, and
war between nature and man. Man has become separate
from nature, he has taken the first step toward becoming
human by becoming an "individual." He has committed
the first act of freedom. The myth emphasizes the suffering
resulting from this act. To transcend nature, to be alienated from nature and from another human being, finds
man naked, ashamed. He is alone and free, yet powerless
and afraid. The newly won freedom appears as a curse; he

is free *from* the sweet bondage of paradise, but he is not free *to* govern himself, to realize his individuality.

"Freedom from" is not identical with positive freedom, with "freedom to." The emergence of man from nature is a long-drawn-out process; to a large extent he remains tied to the world from which he emerged; he remains part of nature—the soil he lives on, the sun and moon and stars, the trees and flowers, the animals, and the group of people with whom he is connected by the ties of blood. Primitive religions bear testimony to man's feeling of oneness with nature. Animate and inanimate nature are part of his human world or, as one may also put it, he is still part of the natural world.

These primary ties block his full human development; they stand in the way of the development of his reason and his critical capacities; they let him recognize himself and others only through the medium of his, or their, participation in a clan, a social or religious community, and not as human beings; in other words, they block his development as a free, self-determining, productive individual. But although this is one aspect, there is another one. This identity with nature, clan, religion, gives the individual security. He belongs to, he is rooted in, a structuralized whole in which he has an unquestionable place. He may suffer from hunger or suppression, but he does not suffer from the worst of all pains—complete aloneness and doubt.

We see that the process of growing human freedom has the same dialectic character that we have noticed in the process of individual growth. On the one hand it is a process of growing strength and integration, mastery of nature, growing power of human reason, and growing solidarity with other human beings. But on the other hand this growing individuation means growing isolation, insecurity, and thereby growing doubt concerning one's own role in the universe, the meaning of one's life, and with all that a growing feeling of one's own powerlessness and insignificance as an individual.

If the process of the development of mankind had been harmonious, if it had followed a certain plan, then both sides of the development—the growing strength and the growing individuation—would have been exactly balanced. As it is, the history of mankind is one of conflict and strife. Each step in the direction of growing individuation threatened people with new insecurities. Primary bonds once severed cannot be mended; once paradise is lost, man cannot return to it. There is only one possible, productive solution for the relationship of individualized man with the world: his active solidarity with all men and his spontaneous activity, love and work, which unite him again with the world, not by primary ties but as a free and independent individual.

However, if the economic, social and political conditions on which the whole process of human individuation depends, do not offer a basis for the realization of individuality in the sense just mentioned, while at the same time people have lost those ties which gave them security, this lag makes freedom an unbearable burden. It then becomes identical with doubt, with a kind of life which lacks meaning and direction. Powerful tendencies arise to escape from this kind of freedom into submission or some kind of relationship to man and the world which promises relief from uncertainty, even if it deprives the individual of his freedom.

European and American history since the end of the Middle Ages is the history of the full emergence of the individual. It is a process which started in Italy, in the Renaissance, and which only now seems to have come to a climax. It took over four hundred years to break down the medieval world and to free people from the most apparent restraints. But while in many respects the individual has grown, has developed mentally and emotionally, and participates in cultural achievements in a degree unheard-of before, the lag between "freedom from" and "freedom to" has grown too. The result of this disproportion between freedom *from* any tie and the lack of possibilities for the positive realization of freedom and individuality has led, in Europe, to a panicky flight from freedom into new ties or at least into complete indifference.

We shall start our study of the meaning of freedom for modern man with an analysis of the cultural scene in Europe during the late Middle Ages and the beginning of the modern era. In this period the economic basis of Western society underwent radical changes which were accompanied by an equally radical change in the personality structure of man. A new concept of freedom developed then, which found its most significant ideological expression in new religious doctrines, those of the Reformation. Any understanding of freedom in modern society must start with that period in which the foundations of modern culture were laid, for this formative stage of modern man permits us, more clearly than any later epoch, to recognize the ambiguous meaning of freedom which was to operate throughout modern culture: on the one hand the growing independence of man from external authorities, on the other hand his growing isolation and the resulting feeling of individual insignificance and powerlessness. Our understanding of the new elements in the personality structure of man is enhanced by the study of their origins, because by analyzing the essential features of capitalism and individualism at their very roots one is able to contrast them with an economic system and a type of personality which was fundamentally different from ours. This very contrast gives a better perspective for the understanding of the peculiarities of the modern social system, of how it has shaped the character structure of people who live in it, and of the new spirit which resulted from this change in personality.

The following chapter will also show that the period of the Reformation is more similar to the contemporary scene than might appear at first glance; as a matter of fact, in spite of all the obvious differences between the two periods, there is probably no period since the sixteenth century which resembles ours as closely in regard to the ambiguous meaning of freedom. The Reformation is one root of the idea of human freedom and autonomy as it is represented in modern democracy. However, while this aspect is always stressed, especially in non-Catholic countries, its other aspect—its emphasis on the wickedness of human nature, the insignificance and powerlessness of the individual, and the necessity for the individual to subordinate himself to a power outside of himself—is neglected. This idea of the unworthiness of the individual, his fundamental inability to rely on himself and his need to submit, is also the main theme of Hitler's ideology, which, however, lacks the emphasis on freedom and moral principles which was inherent in Protestantism.

This ideological similarity is not the only one that makes the study of the fifteenth and sixteenth centuries a particularly fruitful starting point for the understanding of the present scene. There is also a fundamental likeness in the social situation. I shall try to show how this likeness is responsible for the ideological and psychological similarity. Then as now a vast sector of the population was threatened in its traditional way of life by revolutionary changes in the economic and social organization; especially was the middle class, as today, threatened by the power of monopolies and the superior strength of capital, and this threat had an important effect on the spirit and the ideology of the threatened sector of society by enhancing the individual's feeling of aloneness and insignificance.

CHAPTER III

Freedom in the Age of the Reformation

1. MEDIEVAL BACKGROUND AND THE RENAISSANCE

THE picture of the Middle Ages[1] has been distorted in two ways. Modern rationalism has looked upon the Middle Ages as an essentially dark period. It has pointed to the general lack of personal freedom, to the exploitation of the mass of the population by a small minority, to its narrowness which makes the peasant of the surrounding country a dangerous and suspected stranger to the city dweller —not to speak of a person of another country—and to its superstitiousness and ignorance. On the other hand, the Middle Ages have been idealized, for the most part by re-

---

[1] In speaking of "medieval society" and the "spirit of the Middle Ages" in contrast to "capitalistic society" we speak of ideal types. Actually, of course, the Middle Ages did not suddenly end at one point and modern society come to life at another. All the economic and social forces that are characteristic of modern society had already developed within the medieval society of the twelfth, thirteenth, and fourteenth centuries. In the late Middle Ages the role of capital was growing and so was the antagonism between social classes in the towns. As always in history, all the elements of the new social system had already developed in the older order which the new one had superseded. But while it is important to see how many modern elements existed in the late Middle Ages and how many medieval elements continue to exist in modern society, it blocks any theoretical understanding of the historical process if by emphasizing continuity one tries to minimize the fundamental differences between medieval and modern society, or to reject such concepts as "medieval society" and "capitalistic society" for being unscientific constructions. Such attempts, under the guise of scientific objectivity and accuracy, actually reduce social research to the gathering of countless details, and block any understanding of the structure of society and its dynamics.

actionary philosophers but sometimes by progressive critics of modern capitalism. They have pointed to the sense of solidarity, the subordination of economic to human needs, the directness and concreteness of human relations, the supranational principle of the Catholic Church, the sense of security which was characteristic of man in the Middle Ages. Both pictures are right; what makes them both wrong is to draw one of them and shut one's eyes to the other.

What characterizes medieval in contrast to modern society is its lack of individual freedom. Everybody in the earlier period was chained to his role in the social order. A man had little chance to move socially from one class to another, he was hardly able to move even geographically from one town or from one country to another. With few exceptions he had to stay where he was born. He was often not even free to dress as he pleased or to eat what he liked. The artisan had to sell at a certain price and the peasant at a certain place, the market of the town. A guild member was forbidden to divulge any technical secrets of production to anybody who was not a member of his guild and was compelled to let his fellow guild members share in any advantageous buying of raw material. Personal, economic, and social life was dominated by rules and obligations from which practically no sphere of activity was exempted.

But although a person was not free in the modern sense, neither was he alone and isolated. In having a distinct, unchangeable, and unquestionable place in the social world from the moment of birth, man was rooted in a structuralized whole, and thus life had a meaning which left no place, and no need, for doubt. A person was identical with his role in society; he *was* a peasant, an artisan, a knight, and not an *individual* who *happened* to have this or that occupation. The social order was conceived as a natural order, and being a definite part of it gave man a feeling of security and of belonging. There was comparatively little competition. One was born into a certain economic position which guaranteed a livelihood determined by tradition, just as it carried economic obligations to those higher in the social hierarchy. But within the limits of his social sphere the individual actually had much freedom to express his self in his work and in his emotional life. Although there was no individualism in the modern sense of the unrestricted choice between many possible ways of life (a freedom of choice which is largely abstract), there was a great deal of concrete *individualism in real life.*

There was much suffering and pain, but there was also the Church which made this suffering more tolerable by explaining it as a result of the sin of Adam and the individual sins of each person. While the Church fostered a sense of guilt, it also assured the individual of her unconditional love to all her children and offered a way to acquire the conviction of being forgiven and loved by God. The relationship to God was more one of confidence and love than of doubt and fear. Just as a peasant and a town dweller rarely went beyond the limits of the small geographical area which was theirs, so the universe was limited and simple to understand. The earth and man were its center, heaven or hell was the future place of life, and all actions from birth to death were transparent in their causal interrelation.

Although society was thus structuralized and gave man

security, yet it kept him in bondage. It was a different kind of bondage from that which authoritarianism and oppression in later centuries constituted. Medieval society did not deprive the individual of his freedom, because the "individual" did not yet exist; man was still related to the world by primary ties. He did not yet conceive of himself as an individual except through the medium of his social (which then was also his natural) role. He did not conceive of any other persons as "individuals" either. The peasant who came into town was a stranger, and even within the town members of different social groups regarded each other as strangers. Awareness of one's individual self, of others, and of the world as separate entities, had not yet fully developed.

The lack of self-awareness of the individual in medieval society has found classical expression in Jacob Burckhardt's description of medieval culture:

"In the Middle Ages both sides of human consciousness —that which was turned within as that which was turned without—lay dreaming or half awake beneath a common veil. The veil was woven of faith, illusion, and childish prepossession, through which the world and history were seen clad in strange hues. Man was conscious of himself only as member of a race, people, party, family, or corporation— only through some general category."[2]

The structure of society and the personality of man changed in the late Middle Ages. The unity and centralization of medieval society became weaker. Capital, individual economic initiative and competition grew in im-

---

[2] Jacob Burckhardt, The Civilization of the Renaissance in Italy, The Macmillan Co., New York, 1921. P. 129.

portance; a new moneyed class developed. A growing individualism was noticeable in all social classes and affected all spheres of human activity, taste, fashion, art, philosophy, and theology. I should like to emphasize here that this whole process had a different meaning for the small group of wealthy and prosperous capitalists on the one hand, and on the other hand for the masses of peasants and especially for the urban middle class for which this new development meant to some extent wealth and chances for individual initiative, but essentially a threat to its traditional way of life. It is important to bear this difference in mind from the outset because the psychological and ideological reactions of these various groups were determined by this very difference.

The new economic and cultural development took place in Italy more intensely and with more distinct repercussions on philosophy, art, and on the whole style of life than in Western and Central Europe. In Italy, for the first time, the individual emerged from feudal society and broke the ties which had been giving him security and narrowing him at one and the same time. The Italian of the Renaissance became, in Burckhardt's words, "the first-born among the sons of Modern Europe," the first individual.

There were a number of economic and political factors which were responsible for the breakdown of medieval society earlier in Italy than in Central and Western Europe. Among them were the geographical position of Italy and the commercial advantages resulting from it, in a period when the Mediterranean was the great trade route of Europe; the fight between Pope and emperor resulting in the existence of a great number of independent political units;

the nearness to the Orient, as a consequence of which certain skills which were important for the development of industries, as for instance the silk industry, were brought to Italy long before they came to other parts of Europe.

Resulting from these and other conditions, was the rise in Italy of a powerful moneyed class the members of which were filled with a spirit of initiative, power, ambition. Feudal class stratifications became less important. From the twelfth century onwards nobles and burghers lived together within the walls of the cities. Social intercourse began to ignore distinctions of caste. Birth and origin were of less importance than wealth.

On the other hand, the traditional social stratification among the masses was shaken too. Instead of it, we find urban masses of exploited and politically suppressed workers. As early as 1231, as Burckhardt points out, Frederick II's political measures were "aimed at the complete destruction of the feudal state, at the transformation of the people into a multitude destitute of will and of the means of resistance, but profitable in the utmost degree to the exchequer."[3]

The result of this progressive destruction of the medieval social structure was the emergence of the individual in the modern sense. To quote Burckhardt again: "In Italy this veil (of faith, illusion, and childish prepossession) first melted into air; an *objective* treatment and consideration of the state and of all the things of this world became possible. The *subjective* side at the same time asserted itself with corresponding emphasis; man became a spiritual *individual*, and recognized himself as such. In the same way

[3] *op. cit.*, p. 5.

the Greek had once distinguished himself from the bar-
barian, and the Arabian had felt himself an individual at
a time when other Asiatics knew themselves only as members of a race."[4] Burckhardt's description of the spirit of
this new individual illustrates what we have said in the
previous chapter on the emergence of the individual from
primary ties. Man discovers himself and others as individuals, as separate entities; he discovers nature as something
apart from himself in two apects: as an object of theoretical and practical mastery, and in its beauty, as an object
of pleasure. He discovers the world, practically by discovering new continents and spiritually by developing a cos-
mopolitan spirit, a spirit in which Dante can say: "My
country is the whole world."[5]

[4] op. cit., p. 129.
[5] Burckhardt's main thesis has been confirmed and enlarged by some
authors, it has been repudiated by others. More or less in the same direction
go W. Dilthey's (Weltanschauung und Analyse des Menschen seit Renaissance
und Reformation, in Gesammelte Schriften, Teubner, Leipzig, 1914) and E.
Cassirer's study on "Individuum und Cosmos in der Philosophie der Renaissance." On the other hand, Burckhardt has been sharply attacked by others.
J. Huizinga has pointed out (Das Problem der Renaissance in Wege der
Kulturgeschichte, Drei Masken Verlag, München, 1930, p. 89 ff.; cf. also his
Herbst des Mittelalters, Drei Masken Verlag, München, 1924) that Burckhardt has underrated the degree of similarity between the life of the masses
in Italy and in other European countries during the late Middle Ages; that
he assumes the beginning of the Renaissance to be about 1400, while most
of the material he used as an illustration for his thesis is from the fifteenth
or the beginning of the sixteenth century; that he underrates the Christian
character of the Renaissance and overrates the weight of the heathen element
in it; that he assumes that individualism was the dominant trait of Renaissance culture, while it was only one among others; that the Middle Ages
were not lacking individuality to the degree which Burckhardt has assumed
and that therefore his way of contrasting the Middle Ages with the Renaissance is incorrect; that the Renaissance remained devoted to authority as the
Middle Ages had been; that the medieval world was not as hostile to worldly
pleasure and the Renaissance not so optimistic as Burckhardt has assumed;
that of the attitude of modern man, namely his striving for personal accom-
plishments and the development of individuality, nothing but the seeds existed in the Renaissance; that already in the thirteenth century the troubadours

The Renaissance was the culture of a wealthy and pow-erful upper class, on the crest of the wave which was whipped up by the storm of new economic forces. The masses who did not share the wealth and power of the rul-ing group had lost the security of their former status and had become a shapeless mass, to be flattered or to be threatened—but always to be manipulated and exploited by those in power. A new despotism arose side by side with the new individualism. Freedom and tyranny, individuality and disorder, were inextricably interwoven. The Renais-sance was not a culture of small shopkeepers and petty bourgeois but of wealthy nobles and burghers. Their eco-nomic activity and their wealth gave them a feeling of freedom and a sense of individuality. But at the same time, these same people had lost something: the security and

had developed the idea of nobility of the heart, while on the other hand the Renaissance did not break with the medieval concept of personal loyalty and service to somebody superior in the social hierarchy.

It seems to me, however, that even if these arguments are correct in de-tail, they do not invalidate Burckhardt's main thesis. Huizinga's argument actually follows this principle: Burckhardt is wrong because part of the phenomena he claims for the Renaissance existed already in the late Middle Ages in Western and Central Europe, while others came only into existence after the end of the Renaissance period. This is the same kind of argument which has been used against all concepts which contrast medieval feudal with modern capitalistic society; what has been said about this argument above also holds true for the criticism against Burckhardt. Burckhardt has recognized the essential difference between medieval and modern culture. He may have used "Renaissance" and "Middle Ages" too much as ideal types and spoken of differences which are quantitative as though they were quali-tative; yet it seems to me that he had the vision to recognize clearly the peculiarities and dynamics of those trends which were to turn from quantita-tive into qualitative ones in the course of European history. On this whole problem see also the excellent study by Charles E. Trinkhaus, Adversity's Noblemen, Columbia University Press, New York, 1940, which contains a constructive criticism of Burckhardt's work by analyzing the views of the Italian humanists on the problem of happiness in life. With regard to the problems discussed in this book, his remarks concerning insecurity, resigna-tion, and despair as a result of the growing competitive struggle for self-advancement are particularly relevant (p. 18).

feeling of belonging which the medieval social structure
had offered. They were more free, but they were also more
alone. They used their power and wealth to squeeze the
last ounce of pleasure out of life; but in doing so, they had
to use ruthlessly every means, from physical torture to psychological manipulation, to rule over the masses and to
check their competitors within their own class. All human
relationships were poisoned by this fierce life-and-death
struggle for the maintenance of power and wealth. Solidarity with one's fellow men—or at least with the members
of one's own class—was replaced by a cynical detached
attitude; other individuals were looked upon as "objects"
to be used and manipulated, or they were ruthlessly destroyed if it suited one's own ends. The individual was
absorbed by a passionate egocentricity, an insatiable greed
for power and wealth. As a result of all this, the successful
individual's relation to his own self, his sense of security
and confidence were poisoned too. His own self became as
much an object of manipulation to him as other persons
had become. We have reasons to doubt whether the powerful masters of Renaissance capitalism were as happy and
as secure as they are often pictured. It seems that the new
freedom brought two things to them: an increased feeling
of strength and at the same time an increased isolation,
doubt, scepticism,[6] and— resulting from all these—anxiety.
It is the same contradiction that we find in the philosophic
writings of the humanists. Side by side with their emphasis
on human dignity, individuality, and strength, they exhibited insecurity and despair in their philosophy.[7]

[6] Cf. Huizinga, p. 159.
[7] Cf. Dilthey's analysis of Petrarch (*op. cit.*, p. 19 ff.) and Trinkhaus,
Adversity's Noblemen.

This underlying insecurity resulting from the position of an isolated individual in a hostile world tends to explain the genesis of a character trait which was, as Burckhardt has pointed out,[8] characteristic of the individual of the Renaissance and not present, at least in the same intensity, in the member of the medieval social structure: his passionate craving for fame. If the meaning of life has become doubtful, if one's relations to others and to oneself do not offer security, then fame is one means to silence one's doubts. It has a function to be compared with that of the Egyptian pyramids or the Christian faith in immortality: it elevates one's individual life from its limitations and instability to the plane of indestructibility; if one's name is known to one's contemporaries and if one can hope that it will last for centuries, then one's life has meaning and significance by this very reflection of it in the judgments of others. It is obvious that this solution of individual insecurity was only possible for a social group whose members possessed the actual means of gaining fame. It was not a solution which was possible for the powerless masses in that same culture nor one which we shall find in the urban middle class that was the backbone of the Reformation.

We started with the discussion of the Renaissance because this period is the beginning of modern individualism and also because the work done by historians of this period throws some light on the very factors which are significant for the main process which this study analyzes, namely the emergence of man from a preindividualistic existence to one in which he has full awareness of himself as a separate entity. But in spite of the fact that the ideas of the Renais-

[8] op. cit., p. 139.

sance were not without influence on the further development of European thinking, the essential roots of modern
capitalism, its economic structure and its spirit, are not to
be found in the Italian culture of the late Middle Ages,
but in the economic and social situation of Central and
Western Europe and in the doctrines of Luther and
Calvin.

The main difference between the two cultures is this:
the Renaissance period represented a comparatively high
development of commercial and industrial capitalism; it
was a society in which a small group of wealthy and powerful individuals ruled and formed the social basis for the
philosophers and artists who expressed the spirit of this
culture. The Reformation, on the other hand, was essentially a religion of the urban middle and lower classes, and
of the peasants. Germany, too, had its wealthy businessmen, like the Fuggers, but they were not the ones to whom
the new religious doctrines appealed, nor were they the
main basis from which modern capitalism developed. As
Max Weber has shown, it was the urban middle class
which became the backbone of modern capitalistic development in the Western World.[9] According to the entirely
different social background of both movements we must
expect the spirit of the Renaissance and that of the Reformation to be different.[10] In discussing the theology of
Luther and Calvin some of the differences will become
clear by implication. Our attention will be focused on the
question of how the liberation from individual bonds af-

[9] Cf. Max Weber, *The Protestant Ethic and the Spirit of Capitalism*,
Charles Scribner's Sons, New York, 1930. p. 65.

[10] Cf. Ernst Troeltsch, *Renaissance und Reformation*, Vol. IV, *Gesammelte Schriften*, Tübingen, 1923.

fected the character structure of the urban middle class; we shall try to show that Protestantism and Calvinism, while giving expression to a new feeling of freedom, at the same time constituted an escape from the burden of freedom.

We shall first discuss what the economic and social situation in Europe, especially in Central Europe, was in the beginning of the sixteenth century, and then analyze what repercussions this situation had on the personality of the people living in this period, what relation the teachings of Luther and Calvin had to these psychological factors, and what was the relation of these new religious doctrines to the spirit of capitalism.[11]

In *medieval society* the economic organization of the

[11] The following presentation of the economic history of the late Middle Ages and the period of the Reformation is mainly based on:

Lamprecht, *Zum Verständnis der wirtschaftlichen und sozialen Wandlungen in Deutschland vom 14. zum 16. Jahrhundert*, Akademische Verlagsbuchhandlung J.C.B. Mohr, Ztsch. für Sozial- und Wirtschaftsgeschichte, Freiburg i.B. und Leipzig, 1893.

Ehrenberg, *Das Zeitalter der Fugger*, G. Fischer, Jena, 1896.

Sombart, *Der Moderne Kapitalismus*, 1921, 1928.

v. Below, *Probleme der Wirtschaftsgeschichte*, Mohr, Tübingen, 1920.

Kulischer, *Allgemeine Wirtschaftsgeschichte des Mittelalters und der Neuzeit*, Druck und Verlag von R. Oldenbourg, München und Berlin, 1928.

Andreas, *Deutschland vor der Reformation*, Deutsche Verlags-Anstalt, Stuttgart und Berlin, 1932.

Weber, *The Protestant Ethic and the Spirit of Capitalism*, Charles Scribner's Sons, New York, 1930.

Schapiro, *Social Reform and the Reformation*, Thesis, Columbia University, 1909.

Pascal, *The Social Basis of the German Reformation, Martin Luther and His Times*, London, 1933.

Tawney, *Religion and the Rise of Capitalism*, Harcourt, Brace & Co., New York, 1926.

Brentano, *Der wirtschaftende Mensch in der Geschichte*, Meiner, Leipzig, 1923.

Kraus, *Scholastic, Puritanismus und Kapitalismus*, Dunker & Humblot, München, 1930.

city had been relatively static. The craftsmen since the later part of the Middle Ages were united in their guilds. Each master had one or two apprentices and the number of masters was in some relation to the needs of the community. Although there were always some who had to struggle hard to earn enough to survive, by and large the guild member could be sure that he could live by his hand's work. If he made good chairs, shoes, bread, saddles, and so on, he did all that was necessary to be sure of living safely on the level which was traditionally assigned to his social position. He could rely on his "good works," if we use the term here not in its theological but in its simple economic meaning. The guilds blocked any strong competition among their members and enforced co-operation with regard to the buying of raw materials, the techniques of production, and the prices of their products. In contradiction to a tendency to idealize the guild system together with the whole of medieval life, some historians have pointed out that the guilds were always tinged with a monopolistic spirit, which tried to protect a small group and to exclude newcomers. Most authors, however, agree that even if one avoids any idealization of the guilds they were based on mutual co-operation and offered relative security to their members.[12]

Medieval commerce was, in general, as Sombart has pointed out, carried on by a multitude of very small businessmen. Retail and wholesale business were not yet separated and even those traders who went into foreign countries, such as the members of the North German Hanse, were also concerned with retail selling. The accumulation

---

[12] Cf. literature on this problem quoted by J. Kulischer, op. cit., p. 192 ff.

of capital was also very slow up to the end of the fifteenth century. Thus the small businessman had a considerable amount of security compared with the economic situation in the late Middle Ages when large capital and monopolistic commerce assumed increasing importance. "Much that is now mechanical," says Professor Tawney about the life of a medieval city, "was then personal, intimate and direct and there was little room for an organization on a scale too vast for the standards that are applied to individuals, and for the doctrine that silences scruples and closes all accounts with the final plea of economic expediency."[18]

This leads us to a point which is essential for the understanding of the position of the individual in medieval society, the *ethical views* concerning *economic activities* as they were expressed not only in the doctrines of the Catholic Church, but also in secular laws. We follow Tawney's presentation on this point, since his position cannot be suspected of attempting to idealize or romanticize the medieval world. The basic assumptions concerning economic life were two: "*That economic interests are subordinate to the real business of life, which is salvation, and that economic conduct is one aspect of personal conduct, upon which as on other parts of it, the rules of morality are binding.*"

Tawney then elaborates the medieval view on economic activities: "Material riches are necessary; they have secondary importance, since without them men cannot support themselves and help one another . . . But economic motives are suspect. Because they are powerful appetites, men fear them, but they are not mean enough to applaud

---

[18] Tawney, *op. cit.*, p. 28.

them . . . There is no place in medieval theory for economic activity which is not related to a moral end, and to found a science of society upon the assumption that the appetite for economic gain is a constant and measurable force, to be accepted like other natural forces, as an inevitable and self-evident datum, would have appeared to the medieval thinker as hardly less irrational and less immoral than to make the premise of social philosophy the unrestrained operation of such necessary human attributes as pugnacity and the sexual instinct . . . Riches, as St. Antonio says, exist for man, not man for riches . . . At every turn therefore, there are limits, restrictions, warnings against allowing economic interests to interfere with serious affairs. It is right for a man to seek such wealth as is necessary for a livelihood in his station. To seek more is not enterprise, but avarice, and avarice is a deadly sin. Trade is legitimate; the different resources of different countries show that it was intended by Providence. But it is a dangerous business. A man must be sure that he carries it on for the public benefit, and that the profits which he takes are no more than the wages of his labor. Private property is a necessary institution, at least in a fallen world; men work more and dispute less when goods are private than when they are common. But it is to be tolerated as a concession to human frailty, not applauded as desirable in itself; the ideal—if only man's nature could rise to it—is communism. 'Communis enim,' wrote Gratian in his decretum, 'usus omnium quae sunt in hoc mundo, omnibus hominibus esse debuit.' At best, indeed, the estate is somewhat encumbered. It must be legitimately acquired. It must be in the largest possible number of hands. It must provide for the support of the poor. Its use must as far as practicable be common.

Its owners must be ready to share it with those who need, even if they are not in actual destitution."[14]

Although these views expressed norms and were not an exact picture of the reality of economic life, they did reflect to some extent the actual spirit of medieval society.

The relative stability of the position of craftsmen and merchants which was characteristic in the medieval city, was slowly undermined in the late Middle Ages until it completely collapsed in the sixteenth century. Already in the fourteenth century—or even earlier—an increasing differentiation within the guilds had started and it continued in spite of all efforts to stop it. Some guild members had more capital than others and employed five or six journeymen instead of one or two. Soon some guilds admitted only persons with a certain amount of capital. Others became powerful monopolies trying to take every advantage from their monopolistic position and to exploit the customer as much as they could. On the other hand, many guild members became impoverished and had to try to earn some money outside of their traditional occupation; often they became small traders on the side. Many of them had lost their economic independence and security while they desperately clung to the traditional ideal of economic independence.[15]

In connection with this development of the guild system, the situation of the journeymen degenerated from bad to worse. While in the industries of Italy and Flanders a class of dissatisfied workers existed already in the thirteenth century or even earlier, the situation of the journeymen in the craft guilds was still a relatively secure one. Although

[14] op. cit., p. 31 ff.
[15] Cf. Lamprecht, op. cit., p. 207; Andreas, op. cit., p. 303.

it was not true that every journeyman could become a master, many of them did. But as the number of journeymen under one master increased, the more capital was needed to become a master and the more the guilds assumed a monopolistic and exclusive character, the less were the opportunities of journeymen. The deterioration of their economic and social position was shown by their growing dissatisfaction, the formation of organizations of their own, by strikes and even violent insurrections.

What has been said about the increasing capitalistic development of the craft guilds is even more apparent with regard to commerce. While medieval commerce had been mainly a petty intertown business, national and international commerce grew rapidly in the fourteenth and fifteenth centuries. Although historians disagree as to just when the big commercial companies started to develop, they do agree that in the fifteenth century they became more and more powerful and developed into monopolies, which by their superior capital strength threatened the small businessman as well as the consumer. The reform of Emperor Sigismund in the fifteenth century tried to curb the power of the monopolies by means of legislation. But the position of the small dealer became more and more insecure; he "had just enough influence to make his complaint heard but not enough to compel effective action."[16]

The indignation and rage of the small merchant against the monopolies was given eloquent expression by Luther in his pamphlet "On Trading and Usury,"[17] printed in 1524. "They have all commodities under their control and

---

[16] Schapiro, op. cit., p. 59.

[17] Works of Martin Luther, A. J. Holman Company, Philadelphia. Vol. IV, p. 34.

practise without concealment all the tricks that have been mentioned; they raise and lower prices as they please and oppress and ruin all the small merchants, as the pike the little fish in the water, just as though they were lords over God's creatures and free from all the laws of faith and love." These words of Luther's could have been written to-day. The fear and rage which the middle class felt against the wealthy monopolists in the fifteenth and sixteenth centuries is in many ways similar to the feeling which characterizes the attitude of the middle class against monopolies and powerful capitalists in our era.

The role of capital was also growing in *industry*. One remarkable example is the mining industry. Originally the share of each member of a mining guild was in proportion to the amount of work he did. But by the fifteenth century, in many instances, the shares belonged to capitalists who did not work themselves, and increasingly the work was done by workers who were paid wages and had no share in the enterprise. The same capitalistic development occurred in other industries too, and increased the trend which resulted from the growing role of capital in the craft guilds and in commerce: growing division between poor and rich and growing dissatisfaction among the poor classes.

As to the situation of the peasantry the opinions of historians differ. However, the following analysis of Schapiro seems to be sufficiently supported by the findings of most historians. "Notwithstanding these evidences of prosperity, the condition of the peasantry was rapidly deteriorating. At the beginning of the sixteenth century very few indeed were independent proprietors of the land they cultivated, with representation in the local diets, which in the Middle

Ages was a sign of class independence and equality. The vast majority were *Hoerige*, a class personally free but whose land was subject to dues, the individuals being liable to services according to agreement . . . It was the *Hoerige* who were the backbone of all the agrarian uprisings. This middle-class peasant, living in a semi-independent community near the estate of the lord, became aware that the increase of dues and services was transforming him into a state of practical serfdom, and the village common into a part of the lord's manor."[18]

Significant changes in the *psychological atmosphere* accompanied the economic development of capitalism. A spirit of restlessness began to pervade life toward the end of the Middle Ages. The concept of time in the modern sense began to develop. Minutes became valuable; a symptom of this new sense of time is the fact that in Nürnberg the clocks have been striking the quarter hours since the sixteenth century.[19] Too many holidays began to appear as a misfortune. Time was so valuable that one felt one should never spend it for any purpose which was not useful. Work became increasingly a supreme value. A new attitude toward work developed and was so strong that the middle class grew indignant against the economic unproductivity of the institutions of the Church. Begging orders were resented as unproductive, and hence immoral.

The idea of efficiency assumed the role of one of the highest moral virtues. At the same time, the desire for wealth and material success became the all-absorbing passion. "All the world," says the preacher Martin Butzer, "is

[18] Schapiro, *op. cit.*, pp. 54, 55.
[19] Lamprecht, *op. cit.*, p. 200.

running after those trades and occupations that will bring the most gain. The study of the arts and sciences is set aside for the basest kind of manual work. All the clever heads, which have been endowed by God with a capacity for the nobler studies, are engrossed by commerce, which nowadays is so saturated with dishonesty that it is the last sort of business an honorable man should engage in." [20]

One outstanding consequence of the economic changes we have been describing affected everyone. The medieval social system was destroyed and with it the stability and relative security it had offered the individual. Now with the beginning of capitalism all classes of society started to move. There ceased to be a fixed place in the economic order which could be considered a natural, an unquestionable one. *The individual was left alone; everything depended on his own effort, not on the security of his traditional status.*

Each class, however, was affected in a different way by this development. For the poor of the cities, the workers and apprentices, it meant growing exploitation and impoverishment; for the peasants also it meant increased economic and personal pressure; the lower nobility faced ruin, although in a different way. While for these classes the new development was essentially a change for the worse, the situation was much more complicated for the urban middle class. We have spoken of the growing differentiation which took place within its ranks. Large sections of it were put into an increasingly bad position. Many artisans and small traders had to face the superior power of monopolists and other competitors with more capital, and they

[20] Quoted by Schapiro, op. cit., pp. 21, 22.

had greater and greater difficulties in remaining independent. They were often fighting against overwhelmingly strong forces and for many it was a desperate and hopeless fight. Other parts of the middle class were more prosperous and participated in the general upward trend of rising capitalism. But even for these more fortunate ones the increasing role of *capital*, of the *market*, and of *competition*, changed their personal situation into one of insecurity, isolation, and anxiety.

The fact that capital assumed decisive importance meant that a suprapersonal force was determining their economic and thereby their personal fate. Capital "had ceased to be a servant and had become a master. Assuming a separate and independent vitality it claimed the right of a predominant partner to dictate economic organization in accordance with its own exacting requirements."[21]

The new function of the market had a similar effect. The medieval market had been a relatively small one, the functioning of which was readily understood. It brought demand and supply into direct and concrete relation. A producer knew approximately how much to produce and could be relatively sure of selling his products for a proper price. Now it was necessary to produce for an increasingly large market, and one could not determine the possibilities of sale in advance. It was therefore not enough to produce useful goods. Although this was one condition for selling them, the unpredictable laws of the market decided whether the products could be sold at all and at what profit. The mechanism of the new market seemed to resemble the Calvinistic doctrine of predestination, which

[21] Tawney, *op. cit.*, p. 86.

taught that the individual must make every effort to be good, but that even before his birth it had been decided whether or not he is to be saved. The market day became the day of judgment for the products of human effort.

Another important factor in this context was the growing role of competition. While competition was certainly not completely lacking in medieval society, the feudal economic system was based on the principle of co-operation and was regulated—or regimented—by rules which curbed competition. With the rise of capitalism these medieval principles gave way more and more to a principle of individualistic enterprise. Each individual must go ahead and try his luck. He had to swim or to sink. Others were not allied with him in a common enterprise, they became competitors, and often he was confronted with the choice of destroying them or being destroyed.[22]

Certainly the role of capital, the market, and individual competition, was not as important in the sixteenth century as it was to become later on. At the same time, all the decisive elements of modern capitalism had already by that time come into existence, together with their psychological effect upon the individual.

While we have just described one side of the picture, there is also another one: capitalism freed the individual It freed man from the regimentation of the corporative system; it allowed him to stand on his own feet and to try his luck. He became the master of his fate, his was the risk, his the gain. Individual effort could lead him to success

---

[22] Cf this problem of competition with M. Mead, *Cooperation and Competition among Primitive Peoples*, McGraw-Hill Book Company, New York, 1937; L. K. Frank, *The Cost of Competition*, in Plan Age, Vol. VI, November–December, 1940.

and economic independence. Money became the great equalizer of man and proved to be more powerful than birth and caste.

This side of capitalism was only beginning to develop in the early period which we have been discussing. It played a greater role with the small group of wealthy capitalists than with the urban middle class. However, even to the extent to which it was effective then, it had an important effect in shaping the personality of man.

If we try now to sum up our discussion of the impact of the social and economic changes on the individual in the fifteenth and sixteenth centuries we arrive at the following picture:

We find the same ambiguity of freedom which we have discussed before. The individual is freed from the bondage of economic and political ties. He also gains in positive freedom by the active and independent role which he has to play in the new system. But simultaneously he is freed from those ties which used to give him security and a feeling of belonging. Life has ceased to be lived in a closed world the center of which was man; the world has become limitless and at the same time threatening. By losing his fixed place in a closed world man loses the answer to the meaning of his life; the result is that doubt has befallen him concerning himself and the aim of life. He is threatened by powerful suprapersonal forces, capital and the market. His relationship to his fellow men, with everyone a potential competitor, has become hostile and estranged; he is free—that is, he is alone, isolated, threatened from all sides. Not having the wealth or the power which the Renaissance capitalist had, and also having lost the sense of unity with men and the universe, he is overwhelmed with a sense of his individual nothingness and helplessness. Paradise is lost for good, the individual stands alone and faces the world—a stranger thrown into a limitless and threatening world. The new freedom is bound to create a deep feeling of insecurity, powerlessness, doubt, aloneness, and anxiety. These feelings must be alleviated if the individual is to function successfully.

2. THE PERIOD OF THE REFORMATION

At this point of development, *Lutheranism* and *Calvinism* came into existence. The new religions were not the religions of a wealthy upper class but of the urban middle class, the poor in the cities, and the peasants. They carried an appeal to these groups because they gave expression to a new feeling of freedom and independence as well as to the feeling of powerlessness and anxiety by which their members were pervaded. But the new religious doctrines did more than give articulate expression to the feelings engendered by a changing economic order. By their teachings they increased them and at the same time offered solutions which enabled the individual to cope with an otherwise unbearable insecurity.

Before we begin to analyze the social and psychological significance of the new religious doctrines, some remarks concerning the method of our approach may further the understanding of this analysis.

In studying the psychological significance of a religious or political doctrine, we must first bear in mind that the psychological analysis does not imply a judgment concerning the truth of the doctrine one analyzes. This latter question can be decided only in terms of the logical structure of the problem. The analysis of the psychological motivations behind certain doctrines or ideas can never be a substitute for a rational judgment of the validity of the doctrine and of the values which it implies, although such analysis may lead to a better understanding of the real meaning of a doctrine and thereby influence one's value judgment.

What the psychological analysis of doctrines can show is the subjective motivations which make a person aware of certain problems and make him seek for answers in certain directions. Any kind of thought, true or false, if it is more than a superficial conformance with conventional ideas, is motivated by the subjective needs and interests of the person who is thinking. It happens that some interests are furthered by finding the truth, others by destroying it. But in both cases the psychological motivations are important incentives for arriving at certain conclusions. We can go even further and say that ideas which are not rooted in powerful needs of the personality will have little influence on the actions and on the whole life of the person concerned.

If we analyze religious or political doctrines with regard to their psychological significance we must differentiate between two problems. We can study the character structure of the individual who creates a new doctrine and try to understand which traits in his personality are responsible for the particular direction of his thinking. Concretely speaking, this means, for instance, that we must analyze the character structure of Luther or Calvin to find out what trends in their personality made them arrive at certain conclusions and formulate certain doctrines. The other problem is to study the psychological motives, not of the creator of a doctrine, but of the social group to which this doctrine appeals. The influence of any doctrine or idea depends on the extent to which it appeals to psychic needs in the character structure of those to whom it is addressed. Only if the idea answers powerful psychological needs of certain social groups will it become a potent force in history.

Both problems, the psychology of the leader and that of his followers, are, of course, closely linked with each other. If the same ideas appeal to them their character structure must be similar in important aspects. Aside from factors such as the special talent for thinking and action on the part of the leader, his character structure will usually exhibit in a more extreme and clear-cut way the particular personality structure of those to whom his doctrines appeal; he can arrive at a clearer and more outspoken formulation of certain ideas for which his followers are already prepared psychologically. The fact that the character structure of the leader shows more sharply certain traits to be found in his followers, can be due to one of two factors or to a combination of both: first, that his social position is typical for those conditions which mold the personality of the whole group; second, that by the accidental circumstances of his upbringing and his individual experiences these same traits are developed to a marked degree which for the group result from its social position.

In our analysis of the psychological significance of the doctrines of Protestantism and Calvinism we are not discussing Luther's and Calvin's personalities but the psychological situation of the social classes to which their ideas appealed. I want only to mention very briefly before starting with the discussion of Luther's theology, that Luther as a person was a typical representative of the "authoritarian character" as it will be described later on. Having been brought up by an unusually severe father and having experienced little love or security as a child, his personality was torn by a constant ambivalence toward authority; he hated it and rebelled against it, while at the same time he admired it and tended to submit to it. During his whole life there was always one authority against which he was opposed and another which he admired—his father and his superiors in the monastery in his youth; the Pope and the princes later on. He was filled with an extreme feeling of aloneness, powerlessness, wickedness, but at the same time with a passion to dominate. He was tortured by doubts as only a compulsive character can be, and was constantly seeking for something which would give him inner security and relieve him from this torture of uncertainty. He hated others, especially the "rabble," he hated himself, he hated life; and out of all this hatred came a passionate and desperate striving to be loved. His whole being was pervaded by fear, doubt, and inner isolation, and on this personal basis he was to become the champion of social groups which were in a very similar position psychologically.

One more remark concerning the method of the following analysis seems to be warranted. Any psychological analysis of an individual's thoughts or of an ideology aims at the understanding of the psychological roots from which these thoughts or ideas spring. The first condition for such an analysis is to understand fully the logical context of an idea, and what its author consciously wants to say. However, we know that a person, even if he is subjectively sincere, may frequently be driven unconsciously by a motive that is different from the one he believes himself to be driven by; that he may use one concept which logically implies a certain meaning and which to him, unconsciously, means something different from this "official" meaning. Furthermore, we know that he may attempt to harmonize certain contradictions in his own feeling by an ideological construction or to cover up an idea which he represses by a rationalization that expresses its very opposite. The understanding of the operation of unconscious elements has taught us to be sceptical towards words and not to take them at face value.

The analysis of ideas has mainly to do with two tasks: one is to determine the weight that a certain idea has in the whole of an ideological system; the second is to determine whether we deal with a rationalization that differs from the *real* meaning of the thoughts. An example of the first point is the following: In Hitler's ideology, the emphasis on the injustice of the Versailles treaty plays a tremendous role, and it is true that he was genuinely indignant at the peace treaty. However, if we analyze his whole political ideology we see that its foundations are an intense wish for power and conquest, and although he consciously gives much weight to the injustice done to Germany, actually this thought has little weight in the whole of his thinking. An example of the difference between the consciously intended meaning of a thought and its real psychological meaning can be taken from the analysis of Luther's doctrines with which we are dealing in this chapter.

We say that his relation to God is one of submission on the basis of man's powerlessness. He himself speaks of this submission as a voluntary one, resulting not from fear but from love. Logically then, one might argue, this is not submission. Psychologically, however, it follows from the whole structure of Luther's thoughts that his kind of love or faith actually is submission; that although he consciously thinks in terms of the voluntary and loving character of his "submission" to God, he is pervaded by a feeling of powerlessness and wickedness that makes the nature of his relationship to God one of submission. (Exactly as masochistic dependence of one person on another consciously is frequently conceived as "love.") From the viewpoint of a psychological analysis, therefore, the objection that Luther says something different from what we believe he means (although unconsciously) has little weight. We believe that certain contradictions in his system can be understood only by the analysis of the psychological meaning of his concepts.

In the following analysis of the doctrines of Protestantism I have interpreted the religious doctrines according to what they mean from the context of the whole system. I do not quote sentences that contradict some of Luther's or Calvin's doctrines if I have convinced myself that their weight and meaning is such as not to form real contradictions. But the interpretation I give is not founded on a method of picking out particular sentences that fit into my interpretation, but on a study of the whole of Luther's and Calvin's system, of its psychological basis, and following that of an interpretation of its single elements in the light of the psychological structure of the whole system.

If we want to understand what was new in the doctrines of the Reformation we have first to consider what was essential in the theology of the medieval Church.[23] In trying to do so, we are confronted with the same methodological difficulty which we have discussed in connection with such concepts as "medieval society" and "capitalistic society." Just as in the economic sphere there is no sudden change from one structure to the other, so there is no such sudden change in the theological sphere either. Certain doctrines of Luther and Calvin are so similar to those of the medieval church that it is sometimes difficult to see any essential difference between them. Like Protestantism and Calvinism, the Catholic Church had always denied that man, on the strength of his own virtues and merits alone, could find salvation, that he could do without the grace of God as an indispensable means for salvation. However, in spite of all the elements common to the old and the new theology, the spirit of the Catholic Church had been essentially different from the spirit of the Reformation, especially with regard to the problem of human dignity and freedom and the effect of man's actions upon his own fate.

Certain principles were characteristic of Catholic theology in the long period prior to the Reformation: the doctrine that man's nature, though corrupted by the sin of Adam, innately strives for the good; that man's will is free to desire the good; that man's own effort is of avail for his salvation; and that by the sacraments of the Church, based on the merits of Christ's death, the sinner can be saved.

[23] I follow here mainly R. Seeberg's *Lehrbuch der Dogmengeschichte*, Deutsche Verlagsbuchhandlung, Leipzig. Vol. III, 1930; Vol. IV, 1, 1933; Vol. IV, 2, 1920, and B. Bartmann's *Lehrbuch der Dogmatik*, Herder, Freiburg. 1911.

However, some of the most representative theologians like Augustine and Thomas Aquinas, though holding the views just mentioned, at the same time taught doctrines which were of a profoundly different spirit. But although Aquinas teaches a doctrine of predestination, he never ceases to emphasize freedom of will as one of his fundamental doctrines. To bridge the contrast between the doctrine of freedom and that of predestination, he is obliged to use the most complicated constructions; but, although these constructions do not seem to solve the contradictions satisfactorily, he does not retreat from the doctrine of freedom of the will and of human effort, as being of avail for man's salvation, even though the will itself may need the support of God's grace.[24]

On the freedom of will Aquinas says that it would contradict the essence of God's and man's nature to assume that man was not free to decide and that man has even the freedom to refuse the grace offered to him by God.[25]

Other theologians emphasized more than Aquinas the role of man's effort for his salvation. According to Bonaventura, it is God's intention to offer grace to man, but only those receive it who prepare themselves for it by their merits.

This emphasis grew during the thirteenth, fourteenth, and fifteenth centuries in the systems of Duns Scotus, Ockam, and Biel, a particularly important development for

[24] With regard to the latter point, he says: "Whence, the predestined must strive after good works and prayer; because through these means predestination is most certainly fulfilled . . . and therefore predestination can be furthered by creatures, but it cannot be impeded by them." The Summa Theologica of St. Thomas Aquinas, literally translated by Fathers of the English Dominican Province. Second and revised edition, Burns Oates Washbourne, Ltd., London, 1929. Part I, Q. 23, Art. 8.

[25] Cf. Summa contra Gentiles, Vol. III, Chapters 73, 85, 159.

the understanding of the new spirit of the Reformation, since Luther's attacks were directed particularly against the Schoolmen of the late Middle Ages whom he called "Sau Theologen."

Duns Scotus stressed the role of will. The will is free. Through the realization of his will man realizes his individual self, and this self-realization is a supreme satisfaction to the individual. Since it is God's command that will is an act of the individual self, even God has no direct influence on man's decision.

Biel and Ockam stress the role of man's own merits as a condition for his salvation and although they too speak of God's help, its basic significance as it was assumed by the older doctrines was given up by them.[26] Biel assumes that man is free and can always turn to God, whose grace comes to his help. Ockam taught that man's nature has not been really corrupted by sin; to him, sin is only a single act which does not change the substance of man. The Tridentinum very clearly states that the free will co-operates with God's grace but that it can also refrain from this co-operation.[27] The picture of man, as it is presented by Ockam and other late Schoolmen, shows him not as the poor sinner but as a free being whose very nature makes him capable of everything good, and whose will is free from natural or any other external force.

The practice of buying a letter of indulgence, which played an increasing role in the late Middle Ages, and against which one of Luther's main attacks was directed, was related to this increasing emphasis on man's will and the avail of his efforts. By buying the letter of indulgence

[26] R. Seeberg, op. cit., p. 766.
[27] Cf. Bartmann, op. cit., p. 468.

from the Pope's emissary, man was relieved from temporal punishment which was supposed to be a substitute for eternal punishment, and, as Seeberg has pointed out,[28] man had every reason to expect that he would be absolved from all sins.

At first glance it may seem that this practice of buying one's remission from the punishment of purgatory from the Pope contradicted the idea of the efficacy of man's efforts for his salvation, because it implies a dependence on the authority of the Church and its sacraments. But while this is true to a certain extent, it is also true that it contains a spirit of hope and security; if man could free himself from punishment so easily, then the burden of guilt was eased considerably. He could free himself from the weight of the past with relative ease and get rid of the anxiety which had haunted him. In addition to that one must not forget that according to the explicit or implicit theory of the Church, the effect of the letter of indulgence was dependent on the premise that its buyer had repented and confessed.[29]

Those ideas that sharply differ from the spirit of the Reformation are also to be found in the writings of the mystics, in the sermons and in the elaborate rules for the practice of confessors. In them we find a spirit of affirma-

---

[28] op. cit., p. 624.

[29] The practice and theory of the letter of indulgence seems to be a particularly good illustration of the influence of growing capitalism. Not only does the idea that one could buy one's freedom from punishment express a new feeling for the eminent role of money, but the theory of the letter of indulgence as formulated in 1343 by Clemens VI also shows the spirit of the new capitalistic thinking. Clemens VI said that the Pope had in his trust the limitless amount of merits acquired by Christ and the Saints and that he could therefore distribute parts of this treasure to the believers (Cf. R. Seeberg, op. cit., p. 621). We find here the concept of the Po, e as a monopolist owning an immense moral capital and using it for his own financial advantage—for his "customers'" moral advantage.

tion of man's dignity and of the legitimacy of the expression of his whole self. Along with such an attitude we find the notion of the imitation of Christ, widespread as early as the twelfth century, and a belief that man could aspire to be like God. The rules for confessors showed a great understanding of the concrete situation of the individual and gave recognition to subjective individual differences. They did not treat sin as the weight by which the individual should be weighed down and humiliated, but as human frailty for which one should have understanding and respect.[30]

To sum up: the medieval Church stressed the dignity of man, the freedom of his will, and the fact that his efforts were of avail; it stressed the likeness between God and man and also man's right to be confident of God's love. Men were felt to be equal and brothers in their very likeness to God. In the late Middle Ages, in connection with the beginning of capitalism, bewilderment and insecurity arose; but at the same time tendencies that emphasized the role of will and human effort became increasingly stronger. We may assume that both the philosophy of the Renaissance and the Catholic doctrine of the late Middle Ages reflected the spirit prevailing in those social groups whose economic position gave them a feeling of power and independence. On the other hand, Luther's theology gave expression to the feelings of the middle class which, fighting against the authority of the Church and resenting the new moneyed class, felt threatened by rising capitalism and overcome by a feeling of powerlessness and individual insignificance.

[30] I am indebted to Charles Trinkhaus for sharpening my attention to the importance of the mystical and sermon literature and for a number of specific suggestions mentioned in this paragraph.

Luther's system, in so far as it differed from the Catholic tradition, has two sides, one of which has been stressed more than the other in the picture of his doctrines which is usually given in Protestant countries. This aspect points out that he gave man independence in religious matters; that he deprived the Church of her authority and gave it to the individual; that his concept of faith and salvation is one of subjective individual experience, in which all responsibility is with the individual and none with an authority which could give him what he cannot obtain himself. There are good reasons to praise this side of Luther's and of Calvin's doctrines, since they are one source of the development of political and spiritual freedom in modern society; a development which, especially in Anglo-Saxon countries, is inseparably connected with the ideas of Puritanism.

The other aspect of modern freedom is the isolation and powerlessness it has brought for the individual, and this aspect has its roots in Protestantism as much as that of independence. Since this book is devoted mainly to freedom as a burden and danger, the following analysis, being intentionally onesided, stresses that side in Luther's and Calvin's doctrines in which this negative aspect of freedom is rooted: their emphasis on the fundamental evilness and powerlessness of man.

Luther assumed the existence of an innate evilness in man's nature, which directs his will for evil and makes it impossible for any man to perform any good deed on the basis of his nature. Man has an evil and vicious nature ("naturaliter et inevitabiliter mala et vitiata natura"). The depravity of man's nature and its complete lack of freedom to choose the right is one of the fundamental concepts of Luther's whole thinking. In this spirit he begins his comment on Paul's letter to the Romans: "The essence of this letter is: to destroy, to uproot, and to annihilate all wisdom and justice of the flesh, may it appear—in our eyes and in those of others—ever so remarkable and sincere . . . What matters is that our justice and wisdom which unfold before our eyes are being destroyed and uprooted from our heart and from our vain self."[31]

This conviction of man's rottenness and powerlessness to do anything good on his own merits is one essential condition of God's grace. Only if man humiliates himself and demolishes his individual will and pride will God's grace descend upon him. "For God wants to save us not by our own but by extraneous (fremde) justice and wisdom, by a justice that does not come from ourselves and does not originate in ourselves but comes to us from somewhere else . . . That is, a justice must be taught that comes exclusively from the outside and is entirely alien to ourselves."[32]

An even more radical expression of man's powerlessness was given by Luther seven years later in his pamphlet "De servo arbitrio," which was an attack against Erasmus' defense of the freedom of the will. ". . . Thus the human will is, as it were, a beast between the two. If God sit thereon, it wills and goes where God will; as the Psalm saith, 'I was as a beast before thee, nevertheless I am continually with thee.' (Ps. 73. 22, 23.) If Satan sit thereon, it wills and goes as Satan will. Nor is it in the power of its own will to

[31] Martin Luther, Vorlesung über den Römerbrief, Chapter I, i. (My own translation since no English translation exists.)
[32] op. cit., Chapter I, i.

choose, to which rider it will run, nor which it will seek; but the riders themselves contend, which shall have and hold it."[33] Luther declares that if one does not like "to leave out this theme (of free will) altogether (which would be most safe and also most religious) we may, nevertheless, with a good conscience teach that it be used so far as to allow man a 'free will,' not in respect of those who are above him, but in respect only of those beings who are below him . . . God-ward man has no 'free will,' but is a captive, slave, and servant either to the will of God or to the will of Satan."[34] The doctrines that man was a powerless tool in God's hands and fundamentally evil, that his only task was to resign to the will of God, that God could save him as the result of an incomprehensible act of justice —these doctrines were not the definite answer a man was to give who was so much driven by despair, anxiety, and doubt and at the same time by such an ardent wish for certainty as Luther. He eventually found the answer for his doubts. In 1518 a sudden revelation came to him. Man cannot be saved on the basis of his virtues; he should not even meditate whether or not his works were well pleasing to God; but he can have certainty of his salvation if he has faith. Faith is given to man by God; once man has had the indubitable subjective experience of faith he can also be certain of his salvation. The individual is essentially receptive in this relationship to God. Once man receives God's grace in the experience of faith his nature becomes

[33] Martin Luther, *The Bondage of the Will*. Translated by Henry Cole, M.A., B. Erdmans Publishing Co., Grand Rapids, Michigan, 1931. p. 74.

[34] op. cit. p. 79. This dichotomy—submission to powers above and domination over those below—is, as we shall see later, characteristic of the attitude of the authoritarian character.

changed, since in the act of faith he unites himself with Christ, and Christ's justice replaces his own which was lost by Adam's fall. However, man can never become entirely virtuous during his life, since his natural evilness can never entirely disappear.[35]

Luther's doctrine of faith as an indubitable subjective experience of one's own salvation may at first glance strike one as an extreme contradiction to the intense feeling of doubt which was characteristic for his personality and his teachings up to 1518. Yet, psychologically, this change from doubt to certainty, far from being contradictory, has a causal relation. We must remember what has been said about the nature of this doubt: it was not the rational doubt which is rooted in the freedom of thinking and which dares to question established views. It was the irrational doubt which springs from the isolation and powerlessness of an individual whose attitude toward the world is one of anxiety and hatred. This irrational doubt can never be cured by rational answers; it can only disappear if the individual becomes an integral part of a meaningful world. If this does not happen, as it did not happen with Luther and the middle class which he represented, the doubt can only be silenced, driven underground, so to speak, and this can be done by some formula which promises absolute certainty. *The compulsive quest for certainty, as we find with Luther, is not the expression of genuine faith but is rooted in the need to conquer the unbearable doubt.* Luther's solution is one which we find present in many individuals today, who do not think in theological terms: namely to find certainty by elimination of the iso-

[35] Cf. "Sermo de duplici institia" (*Luthers Werke*, Weimar ed. Vol. II).

lated individual self, by becoming an instrument in the hands of an overwhelmingly strong power outside of the individual. For Luther this power was God and in unqualified submission he sought certainty. But although he thus succeeded in silencing his doubts to some extent, they never really disappeared; up to his last day he had attacks of doubt which he had to conquer by renewed efforts toward submission. Psychologically, faith has two entirely different meanings. It can be the expression of an inner relatedness to mankind and affirmation of life; or it can be a reaction formation against a fundamental feeling of doubt, rooted in the isolation of the individual and his negative attitude toward life. Luther's faith had that compensatory quality.

It is particularly important to understand the significance of doubt and the attempts to silence it, because this is not only a problem concerning Luther's and, as we shall see soon, Calvin's theology, but it has remained one of the basic problems of modern man. Doubt is the starting point of modern philosophy; the need to silence it had a most powerful stimulus on the development of modern philosophy and science. But although many rational doubts have been solved by rational answers, the irrational doubt has not disappeared and cannot disappear as long as man has not progressed from negative freedom to positive freedom. The modern attempts to silence it, whether they consist in a compulsive striving for success, in the belief that unlimited knowledge of facts can answer the quest for certainty, or in the submission to a leader who assumes the responsibility for "certainty"—all these solutions can only eliminate the awareness of doubt. The doubt itself will not disappear as long as man does not overcome his isolation and as long as his place in the world has not become a meaningful one in terms of his human needs.

What is the connection of Luther's doctrines with the psychological situation of all but the rich and powerful toward the end of the Middle Ages? As we have seen, the old order was breaking down. The individual had lost the security of certainty and was threatened by new economic forces, by capitalists and monopolies; the corporative principle was being replaced by competition; the lower classes felt the pressure of growing exploitation. The appeal of Lutheranism to the lower classes differed from its appeal to the middle class. The poor in the cities, and even more the peasants, were in a desperate situation. They were ruthlessly exploited and deprived of traditional rights and privileges. They were in a revolutionary mood which found expression in peasant uprisings and in revolutionary movements in the cities. The Gospel articulated their hopes and expectations as it had done for the slaves and laborers of early Christianity, and led the poor to seek for freedom and justice. In so far as Luther attacked authority and made the word of the Gospel the center of his teachings, he appealed to these restive masses as other religious movements of an evangelical character had done before him.

Although Luther accepted their allegiance to him and supported them, he could do so only up to a certain point; he had to break the alliance when the peasants went further than attacking the authority of the Church and merely making minor demands for the betterment of their lot. They proceeded to become a revolutionary class which threatened to overthrow all authority and to destroy the foundations of a social order in whose maintenance the middle class was vitally interested. For, in spite of all the difficulties we earlier described, the middle class, even its lower stratum, had privileges to defend against the demands of the poor; and therefore it was intensely hostile to revolutionary movements which aimed to destroy not only the privileges of the aristocracy, the Church, and the monopolies, but their own privileges as well.

The position of the middle class between the very rich and the very poor made its reaction complex and in many ways contradictory. They wanted to uphold law and order, and yet they were themselves vitally threatened by rising capitalism. Even the more successful members of the middle class were not wealthy and powerful as the small group of big capitalists was. They had to fight hard to survive and make progress. The luxury of the moneyed class increased their feeling of smallness and filled them with envy and indignation. As a whole, the middle class was more endangered by the collapse of the feudal order and by rising capitalism than they were helped.

Luther's picture of man mirrored just this dilemma. Man is free *from* all ties binding him to spiritual authorities, but this very freedom leaves him alone and anxious, overwhelms him with a feeling of his own individual insignificance and powerlessness. This free, isolated individual is crushed by the experience of his individual insignificance. Luther's theology gives expression to this feeling of helplessness and doubt. The picture of man which he draws in religious terms describes the situation of the individual as it was brought about by the current social and economic evolution. The member of the middle class was as helpless in face of the new economic forces as Luther described man to be in his relationship to God.

But Luther did more than bring out the feeling of insignificance which already pervaded the social classes to whom he preached—he offered them a solution. By not only accepting his own insignificance but by humiliating himself to the utmost, by giving up every vestige of individual will, by renouncing and denouncing his individual strength, the individual could hope to be acceptable to God. Luther's relationship to God was one of complete submission. In psychological terms his concept of faith means: if you completely submit, if you accept your individual insignificance, then the all-powerful God may be willing to love you and save you. If you get rid of your individual self with all its shortcomings and doubts by utmost self-effacement, you free yourself from the feeling of your own nothingness and can participate in God's glory. Thus, while Luther freed people from the authority of the Church, he made them submit to a much more tyrannical authority, that of a God who insisted on complete submission of man and annihilation of the individual self as the essential condition to his salvation. Luther's "faith" was the conviction of being loved upon the condition of surrender, a solution which has much in common with the principle of complete submission of the individual to the state and the "leader."

Luther's awe of authority and his love for it appears also in his political convictions. Although he fought against the authority of the Church, although he was filled with indignation against the new moneyed class—part of which was the upper strata of the clerical hierarchy—and although he supported the revolutionary tendencies of the peasants up to a certain point, yet he postulated submission to worldly authorities, the princes, in the most drastic fashion. "Even if those in authority are evil or without faith, nevertheless the authority and its power is good and from God. ... Therefore, where there is power and where it flourishes, there it is and there it remains because God has ordained it."[36] Or he says: "God would prefer to suffer the government to exist no matter how evil, rather than allow the rabble to riot, no matter how justified they are in doing so ... A prince should remain a prince no matter how tyrannical he may be. He beheads necessarily only a few since he must have subjects in order to be a ruler."

The other aspect of his attachment to and awe of authority becomes visible in his hatred and contempt for the powerless masses, the "rabble," especially when they went beyond certain limits in their revolutionary attempts. In one of his diatribes he writes the famous words: "Therefore let everyone who can, smite, slay, and stab, secretly or openly, remembering that nothing can be more poisonous, hurtful, or devilish than a rebel. It is just as when one must kill a mad dog; if you do not strike him he will strike you, and a whole land with you."[37]

Luther's personality as well as his teachings shows ambivalence toward authority. On the one hand he is overawed by authority—that of a worldly authority and that of a tyrannical God—and on the other hand he rebels against

[36] Römerbrief, 13, 1.
[37] "Against the Robbing and Murdering Hordes of Peasants" (1525); Works of Martin Luther, translation: C. M. Jacobs. A. T. Holman Company, Philadelphia, 1931. Vol. X, IV, p. 411. Cf. H. Marcuse's discussion of Luther's attitude toward freedom in Autorität und Familie, F. Alcan, Paris, 1926.

authority—that of the Church. He shows the same ambivalence in his attitude toward the masses. As far as they rebel within the limits he has set he is with them. But when they attack the authorities he approves of, an intense hatred and contempt for the masses comes to the fore. In the chapter which deals with the psychological mechanism of escape we shall show that this simultaneous love for authority and the hatred against those who are powerless are typical traits of the "authoritarian character."

At this point it is important to understand that Luther's attitude towards secular authority was closely related to his religious teachings. In making the individual feel worthless and insignificant as far as his own merits are concerned, in making him feel like a powerless tool in the hands of God, he deprived man of the self-confidence and of the feeling of human dignity which is the premise for any firm stand against oppressing secular authorities. In the course of the historical evolution the results of Luther's teachings were still more far-reaching. Once the individual had lost his sense of pride and dignity, he was psychologically prepared to lose the feeling which had been characteristic of the medieval thinking, namely, that man, his spiritual salvation, and his spiritual aims were the purpose of life; he was prepared to accept a role in which his life became a means to purposes outside of himself, those of economic productivity and accumulation of capital. Luther's views on economic problems were typically medieval, still more so than Calvin's. He would have abhorred the idea that man's life should become a means for economic ends. But while his thinking on economic matters was the traditional one, his emphasis on the nothingness of the individual was in contrast and paved the way for a development in which man not only was to obey secular authorities but had to subordinate his life to the ends of economic achievements. In our day this trend has reached a peak in the Fascist emphasis that it is the aim of life to be sacrificed for "higher" powers, for the leader or the racial community.

Calvin's theology, which was to become as important for the Anglo-Saxon countries as Luther's for Germany, exhibits essentially the same spirit as Luther's, both theologically and psychologically. Although he too opposes the authority of the Church and the blind acceptance of its doctrines, religion for him is rooted in the powerlessness of man; self-humiliation and the destruction of human pride are the *Leitmotiv* of his whole thinking. Only he who despises this world can devote himself to the preparation for the future world.[38]

He teaches that we should humiliate ourselves and that this very self-humiliation is the means to reliance on God's strength. "For nothing arouses us to repose all confidence and assurance of mind on the Lord, so much as diffidence of ourselves, and anxiety arising from a consciousness of our own misery."[39]

He preaches that the individual should not feel that he is his own master. "We are not our own; therefore neither our reason nor our will should predominate in our deliberations and actions. We are not our own; therefore, let us not propose it as our end, to seek what may be expedient

[38] John Calvin's *Institutes of the Christian Religion*, translated by John Allen, Presbyterian Board of Christian Education, Philadelphia, 1928. Book III, Chapter IX, 1.

[39] op. cit., Book III, Chapter II, 23.

for us according to the flesh. We are not our own; therefore, let us, as far as possible, forget ourselves and all things
that are ours. On the contrary, we are God's; to him, therefore, let us live and die. For, as it is the most devastating
pestilence which ruins people if they obey themselves, it is
the only haven of salvation not to know or to want anything oneself but to be guided by God who walks before
us."[40]

Man should not strive for virtue for its own sake. That
would lead to nothing but vanity: "For it is an ancient and
true observation that there is a world of vices concealed in
the soul of man. Nor can you find any other remedy than
to deny yourself and discard all selfish considerations, and
to devote your whole attention to the pursuit of those
things which the Lord requires of you, and which ought to

---

[40] op. cit., Book III, Chapter 7, 1. From "For, as it is . . ." the translation
is mine from the Latin original, *Johannes Calvini Institutio Christianae Re-
ligionis. Editionem curavit A. Tholuk, Berolini, 1835. Par. I, p. 445.* The
reason for this shift is that Allen's translation slightly changes the original
in the direction of softening the rigidity of Calvin's thought. Allen translates
this sentence: "For, as compliance with their own inclinations leads men most
effectually to ruin, so to place no dependence on our own knowledge or will,
but merely to follow the guidance of the Lord, is the only way of safety."
However, the Latin *sibi ipsis obtemperant* is not equivalent to "follow one's
own inclinations" but "to obey oneself." To forbid following one's inclinations has the mild quality of Kantian ethics that man should suppress his
natural inclinations and by doing so follow the orders of his conscience. On
the other hand, the forbiddance to obey oneself is a denial of the autonomy
of man. The same subtle change of meaning is reached by translating *ita
unicus est salutis portis nihil nec sapere, nec velle per se ipsum* as "to place
no dependence on our knowledge or will." While the formulation of the
original straightforwardly contradicts the motto of enlightenment philosophy:
sapere aude—dare to know: Allen's translation warns only of a dependence
on one's own knowledge, a warning which is far less contradictory to modern
thought. I mention these deviations of the translation from the original because they offer a good illustration of the fact that the spirit of an author is
"modernized" and colored—certainly without any intention of doing so—
just by translating him.

be pursued for this sole reason, because they are pleasing to him."[41]

Calvin, too, denies that good works can lead to salvation. We are completely lacking them: "No work of a pious man ever existed which, if it were examined before the strict judgment of God, did not prove to be damnable."[42]

If we try to understand the psychological significance of Calvin's system, the same holds true, in principle, as has been said about Luther's teachings. Calvin, too, preached to the conservative middle class, to people who felt immensely alone and frightened, whose feelings were expressed in his doctrine of the insignificance and powerlessness of the individual and the futility of his efforts. However, we may assume that there was some slight difference; while Germany in Luther's time was in a general state of upheaval, in which not only the middle class, but also the peasants and the poor of urban society, were threatened by the rise of capitalism, Geneva was a relatively prosperous community. It had been one of the important fairs in Europe in the first half of the fifteenth century, and although at Calvin's time it was already overshadowed by Lyons in this respect,[43] it had preserved a good deal of economic solidity.

On the whole, it seems safe to say that Calvin's adherents were recruited mainly from the conservative middle class,[44] and that also in France, Holland, and England his main adherents were not advanced capitalistic groups but

[41] op. cit., Book III, Chapter 7, 2.
[42] op. cit., Book III, Chapter 14, 11.
[43] Cf. J. Kulischer, op. cit., p. 249.
[44] Cf. Georgia Harkness, John Calvin, The Man and His Ethics, Henry Holt & Co., New York, 1931. p. 151 ff.

artisans and small business men, some of whom were already more prosperous than others but who, as a group, were threatened by the rise of capitalism.[45]

To this social class Calvinism had the same psychological appeal that we have already discussed in connection with Lutheranism. It expressed the feeling of freedom but also of insignificance and powerlessness of the individual. It offered a solution by teaching the individual that by complete submission and self-humiliation he could hope to find new security.

There are a number of subtle differences between Calvin's and Luther's teachings which are not important for the main line of thought of this book. Only two points of difference need to be stressed. One is Calvin's doctrine of predestination. In contrast to the doctrine of predestination as we find it in Augustine, Aquinas and Luther, with Calvin it becomes one of the cornerstones, perhaps the central doctrine, of his whole system. He gives it a new version by assuming that God not only predestines some for grace, but decides that others are destined for eternal damnation.[46]

Salvation or damnation are not results of anything good or bad a man does in his life, but are predetermined by God before man ever comes to life. Why God chose the one and condemned the other is a secret into which man must not try to delve. He did so because it pleased him to show his unlimited power in that way. Calvin's God, in spite of all attempts to preserve the idea of God's justice and love, has all the features of a tyrant without any quality

---

[45] Cf. F. Borkenau, *Der Ubergang vom feudalen zum bürgerlichen Welt bild*, Alcan, Paris, 1934. p. 156 ff.

[46] op. cit., Book III, Chapter 21, 5.

of love or even justice. In blatant contradiction to the New Testament, Calvin denies the supreme role of love and says: "For what the Schoolmen advance concerning the priority of charity to faith and hope, is a mere reverie of a distempered imagination. . . ."[47]

The psychological significance of the doctrine of predestination is a twofold one. It expresses and enhances the feeling of individual powerlessness and insignificance. No doctrine could express more strongly than this the worthlessness of human will and effort. The decision over man's fate is taken completely out of his own hands and there is nothing man can do to change this decision. He is a powerless tool in God's hands. The other meaning of this doctrine, like that of Luther's, consists in its function to silence the irrational doubt which was the same in Calvin and his followers as in Luther. At first glance the doctrine of predestination seems to enhance the doubt rather than silence it. Must not the individual be torn by even more torturing doubts than before to learn that he was predestined either to eternal damnation or to salvation before he was born? How can he ever be sure what his lot will be? Although Calvin did not teach that there was any concrete proof of such certainty, he and his followers actually had the conviction that they belonged to the chosen ones. They got this conviction by the same mechanism of self-humiliation which we have analyzed with regard to Luther's doctrine. Having such conviction, the doctrine of predestination implied utmost certainty; one could not do anything which would endanger the state of salvation, since one's salvation

[47] op. cit., Book III, Chapter 2, 41.

did not depend on one's own actions but was decided upon before one was ever born. Again, as with Luther, the fundamental doubt resulted in the quest for absolute certainty; but though the doctrine of predestination gave such certainty, the doubt remained in the background and had to be silenced again and again by an ever-growing fanatic belief that the religious community to which one belonged represented that part of mankind which had been chosen by God.

Calvin's theory of predestination has one implication which should be explicitly mentioned here, since it has found its most vigorous revival in Nazi ideology: the principle of the basic inequality of men. For Calvin there are two kinds of people—those who are saved and those who are destined to eternal damnation. Since this fate is determined before they are born and without their being able to change it by anything they do or do not do in their lives, the equality of mankind is denied in principle. Men are created unequal. This principle implies also that there is no solidarity between men, since the one factor which is the strongest basis for human solidarity is denied: the equality of man's fate. The Calvinists quite naïvely thought that they were the chosen ones and that all others were those whom God had condemned to damnation. It is obvious that this belief represented psychologically a deep contempt and hatred for other human beings—as a matter of fact, the same hatred with which they had endowed God. While modern thought has led to an increasing assertion of the equality of men, the Calvinists' principle has never been completely mute. The doctrine that men are basically unequal according to their racial background is confirmation of the same principle with a different rationalization. The psychological implications are the same.

Another and very significant difference from Luther's teachings is the greater emphasis on the importance of moral effort and a virtuous life. Not that the individual can change his fate by any of his works, but the very fact that he is able to make the effort is one sign of his belonging to the saved. The virtues man should acquire are: modesty and moderation (sobrietas), justice (iustitia) in the sense of everybody being given what is his due share, and piousness (pietas) which unites man with God.[48] In the further development of Calvinism, the emphasis on a virtuous life and on the significance of an unceasing effort gains in importance, particularly the idea that success in worldly life, as a result of such efforts, is a sign of salvation.[49]

But the particular emphasis on a virtuous life which was characteristic for Calvinism had also a particular psychological significance. Calvinism emphasized the necessity of unceasing human effort. Man must constantly try to live according to God's word and never lapse in his effort to do so. This doctrine appears to be a contradiction of the doctrine that human effort is of no avail with regard to man's salvation. The fatalistic attitude of not making any effort might seem like a much more appropriate response. Some psychological considerations, however, show that this is not so. The state of anxiety, the feeling of power-

[48] op. cit., Book III, Chapter 7, 3.
[49] This latter point has found particular attention in M. Weber's work as being one important link between Calvin's doctrine and the spirit of capitalism.

lessness and insignificance, and especially the doubt concerning one's future after death, represent a state of mind which is practically unbearable for anybody. Almost no one stricken with this fear would be able to relax, enjoy life, and be indifferent as to what happened afterwards. One possible way to escape this unbearable state of uncertainty and the paralyzing feeling of one's own insignificance is the very trait which became so prominent in Calvinism: the development of a frantic activity and a striving to do *something*. Activity in this sense assumes a compulsory quality: *the individual has to be active in order to overcome his feeling of doubt and powerlessness.* This kind of effort and activity is not the result of inner strength and self-confidence; it is a desperate escape from anxiety.

This mechanism can be easily observed in attacks of anxiety panic in individuals. A man who expects to receive within a few hours the doctor's diagnosis of his illness—which may be fatal—quite naturally is in a state of anxiety. Usually he will not sit down quietly and wait. Most frequently his anxiety, if it does not paralyze him, will drive him to some sort of more or less frantic activity. He may pace up and down the floor, start asking questions and talk to everybody he can get hold of, clean up his desk, write letters. He may continue his usual kind of work but with added activity and more feverishly. Whatever form his effort assumes it is prompted by anxiety and tends to overcome the feeling of powerlessness by frantic activity.

Effort in the Calvinist doctrine had still another psychological meaning. The fact that one did not tire in that unceasing effort and that one succeeded in one's moral as well as one's secular work was a more or less distinct sign of being one of the chosen ones. The irrationality of such compulsive effort is that *the activity is not meant to create a desired end but serves to indicate whether or not something will occur which has been determined beforehand,* independent of one's own activity or control. This mechanism is a well-known feature of compulsive neurotics. Such persons when afraid of the outcome of an important undertaking may, while awaiting an answer, count the windows of houses or trees on the street. If the number is even, a person feels that things will be all right; if it is uneven, it is a sign that he will fail. Frequently this doubt does not refer to a specific instance but to a person's whole life, and the compulsion to look for "signs" will pervade it accordingly. Often the connection between counting stones, playing solitaire, gambling, and so on, and anxiety and doubt, is not conscious. A person may play solitaire out of a vague feeling of restlessness and only an analysis might uncover the hidden function of his activity: to reveal the future.

In Calvinism this meaning of effort was part of the religious doctrine. Originally it referred essentially to moral effort, but later on the emphasis was more and more on effort in one's occupation and on the results of this effort, that is, success or failure in business. Success became the sign of God's grace; failure, the sign of damnation.

These considerations show that the compulsion to unceasing effort and work was far from being in contradiction to a basic conviction of man's powerlessness; rather was it the psychological result. Effort and work in this sense assumed an entirely irrational character. They were not to change fate since this was predetermined by God, regardless of any effort on the part of the individual. They served only as a means of forecasting the predetermined fate; while at the same time the frantic effort was a reassurance against an otherwise unbearable feeling of powerlessness.

This new attitude towards effort and work as an aim in itself may be assumed to be the most important psychological change which has happened to man since the end of the Middle Ages. In every society man has to work if he wants to live. Many societies solved the problem by having the work done by slaves, thus allowing the free man to devote himself to "nobler" occupations. In such societies, work was not worthy of a free man. In medieval society, too, the burden of work was unequally distributed among the different classes in the social hierarchy, and there was a good deal of crude exploitation. But the attitude toward work was different from that which developed subsequently in the modern era. Work did not have the abstract character of producing some commodity which might be profitably sold on the market. One worked in response to a concrete demand and with a concrete aim: to earn one's livelihood. There was, as Max Weber particularly has shown, no urge to work more than was necessary to maintain the traditional standard of living. It seems that for some groups of medieval society work was enjoyed as a realization of productive ability; that many others worked because they *had* to and felt this necessity was conditioned by pressure from the outside. What was new in modern society was that men came to be driven to work not so much by external pressure but by an internal compulsion, which made them work as only a very strict master could have made people do in other societies.

The inner compulsion was more effective in harnessing

all energies to work than any outer compulsion can ever be. Against external compulsion there is always a certain amount of rebelliousness which hampers the effectiveness of work or makes people unfit for any differentiated task requiring intelligence, initiative, and responsibility. The compulsion to work by which man was turned into his own slave driver did not hamper these qualities. Undoubtedly capitalism could not have been developed had not the greatest part of man's energy been channeled in the direction of work. There is no other period in history in which free men have given their energy so completely for the one purpose: work. The drive for relentless work was one of the fundamental productive forces, no less important for the development of our industrial system than steam and electricity.

We have so far spoken mainly of the anxiety and of the feeling of powerlessness pervading the personality of the member of the middle class. We must now discuss another trait which we have only touched upon very briefly: his *hostility* and *resentment*. That the middle class developed intense hostility is not surprising. Anybody who is thwarted in emotional and sensual expression and who is also threatened in his very existence will normally react with hostility; as we have seen, the middle class as a whole and especially those of its members who were not yet enjoying the advantages of rising capitalism were thwarted and seriously threatened. Another factor was to increase their hostility: the luxury and power which the small group of capitalists, including the higher dignitaries of the Church, could afford to display. An intense envy against them was the natural result. But while hostility and envy developed, the members of the middle class could not find the direct expression which was possible for the lower classes. These hated the rich who exploited them, they wanted to overthrow their power, and could thus afford to feel and to express their hatred. The upper class also could afford to express aggressiveness directly in the wish for power. The members of the middle class were essentially conservative; they wanted to stabilize society and not uproot it; each of them hoped to become more prosperous and to participate in the general development. Hostility, therefore, was not to be expressed overtly, nor could it even be felt consciously; it had to be repressed. Repression of hostility, however, only removes it from conscious awareness, it does not abolish it. Moreover, the pent-up hostility, not finding any direct expression, increases to a point where it pervades the whole personality, one's relationship to others and to oneself—but in rationalized and disguised forms.

Luther and Calvin portray this all-pervading hostility. Not only in the sense that these two men, personally, belonged to the ranks of the greatest haters among the leading figures of history, certainly among religious leaders; but, which is more important, in the sense that their doctrines were colored by this hostility and could only appeal to a group itself driven by an intense, repressed hostility. The most striking expression of this hostility is found in their concept of God, especially in Calvin's doctrine. Although we are all familiar with this concept, we often do not fully realize what it means to conceive of God as being as arbitrary and merciless as Calvin's God, who destined part of mankind to eternal damnation without any justification or reason except that this act was an expression of

God's power. Calvin himself was, of course, concerned with the obvious objections which could be made against this conception of God; but the more or less subtle constructions he made to uphold the picture of a just and loving God do not sound in the least convincing. This picture of a despotic God, who wants unrestricted power over men and their submission and humiliation, was the projection of the middle class's own hostility and envy.

Hostility or resentment also found expression in the character of relationships to others. The main form which it assumed was moral indignation, which has invariably been characteristic for the lower middle class from Luther's time to Hitler's. While this class was actually envious of those who had wealth and power and could enjoy life, they rationalized this resentment and envy of life in terms of moral indignation and in the conviction that these superior people would be punished by eternal suffering.[50] But the hostile tension against others found expression in still other ways. Calvin's regime in Geneva was characterized by suspicion and hostility on the part of everybody against everybody else, and certainly little of the spirit of love and brotherliness could be discovered in his despotic regime. Calvin distrusted wealth and at the same time had little pity for poverty. In the later development of Calvinism warnings against friendliness towards the stranger, a cruel attitude towards the poor, and a general atmosphere of suspiciousness often appeared.[51]

[50] Cf. Ranulf's *Moral Indignation and Middle Class Psychology*, a study which is an important contribution to the thesis that moral indignation is a trait typical of the middle class, especially the lower middle class.

[51] Cf. Max Weber; *op. cit.*, p. 102; Tawney, *op. cit.*, p. 190; Ranulf, *op. cit.*, p. 66 ff.

Aside from the projection of hostility and jealousy onto God and their indirect expression in the form of moral indignation, one other way in which hostility found expression was in turning it against oneself. We have seen how ardently both Luther and Calvin emphasized the wickedness of man and taught self-humiliation and self-abasement as the basis of all virtue. What they consciously had in mind was certainly nothing but an extreme degree of humility. But to anybody familiar with the psychological mechanisms of self-accusation and self-humiliation there can be no doubt that this kind of "humility" is rooted in a violent hatred which, for some reason or other, is blocked from being directed toward the world outside and operates against one's own self. In order to understand this phenomenon fully, it is necessary to realize that the attitudes toward others and toward oneself, far from being contradictory, in principle run parallel. But while hostility against others is often conscious and can be expressed overtly, hostility against oneself is usually (except in pathological cases) unconscious, and finds expression in indirect and rationalized forms. One is a person's active emphasis on his own wickedness and insignificance, of which we have just spoken; another appears under the guise of conscience or duty. Just as there exists humility which has nothing to do with self-hatred, so there exist genuine demands of conscience and a sense of duty which are not rooted in hostility. This genuine conscience forms a part of integrated personality and the following of its demands is an affirmation of the whole self. However, the sense of "duty" as we find it pervading the life of modern man from the period of the Reformation up to the present in religious or secular rationalizations, is intensely colored by hostility against the self. "Conscience" is a slave driver, put into man by himself. It drives him to act according to wishes and aims which he *believes* to be his own, while they are actually the internalization of external social demands. It drives him with harshness and cruelty, forbidding him pleasure and happiness, making his whole life the atonement for some mysterious sin.[52] It is also the basis of the "inner worldly asceticism" which is so characteristic in early Calvinism and later Puritanism. The hostility in which this modern kind of humility and sense of duty is rooted explains also one otherwise rather baffling contradiction: that such humility goes together with contempt for others, and that self-righteousness has actually replaced love and mercy. Genuine humility and a genuine sense of duty towards one's fellow men could not do this; but self-humiliation and a self-negating "conscience" are only one side of an hostility, the other side of which is contempt for and hatred against others.

On the basis of this brief analysis of the meaning of freedom in the period of the Reformation, it seems appropriate to sum up the conclusions which we have reached with regard to the specific problem of freedom and the general problem of the interaction of economic, psychological, and ideological factors in the social process.

---

[52] Freud has seen the hostility of man against himself which is contained in what he called the superego. He also saw that the superego was originally the internalization of an external and dangerous authority. But he did not distinguish between spontaneous ideals which are part of the self, and internalized commands which rule the self . . . The viewpoint presented here is discussed in greater detail in my study on the psychology of authority (*Authorität und Familie*, ed. M. Horkheimer, Alcan, Paris, 1934). Karen Horney has pointed out the compulsive character of the demands of the superego in *New Ways in Psychoanalysis*.

The breakdown of the medieval system of feudal society had one main significance for all classes of society: the individual was left alone and isolated. He was free. This freedom had a twofold result. Man was deprived of the security he had enjoyed, of the unquestionable feeling of belonging, and he was torn loose from the world which had satisfied his quest for security both economically and spiritually. He felt alone and anxious. But he was also free to act and to think independently, to become his own master and do with his life as he could—not as he was told to do.

However, according to the real life situation of the members of different social classes, these two kinds of freedom were of unequal weight. Only the most successful class of society profited from rising capitalism to an extent which gave them real wealth and power. They could expand, conquer, rule, and amass fortunes as a result of their own activity and rational calculations. This new aristocracy of money, combined with that of birth, was in a position where they could enjoy the fruits of the new freedom and acquire a new feeling of mastery and individual initiative. On the other hand, they had to dominate the masses and to fight against each other, and thus their position, too, was not free from a fundamental insecurity and anxiety. But, on the whole, the positive meaning of freedom was dominant for the new capitalist. It was expressed in the culture which grew on the soil of the new aristocracy, the culture of the Renaissance. In its art and in its philosophy it expressed the new spirit of human dignity, will, and mastery, although often enough despair and scepticism also. The same emphasis on the strength of individual activity and will is to be found in the theological teachings of the

Catholic Church in the late Middle Ages. The Schoolmen of that period did not rebel against authority, they accepted its guidance; but they stressed the positive meaning of freedom, man's share in the determination of his fate, his strength, his dignity, and the freedom of his will.

On the other hand, the lower classes, the poor population of the cities, and especially the peasants, were impelled by a new quest for freedom and an ardent hope to end the growing economic and personal oppression. They had little to lose and much to gain. They were not interested in dogmatic subtleties, but rather in the fundamental principles of the Bible: brotherliness and justice. Their hopes took active form in a number of political revolts and in religious movements which were characterized by the uncompromising spirit typical of the very beginning of Christianity.

Our main interest, however, has been taken up by the reaction of the middle class. Rising capitalism, although it made also for their increased independence and initiative, was greatly a threat. In the beginning of the sixteenth century the individual of the middle class could not yet gain much power and security from the new freedom. Freedom brought isolation and personal insignificance more than strength and confidence. Besides that, he was filled with burning resentment against the luxury and power of the wealthy classes, including the hierarchy of the Roman Church. Protestantism gave expression to the feelings of insignificance and resentment; it destroyed the confidence of man in God's unconditional love; it taught man to despise and distrust himself and others; it made him a tool instead of an end; it capitulated before secular power and relinquished the principle that secular power is not justified because of its mere existence if it contradicts moral principles; and in doing all this it relinquished elements that had been the foundations of Judaeo-Christian tradition. Its doctrines presented a picture of the individual, God, and the world, in which these feelings were justified by the belief that the insignificance and powerlessness which an individual felt came from the qualities of man as such and that he *ought* to feel as he felt.

Thereby the new religious doctrines not only gave expression to what the average member of the middle class felt, but, by rationalizing and systematizing this attitude, they also increased and strengthened it. However, they did more than that; they also showed the individual a way to cope with his anxiety. They taught him that by fully accepting his powerlessness and the evilness of his nature, by considering his whole life an atonement for his sins, by the utmost self-humiliation, and also by unceasing effort, he could overcome his doubt and his anxiety; that by complete submission he could be loved by God and could at least hope to belong to those whom God had decided to save. Protestantism was the answer to the human needs of the frightened, uprooted, and isolated individual who had to orient and to relate himself to a new world. The new character structure, resulting from economic and social changes and intensified by religious doctrines, became in its turn an important factor in shaping the further social and economic development. Those very qualities which were rooted in this character structure—compulsion to work, passion for thrift, the readiness to make one's life a tool for the purposes of an extra personal power, asceticism, and a compulsive sense of duty—were character traits which became productive forces in capitalistic society and without which modern economic and social development are unthinkable; they were the specific forms into which human energy was shaped and in which it became one of the productive forces within the social process. To act in accord with the newly formed character traits was advantageous from the standpoint of economic necessities; it was also satisfying psychologically, since such action answered the needs and anxieties of this new kind of personality. To put the same principle in more general terms: the social process, by determining the mode of life of the individual, that is, his relation to others and to work, molds his character structure; new ideologies—religious, philosophical, or political—result from and appeal to this changed character structure and thus intensify, satisfy, and stabilize it; the newly formed character traits in their turn become important factors in further economic development and influence the social process; while originally they have developed as a reaction to the threat of new economic forces, they slowly become productive forces furthering and intensifying the new economic development.[53]

[53] A more detailed discussion of the interaction between socioeconomic, ideological, and psychological factors is given in the Appendix.

CHAPTER IV

The Two Aspects of Freedom for Modern Man

THE previous chapter has been devoted to an analysis of the psychological meaning of the main doctrines of Protestantism. It showed that the new religious doctrines were an answer to psychic needs which in themselves were brought about by the collapse of the medieval social system and by the beginnings of capitalism. The analysis centered about the problem of freedom in its twofold meaning; it showed that freedom *from* the traditional bonds of medieval society, though giving the individual a new feeling of independence, at the same time made him feel alone and isolated, filled him with doubt and anxiety, and drove him into new submission and into a compulsive and irrational activity.

In this chapter, I wish to show that the further development of capitalistic society affected personality in the same direction which it had started to take in the period of the Reformation.

By the doctrines of Protestantism, man was psychologically prepared for the role he was to play under the modern industrial system. This system, its practice, and the spirit which grew out of it, reaching every aspect of life, molded the whole personality of man and accentuated the contradictions which we have discussed in the previous chapter: it developed the individual—and made him more helpless; it increased freedom—and created dependencies of a new kind. We do not attempt to describe the effect of capitalism on the whole character structure of man, since we are focused only on one aspect of this general problem: the dialectic character of the process of growing freedom. Our aim will be to show that the structure of modern society affects man in two ways simultaneously: he becomes more independent, self-reliant, and critical, and he becomes more isolated, alone, and afraid. The understanding of the whole problem of freedom depends on the very ability to see both sides of the process and not to lose track of one side while following the other.

This is difficult because conventionally we think in non-dialectical terms and are prone to doubt whether two contradictory trends can result simultaneously from one cause. Furthermore, the negative side of freedom, the burden which it puts upon man, is difficult to realize, especially for those whose heart is with the cause of freedom. Because in the fight for freedom in modern history the attention was focused upon combating *old* forms of authority and restraint, it was natural that one should feel that the more these traditional restraints were eliminated, the more freedom one had gained. We fail sufficiently to recognize, however, that although man has rid himself from old enemies of freedom, new enemies of a different nature have arisen; enemies which are not essentially external restraints, but internal factors blocking the full realization of the freedom of personality. We believe, for instance, that freedom of worship constitutes one of the final victories for freedom. We do not sufficiently recognize that while it is a victory against those powers of Church and State which

did not allow man to worship according to his own conscience, the modern individual has lost to a great extent
the inner capacity to have faith in anything which is not
provable by the methods of the natural sciences. Or, to
choose another example, we feel that freedom of speech is
the last step in the march of victory of freedom. We forget
that, although freedom of speech constitutes an important
victory in the battle against old restraints, modern man is
in a position where much of what "he" thinks and says are
the things that everybody else thinks and says; that he has
not acquired the ability to think originally—that is, for himself—which alone gives meaning to his claim that nobody
can interfere with the expression of his thoughts. Again,
we are proud that in his conduct of life man has become
free from external authorities, which tell him what to do
and what not to do. We neglect the role of the anonymous
authorities like public opinion and "common sense,"
which are so powerful because of our profound readiness
to conform to the expectations everybody has about ourselves and our equally profound fear of being different. In
other words, we are fascinated by the growth of freedom
from powers outside of ourselves and are blinded to the fact
of inner restraints, compulsions, and fears, which tend to
undermine the meaning of the victories freedom has won
against its traditional enemies. We therefore are prone to
think that the problem of freedom is exclusively that of
gaining still more freedom of the kind we have gained in
the course of modern history, and to believe that the defense of freedom against such powers that deny such freedom is all that is necessary. We forget that, although each
of the liberties which have been won must be defended

with utmost vigor, the problem of freedom is not only a quantitative one, but a qualitative one; that we not only have to preserve and increase the traditional freedom, but that we have to gain a new kind of freedom, one which enables us to realize our own individual self, to have faith in this self and in life.

Any critical evaluation of the effect which the industrial system had on this kind of inner freedom must start with the full understanding of the enormous progress which capitalism has meant for the development of human personality. As a matter of fact, any critical appraisal of modern society which neglects this side of the picture must prove to be rooted in an irrational romanticism and is suspect of criticizing capitalism, not for the sake of progress, but for the sake of the destruction of the most important achievements of man in modern history.

What Protestantism had started to do in freeing man spiritually, capitalism continued to do mentally, socially, and politically. Economic freedom was the basis of this development, the middle class was its champion. The individual was no longer bound by a fixed social system, based on tradition and with a comparatively small margin for personal advancement beyond the traditional limits. He was allowed and expected to succeed in personal economic gains as far as his diligence, intelligence, courage, thrift, or luck would lead him. His was the chance of success, his was the risk to lose and to be one of those killed or wounded in the fierce economic battle in which each one fought against everybody else. Under the feudal system the limits of his life expansion had been laid out before he was born; but under the capitalistic system the individual, particularly the member of the middle class, had a chance—in spite of many limitations—to succeed on the basis of his own merits and actions. He saw a goal before his eyes toward which he could strive and which he often had a good chance to attain. He learned to rely on himself, to make responsible decisions, to give up both soothing and terrifying superstitions. Man became increasingly free from the bondage of nature; he mastered natural forces to a degree unheard and undreamed of in previous history. Men became equal, differences of caste and religion, which once had been natural boundaries blocking the unification of the human race, disappeared, and men learned to recognize each other as human beings. The world became increasingly free from mystifying elements; man began to see himself objectively and with fewer and fewer illusions. Politically freedom grew too. On the strength of its economic position the rising middle class could conquer political power and the newly won political power created increased possibilities for economic progress. The great revolutions in England and France and the fight for American independence are the milestones marking this development. The peak in the evolution of freedom in the political sphere was the modern democratic state based on the principle of equality of all men and the equal right of everybody to share in the government by representatives of his own choosing. Each one was supposed to be able to act according to his own interest and at the same time with a view to the common welfare of the nation.

In one word, capitalism not only freed man from traditional bonds, but it also contributed tremendously to the increasing of positive freedom, to the growth of an active, critical, responsible self.

However, while this was one effect capitalism had on the process of growing freedom, at the same time it made the individual more alone and isolated and imbued him with a feeling of insignificance and powerlessness.

The first factor to be mentioned here is one of the general characteristics of capitalistic economy: the principle of individualistic activity. In contrast to the feudal system of the Middle Ages under which everybody had a fixed place in an ordered and transparent social system, capitalistic economy put the individual entirely on his own feet. What he did, how he did it, whether he succeeded or whether he failed, was entirely his own affair. That this principle furthered the process of individualization is obvious and is always mentioned as an important item on the credit side of modern culture. But in furthering "freedom from," this principle helped to sever all ties between one individual and the other and thereby isolated and separated the individual from his fellow men. This development had been prepared by the teachings of the Reformation. In the Catholic Church the relationship of the individual to God had been based on membership in the Church. The Church was the link between him and God, thus on the one hand restricting his individuality, but on the other hand letting him face God as an integral part of a group. Protestantism made the individual face God alone. Faith in Luther's sense was an entirely subjective experience and with Calvin the conviction of salvation also had this same subjective quality. The individual facing God's might alone could not

help feeling crushed and seeking salvation in complete submission. Psychologically this spiritual individualism is not
too different from the economic individualism. In both instances the individual is completely alone and in his isolation faces the superior power, be it of God, of competitors,
or of impersonal economic forces. *The individualistic relationship to God was the psychological preparation for the
individualistic character of man's secular activities.*

While the individualistic character of the economic system is an undisputed fact and only the effect this economic
individualism has in increasing the individual's aloneness
may appear doubtful, the point we are going to discuss
now contradicts some of the most widespread conventional
concepts about capitalism. These concepts assume that in
modern society man has become the center and purpose of
all activity, that what he does he does for himself, that the
principle of self-interest and egotism are the all-powerful
motivations of human activity. It follows from what has
been said in the beginning of this chapter that we believe
this to be true to some extent. Man has done much for
himself, for his own purposes, in these last four hundred
years. Yet much of what seemed to him to be *his* purpose
was not his, if we mean by "him," not "the worker," "the
manufacturer," but the concrete human being with all his
emotional, intellectual, and sensuous potentialities. Besides
the affirmation of the individual which capitalism brought
about, it also led to a self-negation and asceticism which is
the direct continuation of the Protestant spirit.

In order to explain this thesis we must mention first a
fact which has been already stated in the previous chapter.
In the medieval system capital was the servant of man, but

in the modern system it became his master. In the medieval world economic activities were a means to an end; the
end was life itself, or—as the Catholic Church understood
it—the spiritual salvation of man. Economic activities are
necessary, even riches can serve God's purposes, but all
external activity has only significance and dignity as far as
it furthers the aims of life. Economic activity and the wish
for gain for its own sake appeared as irrational to the medieval thinker as their absence appears to modern thought.
 In capitalism economic activity, success, material gains,
become ends in themselves. It becomes man's fate to contribute to the growth of the economic system, to amass
capital, not for purposes of his own happiness or salvation,
but as an end in itself. Man became a cog in the vast economic machine—an important one if he had much capital,
an insignificant one if he had none—but always a cog to
serve a purpose outside of himself. This readiness for submission of one's self to extrahuman ends was actually prepared by Protestantism, although nothing was further from
Luther's or Calvin's mind than the approval of such su-
premacy of economic activities. But in their theological
teaching they had laid the ground for this development by
breaking man's spiritual backbone, his feeling of dignity
and pride, by teaching him that activity had to further aims
outside of himself.

As we have seen in the previous chapter, one main point
in Luther's teachings was his emphasis on the evilness of
human nature, the uselessness of his will and of his efforts.
Calvin placed the same emphasis on the wickedness of
man and put in the center of his whole system the idea
that man must humiliate his self-pride to the utmost; and

furthermore, that the purpose of man's life is exclusively God's glory and nothing of his own. Thus Luther and Calvin psychologically prepared man for the role which he had to assume in modern society: of feeling his own self to be insignificant and of being ready to subordinate his life exclusively for purposes which were not his own. Once man was ready to become nothing but the means for the glory of a God who represented neither justice nor love, he was sufficiently prepared to accept the role of a servant to the economic machine—and eventually a "Führer."

The subordination of the individual as a means to economic ends is based on the peculiarities of the capitalistic mode of production, which makes the accumulation of capital the purpose and aim of economic activity. One works for profit's sake, but the profit one makes is not made to be spent but to be invested as new capital; this increased capital brings new profits which again are invested, and so on in a circle. There were of course always capitalists who spent money for luxuries or as "conspicuous waste"; but the classic representatives of capitalism enjoyed working—not spending. This principle of accumulating capital instead of using it for consumption is the premise of the grandiose achievements of our modern industrial system. If man had not had the ascetic attitude to work and the desire to invest the fruits of his work for the purpose of developing the productive capacities of the economic system, our progress in mastering nature never could have been made; it is this growth of the productive forces of society which for the first time in history permits us to visualize a future in which the continual struggle for the satisfaction of material needs will cease. Yet, while the principle of work for the sake of the accumulation of capital objectively is of enormous value for the progress of mankind, subjectively it has made man work for extrapersonal ends, made him a servant to the very machine he built, and thereby has given him a feeling of personal insignificance and powerlessness.

So far we have discussed those individuals in modern society who had capital and were able to turn their profits into new capital investment. Regardless of whether they were big or small capitalists, their life was devoted to the fulfillment of their economic function, the amassing of capital. But what about those who had no capital and who had to earn a living by selling their labor? The psychological effect of their economic position was not much different from that of the capitalist. In the first place, being employed meant that they were dependent on the laws of the market, on prosperity and depression, on the effect of technical improvements in the hands of their employer. They were manipulated directly by him, and to them he became the representative of a superior power to which they had to submit. This was especially true for the position of workers up to and during the nineteenth century. Since then the trade-union movement has given the worker some power of his own and thereby is changing the situation in which he is nothing but an object of manipulation.

But aside from this direct and personal dependence of the worker on the employer, he, like the whole of society, has been imbued by the spirit of asceticism and submission to extrapersonal ends which we have described as characteristic for the owner of capital. This is not surprising. In any society the spirit of the whole culture is determined by the spirit of those groups that are most powerful in that society. This is so partly because these groups have the power to control the educational system, schools, church, press, theater, and thereby to imbue the whole population with their own ideas; furthermore, these powerful groups carry so much prestige that the lower classes are more than ready to accept and imitate their values and to identify themselves psychologically.

Up to this point we have maintained that the mode of capitalistic production made man an instrument for suprapersonal economic purposes, and increased the spirit of asceticism and individual insignificance for which Protestantism had been the psychological preparation. This thesis, however, conflicts with the fact that modern man seems to be motivated not by an attitude of sacrifice and asceticism but, on the contrary, by an extreme degree of egotism and by the pursuit of self-interest. How can we reconcile the fact that objectively he became a servant to ends which were not his, and yet that subjectively he believed himself to be motivated by his self-interest? How can we reconcile the spirit of Protestantism and its emphasis on unselfishness with the modern doctrine of egotism which claims, to use Machiavelli's formulation, that egotism is the strongest motive power of human behavior, that the desire for personal advantage is stronger than all moral considerations, that a man would rather see his own father die than lose his fortune? Can this contradiction be explained by the assumption that the emphasis on unselfishness was only an ideology to cover up the underlying egotism? Although this may be true to some extent, we do not believe that this is the full answer. To indicate in what direction the answer seems to lie, we have to concern ourselves with the psychological intricacies of the problem of selfishness.[1]

The assumption underlying the thinking of Luther and Calvin and also that of Kant and Freud, is: Selfishness is identical with self-love. To love others is a virtue, to love oneself is a sin. Furthermore, love for others and love for oneself are mutually exclusive.

Theoretically we meet here with a fallacy concerning the nature of love. Love is not primarily "caused" by a specific object, but a lingering quality in a person which is only actualized by a certain "object." Hatred is a passionate wish for destruction; love is a passionate affirmation of an "object"; it is not an "affect" but an active striving and inner relatedness, the aim of which is the happiness, growth, and freedom of its object.[2] It is a readiness which, in principle, can turn to any person and object including ourselves. Exclusive love is a contradiction in itself. To be sure, it is not accidental that a certain person becomes the "object" of manifest love. The factors conditioning such a specific choice are too numerous and too complex to be discussed here. The important point, however, is that love for a particular "object" is only the actualization and concentration of lingering love with regard to one person; it is not, as the idea of romantic love would have it, that there is only the one person in the world whom one can love, that it is the

---

[1] For a detailed discussion of this problem compare the writer's "Selfishness and Self-Love," *Psychiatry*, Vol. 2, No. 4, November, 1939.

[2] Sullivan has approached this formulation in his lectures. He states that the era of preadolescence is characterized by the appearance of impulses in interpersonal relations which make for a new type of satisfaction in place of the other person (the chum). Love, according to him, is a situation in which the satisfaction of the loved one is exactly as significant and desirable as that of the lover.

great chance of one's life to find that person, and that love for him results in a withdrawal from all others. The kind of love which can only be experienced with regard to one person demonstrates by this very fact that it is not love but a sado-masochistic attachment. The basic affirmation contained in love is directed toward the beloved person as an incarnation of essentially human qualities. Love for one person implies love for man as such. Love for man as such is not, as it is frequently supposed to be, an abstraction coming "after" the love for a specific person, or an enlargement of the experience with a specific "object"; it is its premise, although, genetically, it is acquired in the contact with concrete individuals.

From this it follows that my own self, in principle, is as much an object of my love as another person. The affirmation of my own life, happiness, growth, freedom, is rooted in the presence of the basic readiness of and ability for such an affirmation. If an individual has this readiness, he has it also toward himself; if he can only "love" others, he cannot love at all.

Selfishness is not identical with self-love but with its very opposite. Selfishness is one kind of greediness. Like all greediness, it contains an insatiability, as a consequence of which there is never any real satisfaction. Greed is a bottomless pit which exhausts the person in an endless effort to satisfy the need without ever reaching satisfaction. Close observation shows that while the selfish person is always anxiously concerned with himself, he is never satisfied, is always restless, always driven by the fear of not getting enough, of missing something, of being deprived of something. He is filled with burning envy of anyone who might have more. If we observe still closer, especially the unconscious dynamics, we find that this type of person is basically not fond of himself, but deeply dislikes himself.

The puzzle in this seeming contradiction is easy to solve. Selfishness is rooted in this very lack of fondness for oneself. The person who is not fond of himself, who does not approve of himself, is in constant anxiety concerning his own self. He has not the inner security which can exist only on the basis of genuine fondness and affirmation. He must be concerned about himself, greedy to get everything for himself, since basically he lacks security and satisfaction. The same holds true with the so-called narcissistic person, who is not so much concerned with getting things for himself as with admiring himself. While on the surface it seems that these persons are very much in love with themselves, they actually are not fond of themselves, and their narcissism—like selfishness—is an overcompensation for the basic lack of self-love. Freud has pointed out that the narcissistic person has withdrawn his love from others and turned it toward his own person. Although the first part of this statement is true, the second is a fallacy. He loves neither others nor himself.

Let us return now to the question which led us into this psychological analysis of selfishness. We found ourselves confronted with the contradiction that modern man believes himself to be motivated by self-interest and yet that actually his life is devoted to aims which are not his own; in the same way that Calvin felt that the only purpose of man's existence was to be not himself but God's glory. We tried to show that selfishness is rooted in the lack of affirmation and love for the real self, that is, for the whole concrete human being with all his potentialities. The "self" in the interest of which modern man acts is the social self, a self which is essentially constituted by the role the individual is supposed to play and which in reality is merely the subjective disguise for the objective social function of man in society. Modern selfishness is the greed that is rooted in the frustration of the real self and whose object is the social self. While modern man seems to be characterized by utmost assertion of the self, actually his self has been weakened and reduced to a segment of the total self—intellect and will power—to the exclusion of all other parts of the total personality.

Even if this is true, has not the increasing mastery over nature resulted in an increased strength of the individual self? This is true to some extent, and inasmuch as it is true it concerns the positive side of individual development which we do not want to lose track of. But although man has reached a remarkable degree of mastery of nature, society is not in control of the very forces it has created. The rationality of the system of production, in its technical aspects, is accompanied by the irrationality of our system of production in its social aspects. Economic crises, unemployment, war, govern man's fate. Man has built his world; he has built factories and houses, he produces cars and clothes, he grows grain and fruit. But he has become estranged from the product of his own hands, he is not really the master any more of the world he has built; on the contrary, this man-made world has become his master, before whom he bows down, whom he tries to placate or to manipulate as best he can. The work of his own hands has become his God. He seems to be driven by self-interest, but in reality his total self with all its concrete potentialities has become an instrument for the purposes of the very machine his hands have built. He keeps up the illusion of being the center of the world, and yet he is pervaded by an intense sense of insignificance and powerlessness which his ancestors once consciously felt toward God.

Modern man's feeling of isolation and powerlessness is increased still further by the character which all his human relationships have assumed. The concrete relationship of one individual to another has lost its direct and human character and has assumed a spirit of manipulation and instrumentality. In all social and personal relations the laws of the market are the rule. It is obvious that the relationship between competitors has to be based on mutual human indifference. Otherwise any one of them would be paralyzed in the fulfillment of his economic tasks—to fight each other and not to refrain from the actual economic destruction of each other if necessary.

The relationship between employer and employee is permeated by the same spirit of indifference. The word "employer" contains the whole story: the owner of capital employs another human being as he "employs" a machine. They both use each other for the pursuit of their economic interests; their relationship is one in which both are means to an end, both are instrumental to each other. It is not a relationship of two human beings who have any interest in the other outside of this mutual usefulness. The same instrumentality is the rule in the relationship between the businessman and his customer. The customer is an object to be manipulated, not a concrete person whose aims the businessman is interested to satisfy. The attitude toward work has the quality of instrumentality; in contrast to a medieval artisan the modern manufacturer is not primarily interested in what he produces; he produces essentially in order to make a profit from his capital investment, and what he produces depends essentially on the market which promises that the investment of capital in a certain branch will prove to be profitable.

Not only the economic, but also the personal relations between men have this character of alienation; instead of relations between human beings, they assume the character of relations between things. But perhaps the most important and the most devastating instance of this spirit of instrumentality and alienation is the individual's relationship to his own self.[3] Man does not only sell commodities, he sells himself and feels himself to be a commodity. The manual laborer sells his physical energy; the businessman, the physician, the clerical employee, sell their "personality." They have to have a "personality" if they are to sell their products or services. This personality should be pleasing, but besides that its possessor should meet a number of other requirements: he should have energy, initiative, this, that, or the other, as his particular position may require. As with any other commodity it is the market which decides the value of these human qualities, yes, even their very existence. If there is no use for the qualities a person offers, he *has* none; just as an unsalable commodity is valueless though it might have its use value. Thus, the self-confidence, the "feeling of self," is merely an indication of what others think of the person.

[3] Hegel and Marx have laid the foundations for the understanding of the problem of alienation. Cf. in particular Marx's concept of the "fetishism of commodities" and of the "alienation of labor."

It is not *he* who is convinced of his value regardless of popularity and his success on the market. If he is sought after, he is somebody; if he is not popular, he is simply nobody. This dependence of self-esteem on the success of the "personality" is the reason why for modern man popularity has this tremendous importance. On it depends not only whether or not one goes ahead in practical matters, but also whether one can keep up one's self-esteem or whether one falls into the abyss of inferiority feelings.[4]

We have tried to show that the new freedom which capitalism brought for the individual added to the effect which the religious freedom of Protestantism already had had upon him. The individual became more alone, isolated, became an instrument in the hands of overwhelmingly strong forces outside of himself; he became an "individual," but a bewildered and insecure individual. There were factors to help him overcome the overt manifestations of this underlying insecurity. In the first place his self was backed up by the possession of property. "He" as a person and the property he owned could not be separated. A man's clothes or his house were parts of his self just as much as his body. The less he felt he was being somebody the more he needed to have possessions. If the individual had no property or lost it, he was lacking an important part of his "self" and to a certain extent was not considered to be a full-fledged person, either by others or by himself.

Other factors backing up the self were prestige and power. They are partly the outcome of the possession of property, partly the direct result of success in the fields of

[4] This analysis of self-esteem has been stated clearly and explicitly by Ernest Schachtel in an unpublished lecture on "Self-feeling and the 'Sale' of Personality."

competition. The admiration by others and the power over them, added to the support which property gave, backed up the insecure individual self.

For those who had little property and social prestige, the family was a source of individual prestige. There the individual could feel like "somebody." He was obeyed by wife and children, he was the center of the stage, and he naïvely accepted his role as his natural right. He might be a nobody in his social relations, but he was a king at home. Aside from the family, the national pride (in Europe frequently class-pride) gave him a sense of importance also. Even if he was nobody personally, he was proud to belong to a group which he could feel was superior to other comparable groups.

These factors supporting the weakened self must be distinguished from those factors which we spoke of at the beginning of this chapter: the factual economic and political freedom, the opportunity for individual initiative, the growing rational enlightenment. These latter factors actually strengthened the self and led to the development of individuality, independence, and rationality. The supporting factors, on the other hand, only helped to compensate for insecurity and anxiety. They did not uproot them but covered them up, and thus helped the individual to feel secure consciously; but this feeling was partly only on the surface and lasted only to the extent to which the supporting factors were present.

Any detailed analysis of European and American history of the period between the Reformation and our own day could show how the two contradictory trends inherent in the evolution of "freedom from to freedom to" run parallel—or rather, are continuously interwoven. Unfortunately such an analysis goes beyond the scope of this book and must be reserved for another publication. At some periods and in certain social groups human freedom in its positive sense—strength and dignity of the self—was the dominant factor; broadly speaking this happened in England, France, America, and Germany when the middle class won its victories, economically and politically, over the representatives of an older order. In this fight for positive freedom the middle class could recur to that side of Protestantism which emphasized human autonomy and dignity; while the Catholic Church allied herself with those groups which had to fight the liberation of man in order to preserve their own privileges.

In the philosophical thinking of the modern era we find also that the two aspects of freedom remain interwoven as they had already been in the theological doctrines of the Reformation. Thus for Kant and Hegel autonomy and freedom of the individual are the central postulates of their systems, and yet they make the individual subordinate to the purposes of an all-powerful state. The philosophers of the period of the French Revolution, and in the nineteenth century Feuerbach, Marx, Stirner, and Nietzsche, have again in an uncompromising way expressed the idea that the individual should not be subject to any purposes external to his own growth or happiness. The reactionary philosophers of the same century, however, explicity postulated the subordination of the individual under spiritual and secular authority. The second half of the nineteenth century and the beginning of the twentieth show the trend for human freedom in its positive sense at its peak. Not

only did the middle class participate in it, but also the
working class became an active and free agent, fighting
for its own economic aims and at the same time for the
broader aims of humanity.

With the monopolistic phase of capitalism as it developed increasingly in the last decades, the respective
weight of both trends for human freedom seems to have
changed. Those factors which tend to weaken the individual self have gained, while those strengthening the individual have relatively lost in weight. The individual's feeling
of powerlessness and aloneness has increased, his "freedom" from all traditional bonds has become more pro-
nounced, his possibilities for individual economic achievement have narrowed down. He feels threatened by gigantic
forces and the situation resembles in many ways that of
the fifteenth and sixteenth centuries.

The most important factor in this development is the
increasing power of monopolistic capital. The concentration of capital (not of wealth) in certain sectors of our
economic system restricted the possibilities for the success
of individual initiative, courage, and intelligence. In those
sectors in which monopolistic capital has won its victories
the economic independence of many has been destroyed.
For those who struggle on, especially for a large part of
the middle class, the fight assumes the character of a battle
against such odds that the feeling of confidence in personal
initiative and courage is replaced by a feeling of powerlessness and hopelessness. An enormous though secret power
over the whole of society is exercised by a small group,
on the decisions of which depends the fate of a large part
of society. The inflation in Germany, 1923, or the Amer-

ican crash, 1929, increased the feeling of insecurity and shattered for many the hope of getting ahead by one's own efforts and the traditional belief in the unlimited possibilities of success.

The small or middle-sized businessman who is virtually threatened by the overwhelming power of superior capital may very well continue to make profits and to preserve his independence; but the threat hanging over his head has increased his insecurity and powerlessness far beyond what it used to be. In his fight against monopolistic competitors he is staked against giants, whereas he used to fight against equals. But the psychological situation of those independent businessmen for whom the development of modern industry has created new economic functions is also different from that of the old independent businessmen. One illustration of this difference is seen in a type of independent businessman who is sometimes quoted as an example of the growth of a new type of middle-class existence: the owners of gas stations. Many of them are economically independent. They own their business just like a man who owned a grocery store or the tailor who made men's suits. But what a difference between the old and the new type of independent businessman. The grocery-store owner needed a good deal of knowledge and skill. He had a choice of a number of wholesale merchants to buy from and he could pick them according to what he deemed the best prices and qualities; he had many individual customers whose needs he had to know, whom he had to advise in their buying, and with regard to whom he had to decide whether or not to give them credit. On the whole, the role of the old-fashioned businessman was not only one of independence but also one requiring skill, individualized service, knowledge, and activity. The situation of the gas-station owner, on the other hand, is entirely different. There is the one merchandise he sells; oil and gas. He is limited in his bargaining position with the oil companies. He mechanically repeats the same act of filling in gasoline and oil, again and again. There is less room for skill, initiative, individual activity, than the old-time grocery-store owner had. His profit is determined by two factors: the price he has to pay for the gasoline and oil, and the number of motorists who stop at his gas station. Both factors are largely outside of his control; he just functions as an agent between wholesaler and customer. Psychologically it makes little difference whether he is employed by the concern or whether he is an "independent" businessman; he is merely a cog in the vast machine of distribution.

As to the new middle class consisting of white-collar workers, whose numbers have grown with the expansion of big business, it is obvious that their position is very different from that of the old-type, small, independent businessman. One might argue that although they are not independent any longer in a formal sense, actually the opportunities for the development of initiative and intelligence as a basis for success are as great as or even greater than they were for the old-fashioned tailor or grocery-store owner. This is certainly true in a sense, although it may be doubtful to what extent. But psychologically the white collar worker's situation is different. He is part of a vast economic machine, has a highly specialized task, is in fierce competition with hundreds of others who are in the same position, and is mercilessly fired if he falls behind. In short, even if his chances for success are sometimes greater, he has lost a great deal of the security and independence of the old businessman; and he has been turned into a cog, sometimes small, sometimes larger, of a machinery which forces its tempo upon him, which he cannot control, and in comparison with which he is utterly insignificant.

The psychological effect of the vastness and superior power of big enterprise has also its effect on the worker. In the smaller enterprise of the old days, the worker knew his boss personally and was familiar with the whole enterprise which he was able to survey; although he was hired and fired according to the law of the market, there was some concrete relation to his boss and the business which gave him a feeling of knowing the ground on which he stood. The man in a plant which employs thousands of workers is in a different position. The boss has become an abstract figure —he never sees him; the "management" is an anonymous power with which he deals indirectly and toward which he as an individual is insignificant. The enterprise has such proportions that he cannot see beyond the small sector of it connected with his particular job.

This situation has been somewhat balanced by the trade unions. They have not only improved the economic position of the worker, but have also had the important psychological effect of giving him a feeling of strength and significance in comparison with the giants he is dealing with. Unfortunately many unions themselves have grown into mammoth organizations in which there is little room for the initiative of the individual member. He pays his dues and votes from time to time but here again he is a small cog in a large machine. It is of utmost importance that the unions become organs supported by the active co-operation of each member and of organizing them in such a way that each member may actively participate in the life of the organization and feel responsible for what is going on.

The insignificance of the individual in our era concerns not only his role as a businessman, employee, or manual laborer, but also his role as a customer. A drastic change has occurred in the role of the customer in the last decades. The customer who went into a retail store owned by an independent businessman was sure to get personal attention: his individual purchase was important to the owner of the store; he was received like somebody who mattered, his wishes were studied; the very act of buying gave him a feeling of importance and dignity. How different is the relationship of a customer to a department store. He is impressed by the vastness of the building, the number of employees, the profusion of commodities displayed; all this makes him feel small and unimportant by comparison. As an individual he is of no importance to the department store. He is important as "a" customer; the store does not want to lose him, because this would indicate that there was something wrong and it might mean that the store would lose other customers for the same reason. As an abstract customer he is important; as a concrete customer he is utterly unimportant. There is nobody who is glad about his coming, nobody who is particularly concerned about his wishes. The act of buying has become similar to going to the post office and buying stamps.

This situation is still more emphasized by the methods of modern advertising. The sales talk of the old-fashioned businessman was essentially rational. He knew his merchandise, he knew the needs of the customer, and on the basis of this knowledge he tried to sell. To be sure, his sales talk was not entirely objective and he used persuasion as much as he could; yet, in order to be efficient, it had to be a rather rational and sensible kind of talk. A vast sector of modern advertising is different; it does not appeal to reason but to emotion; like any other kind of hypnoid suggestion, it tries to impress its objects emotionally and then make them submit intellectually. This type of advertising impresses the customer by all sorts of means: by repetition of the same formula again and again; by the influence of an authoritative image, like that of a society lady or of a famous boxer, who smokes a certain brand of cigarette; by attracting the customer and at the same time weakening his critical abilities by the sex appeal of a pretty girl; by terrorizing him with the threat of "b.o." or "halitosis"; or yet again by stimulating daydreams about a sudden change in one's whole course of life brought about by buying a certain shirt or soap. All these methods are essentially irrational; they have nothing to do with the qualities of the merchandise, and they smother and kill the critical capacities of the customer like an opiate or outright hypnosis. They give him a certain satisfaction by their daydreaming qualities just as the movies do, but at the same time they increase his feeling of smallness and powerlessness.

As a matter of fact, these methods of dulling the capacity for critical thinking are more dangerous to our democracy than many of the open attacks against it, and more immoral—in terms of human integrity—than the indecent literature, publication of which we punish. The consumer movement has attempted to restore the customer's critical ability, dignity, and sense of significance, and thus operates in a direction similar to the trade-union movement. So far, however, its scope has not grown beyond modest beginnings.

What holds true in the economic sphere is also true in the political sphere. In the early days of democracy there were various kinds of arrangements in which the individual would concretely and actively participate in voting for a certain decision or for a certain candidate for office. The questions to be decided were familiar to him, as were the candidates; the act of voting, often done in a meeting of the whole population of a town, had a quality of concreteness in which the individual really counted. Today the voter is confronted by mammoth parties which are just as distant and as impressive as the mammoth organizations of industry. The issues are complicated and made still more so by all sorts of methods to befog them. The voter may see something of his candidate around election time; but since the days of the radio, he is not likely to see him so often, thus losing one of the last means of sizing up "his" candidate. Actually he is offered a choice between two or three candidates by the party machines; but these candidates are not of "his" choosing, he and they know little of each other, and their relationship is as abstract as most other relationships have become.

Like the effect of advertising upon the customer, the methods of political propaganda tend to increase the feeling of insignificance of the individual voter. Repetition of slogans and emphasis on factors which have nothing to do with the issue at stake numb his critical capacities. The clear and rational appeal to his thinking are rather the exception than the rule in political propaganda—even in democratic countries. Confronted with the power and size of the parties as demonstrated in their propaganda, the individual voter cannot help feeling small and of little significance.

All this does not mean that advertising and political propaganda overtly stress the individual's insignificance. Quite the contrary; they flatter the individual by making him appear important, and by pretending that they appeal to his critical judgment, to his sense of discrimination. But these pretenses are essentially a method to dull the individual's suspicions and to help him fool himself as to the individual character of his decision. I need scarcely point out that the propaganda of which I have been speaking is not wholly irrational, and that there are differences in the weight of rational factors in the propaganda of different parties and candidates respectively.

Other factors have added to the growing powerlessness of the individual. The economic and political scene is more complex and vaster than it used to be; the individual has less ability to look through it. The threats which he is confronted with have grown in dimensions too. A structural unemployment of many millions has increased the sense of insecurity. Although the support of the unemployed by public means has done much to counteract the results of unemployment, not only economically but also psychologically, the fact remains that for the vast majority of people the burden of being unemployed is very hard to bear psychologically and the dread of it overshadows their whole life. To have a job—regardless of what kind of a job it is—seems to many all they could want of life and something they should be grateful for. Unemployment has also increased the threat of old age. In many jobs only the young and even inexperienced person who is still adaptable is wanted; that means, those who can still be molded without difficulty into the little cogs which are required in that particular setup.

The threat of war has also added to the feeling of individual powerlessness. To be sure, there were wars in the nineteenth century too. But since the last war the possibilities of destruction have increased so tremendously—the range of people to be affected by war has grown to such an extent as to comprise everybody without any exception —that the threat of war has become a nightmare which, though it may not be conscious to many people before their nation is actually involved in the war, has overshadowed their lives and increased their feeling of fright and individual powerlessness.

The "style" of the whole period corresponds to the picture I have sketched. Vastness of cities in which the individual is lost, buildings that are as high as mountains, constant acoustic bombardment by the radio, big headlines changing three times a day and leaving one no choice to decide what is important, shows in which one hundred girls demonstrate their ability with clocklike precision to eliminate the individual and act like a powerful though smooth machine, the beating rhythm of jazz—these and many other details are expressions of a constellation in which the individual is confronted by uncontrollable dimensions in comparison with which he is a small particle. All he can do is to fall in step like a marching soldier or a worker on the endless belt. He can act; but the sense of independence, significance, has gone.

The extent to which the average person in America is filled with the same sense of fear and insignificance seems to find a telling expression in the fact of the popularity of the Mickey Mouse pictures. There the one theme—in so many variations—is always this: something little is persecuted and endangered by something overwhelmingly strong, which threatens to kill or swallow the little thing. The little thing runs away and eventually succeeds in escaping or even in harming the enemy. People would not be ready to look continually at the many variations of this one theme unless it touched upon something very close to their own emotional life. Apparently the little thing threatened by a powerful, hostile enemy is the spectator himself; that is how he feels and that is the situation with which he can identify himself. But of course, unless there were a happy ending there would be no continuous attraction. As it is, the spectator lives through all his own fears and feelings of smallness and at the end gets the comforting feeling that, in spite of all, he will be saved and will even conquer the strong one. However—and this is the significant and sad part of this "happy end"—his salvation lies mostly in his ability to run away and in the unforeseen accidents which make it impossible for the monster to catch him.

The position in which the individual finds himself in our period had already been foreseen by visionary thinkers in the nineteenth century. Kierkegard describes the helpless individual torn and tormented by doubts, overwhelmed by the feeling of aloneness and insignificance. Nietzsche visualizes the approaching nihilism which was to become manifest in Nazism and paints a picture of a "superman" as the negation of the insignificant, directionless individual he saw in reality. The theme of the powerlessness of man has found a most precise expression in Franz Kaffka's work. In his *Castle* he describes the man who wants to get in touch with the mysterious inhabitants of a castle, who are supposed to tell him what to do and show him his place in the world. All his life consists in his frantic effort to get into touch with them, but he never succeeds and is left alone with a sense of utter futility and helplessness.

The feeling of isolation and powerlessness has been beautifully expressed in the following passage by Julian Green: "I knew that we counted little in comparison with the universe, I knew that we were nothing; but to be so immeasurably nothing seems in some way both to overwhelm and at the same time to reassure. Those figures, those dimensions beyond the range of human thought, are utterly overpowering. Is there anything whatsoever to which we can cling? Amid that chaos of illusions into which we are cast headlong, there is one thing that stands out as true, and that is—love. All the rest is nothingness, an empty void. We peer down into a huge dark abyss. And we are afraid."[5]

However, this feeling of individual isolation and power-

---

[5] Julian Green, *Personal Record, 1928–1939,* translated by J. Godefroi Harper & Brothers, New York, 1939.

lessness as it has been expressed by these writers and as it is felt by many so-called neurotic people, is nothing the average normal person is aware of. It is too frightening for that. It is covered over by the daily routine of his activities, by the assurance and approval he finds in his private or social relations, by success in business, by any number of distractions, by "having fun," "making contacts," "going places." But whistling in the dark does not bring light. Aloneness, fear, and bewilderment remain; people cannot stand it for ever. They cannot go on bearing the burden of "freedom from"; they must try to escape from freedom altogether unless they can progress from negative to positive freedom. The principal social avenues of escape in our time are the submission to a leader, as has happened in Fascist countries, and the compulsive conforming as is prevalent in our own democracy. Before we come to describe these two socially patterned ways of escape, I must ask the reader to follow me into the discussion of the intricacies of these psychological mechanisms of escape. We have dealt with some of these mechanisms already in the previous chapters; but in order to understand fully the psychological significance of Fascism and the automatization of man in modern democracy, it is necessary to understand the psychological phenomena not only in a general way but in the very detail and concreteness of their operation. This may appear to be a detour; but actually it is a necessary part of our whole discussion. Just as one cannot properly understand psychological problems without their social and cultural background, neither can one understand social phenomena without the knowledge of the underlying psychological mechanisms. The following chapter attempts to analyze these mechanisms, to reveal what is going on in the individual, and to show how, in our effort to escape from aloneness and powerlessness, we are ready to get rid of our individual self either by submission to new forms of authority or by a compulsive conforming to accepted patterns.

CHAPTER V

Mechanisms of Escape

WE have brought our discussion up to the present period and would now proceed to discuss the psychological significance of Fascism and the meaning of freedom in the authoritarian systems and in our own democracy. However, since the validity of our whole argument depends on the validity of our psychological premises, it seems desirable to interrupt the general trend of thought and devote a chapter to a more detailed and concrete discussion of those psychological mechanisms which we have already touched upon and which we are later going to discuss. These premises require a detailed discussion because they are based on concepts which deal with unconscious forces and the ways in which they find expression in rationalizations and character traits, concepts which for many readers will seem, if not foreign, at least to warrant elaboration.

In this chapter I intentionally refer to individual psychology and to observations that have been made in the minute studies of individuals by the psychoanalytic procedure. Although psychoanalysis does not live up to the ideal which for many years was the ideal of academic psychology, that is, the approximation of the experimental methods of the natural sciences, it is nevertheless a thoroughly empirical method, based on the painstaking observation of an individual's uncensored thoughts, dreams, and phantasies. Only a psychology which utilizes the concept of unconscious forces can penetrate the confusing rationalizations we are confronted with in analyzing either an individual or a culture. A great number of apparently insoluble problems disappear at once if we decide to give up the notion that the motives by which people *believe* themselves to be motivated are necessarily the ones which actually drive them to act, feel, and think as they do.

Many a reader will raise the question whether findings won by the observation of individuals can be applied to the psychological understanding of groups. Our answer to this question is an emphatic affirmation. Any group consists of individuals and nothing but individuals, and psychological mechanisms which we find operating in a group can therefore only be mechanisms that operate in individuals. In studying individual psychology as a basis for the understanding of social psychology, we do something which might be compared with studying an object under the microscope. This enables us to discover the very details of psychological mechanisms which we find operating on a large scale in the social process. If our analysis of socio-psychological phenomena is not based on the detailed study of individual behavior, it lacks empirical character and, therefore, validity.

But even admitted that the study of individual behavior has such significance, one might question whether the study of individuals who are commonly labeled as neurotics can be of any use in considering the problems of social psychology. Again, we believe that this question must be answered in the affirmative. The phenomena which we observe in the neurotic person are in principle not different from those we find in the normal. They are only more accentuated, clearcut, and frequently more accessible to the awareness of the neurotic person than they are in the normal who is not aware of any problem which warrants study.

In order to make this clearer, a brief discussion of the terms neurotic and normal, or healthy, seems to be useful.

The term normal or healthy can be defined in two ways. Firstly, from the standpoint of a functioning society, one can call a person normal or healthy if he is able to fulfill the social role he is to take in that given society. More concretely, this means that he is able to work in the fashion which is required in that particular society, and furthermore that he is able to participate in the reproduction of society, that is, that he can raise a family. Secondly, from the standpoint of the individual, we look upon health or normalcy as the optimum of growth and happiness of the individual.

If the structure of a given society were such that it offered the optimum possibility for individual happiness, both viewpoints would coincide. However, this is not the case in most societies we know, including our own. Although they differ in the degree to which they promote the aims of individual growth, there is a discrepancy between the aims of the smooth functioning of society and of the full development of the individual. This fact makes it imperative to differentiate sharply between the two concepts of health. The one is governed by social necessities, the other by values and norms concerning the aim of individual existence.

Unfortunately, this differentiation is often neglected.

Most psychiatrists take the structure of their own society so much for granted that to them the person who is not well adapted assumes the stigma of being less valuable. On the other hand, the well-adapted person is supposed to be the more valuable person in terms of a scale of human values. If we differentiate the two concepts of normal and neurotic, we come to the following conclusion: the person who is normal in terms of being well adapted is often less healthy than the neurotic person in terms of human values. Often he is well adapted only at the expense of having given up his self in order to become more or less the person he believes he is expected to be. All genuine individuality and spontaneity may have been lost. On the other hand, the neurotic person can be characterized as somebody who was not ready to surrender completely in the battle for his self. To be sure, his attempt to save his individual self was not successful, and instead of expressing his self productively he sought salvation through neurotic symptoms and by withdrawing into a phantasy life. Nevertheless, from the standpoint of human values, he is less crippled than the kind of normal person who has lost his individuality altogether. Needless to say there are persons who are not neurotic and yet have not drowned their individuality in the process of adaptation. But the stigma attached to the neurotic person seems to us to be unfounded and justified only if we think of neurotic in terms of social efficiency. As for a whole society, the term neurotic cannot be applied in this latter sense, since a society could not exist if its members did not function socially. From a standpoint of human values, however, a society could be called neurotic in the sense that its members are crippled in the growth of their personality. Since the term neurotic is so often used to denote lack of social functioning, we would prefer not to speak of a society in terms of its being neurotic, but rather in terms of its being adverse to human happiness and self-realization.

The mechanisms we shall discuss in this chapter are mechanisms of escape, which result from the insecurity of the isolated individual.

Once the primary bonds which gave security to the individual are severed, once the individual faces the world outside of himself as a completely separate entity, two courses are open to him since he has to overcome the unbearable state of powerlessness and aloneness. By one course he can progress to "positive freedom"; he can relate himself spontaneously to the world in love and work, in the genuine expression of his emotional, sensuous, and intellectual capacities; he can thus become one again with man, nature, and himself, without giving up the independence and integrity of his individual self. The other course open to him is to fall back, to give up his freedom, and to try to overcome his aloneness by eliminating the gap that has arisen between his individual self and the world. This second course never reunites him with the world in the way he was related to it before he merged as an "individual," for the fact of his separateness cannot be reversed; it is an escape from an unbearable situation which would make life impossible if it were prolonged. This course of escape, therefore, is characterized by its compulsive character, like every escape from threatening panic; it is also characterized by the more or less complete surrender of individuality and the integrity of the self. Thus it is not a solution which leads to happiness and positive freedom; it is, in principle, a solution which is to be found in all neurotic phenomena. It assuages an unbearable anxiety and makes life possible by avoiding panic; yet it does not *solve* the underlying problem and is paid for by a kind of life that often consists only of automatic or compulsive activities.

Some of these mechanisms of escape are of relatively small social import; they are to be found in any marked degree only in individuals with severe mental and emotional disturbances. In this chapter I shall discuss only those mechanisms which are culturally significant and the understanding of which is a necessary premise for the psychological analysis of the social phenomena with which we shall deal in the following chapters: the Fascist system, on one hand, modern democracy, on the other.[1]

1. AUTHORITARIANISM

The first mechanism of escape from freedom I am going to deal with is the tendency to give up the independence of one's own individual self and to fuse one's self with somebody or something outside of oneself in order to acquire the strength which the individual self is lacking. Or, to put it in different words, to seek for new, "secondary bonds" as a substitute for the primary bonds which have been lost.

The more distinct forms of this mechanism are to be

[1] From a different viewpoint K. Horney in her "neurotic trends" (*New Ways in Psychoanalysis*) has arrived at a concept which has certain similarities with my concept of the "mechanisms of escape." The main differences between the two concepts are these: the neurotic trends are the driving forces in individual neurosis while the mechanisms of escape are driving forces in normal man. Furthermore, Horney's main emphasis is on anxiety while mine is on the isolation of the individual.

found in the striving for submission and domination, or, as we would rather put it, in the masochistic and sadistic strivings as they exist in varying degrees in normal and neurotic persons respectively. We shall first describe these tendencies and then try to show that both of them are an escape from an unbearable aloneness.

The most frequent forms in which *masochistic* strivings appear are feelings of inferiority, powerlessness, individual insignificance. The analysis of persons who are obsessed by these feelings shows that, while they consciously complain about these feelings and want to get rid of them, unconsciously some power within themselves drives them to feel inferior or insignificant. Their feelings are more than realizations of actual shortcomings and weaknesses (although they are usually rationalized as though they were); these persons show a tendency to belittle themselves, to make themselves weak, and not to master things. Quite regularly these people show a marked dependence on powers outside of themselves, on other people, or institutions, or nature. They tend not to assert themselves, not to do what they want, but to submit to the factual or alleged orders of these outside forces. Often they are quite incapable of experiencing the feeling "I want" or "I am." Life, as a whole, is felt by them as something overwhelmingly powerful, which they cannot master or control.

In the more extreme cases—and there are many—one finds besides these tendencies to belittle oneself and to submit to outside forces a tendency to hurt oneself and to make oneself suffer.

This tendency can assume various forms. We find that there are people who indulge in self-accusation and self-criticism which even their worst enemies would scarcely bring against them. There are others, such as certain compulsive neurotics, who tend to torture themselves with compulsory rites and thoughts. In a certain type of neurotic personality, we find a tendency to become physically ill, and to wait, consciously or unconsciously, for an illness as if it were a gift of the gods. Often they incur accidents which would not have happened had there not been at work an unconscious tendency to incur them. These tendencies directed against themselves are often revealed in still less overt or dramatic forms. For instance, there are persons who are incapable of answering questions in an examination when the answers are vey well known to them at the time of the examination and even afterwards. There are others who say things which antagonize those whom they love or on whom they are dependent, although actually they feel friendly toward them and did not intend to say those things. With such people, it almost seems as if they were following advice given them by an enemy to behave in such a way as to be most detrimental to themselves.

The masochistic trends are often felt as plainly pathological or irrational. More frequently they are rationalized. Masochistic dependency is conceived as love or loyalty, inferiority feelings as an adequate expression of actual shortcomings, and one's suffering as being entirely due to unchangeable circumstances.

Besides these masochistic trends, the very opposite of them, namely, sadistic tendencies, are regularly to be found in the same kind of characters. They vary in strength, are more or less conscious, yet they are never missing. We find three kinds of sadistic tendencies, more or less closely knit together. One is to make others dependent on oneself and to have absolute and unrestricted power over them, so as to make of them nothing but instruments, "clay in the potter's hand." Another consists of the impulse not only to rule over others in this absolute fashion, but to exploit them, to use them, to steal from them, to disembowel them, and, so to speak, to incorporate anything eatable in them. This desire can refer to material things as well as to immaterial ones, such as the emotional or intellectual qualities a person has to offer. A third kind of sadistic tendency is the wish to make others suffer or to see them suffer. This suffering can be physical, but more often it is mental suffering. Its aim is to hurt actively, to humiliate, embarrass others, or to see them in embarrassing and humiliating situations.

Sadistic tendencies for obvious reasons are usually less conscious and more rationalized than the socially more harmless masochistic trends. Often they are entirely covered up by reaction formations of overgoodness or over-concern for others. Some of the most frequent rationalizations are the following: "I rule over you because I know what is best for you, and in your own interest you should follow me without opposition." Or, "I am so wonderful and unique, that I have a right to expect that other people become dependent on me." Another rationalization which often covers the exploiting tendencies is: "I have done so much for you, and now I am entitled to take from you what I want." The more aggressive kind of sadistic impulses finds its most frequent rationalization in two forms: "I have been hurt by others and my wish to hurt them is nothing but retaliation," or, "By striking first I am defending myself or my friends against the danger of being hurt."

There is one factor in the relationship of the sadistic person to the object of his sadism which is often neglected and therefore deserves especial emphasis here: his dependence on the object of his sadism.

While the masochistic person's dependence is obvious, our expectation with regard to the sadistic person is just the reverse: he seems so strong and domineering, and the object of his sadism so weak and submissive, that it is difficult to think of the strong one as being dependent on the one over whom he rules. And yet close analysis shows that this is true. The sadist needs the person over whom he rules, he needs him very badly, since his own feeling of strength is rooted in the fact that he is the master over some one. This dependence may be entirely unconscious. Thus, for example, a man may treat his wife very sadistically and tell her repeatedly that she can leave the house any day and that he would be only too glad if she did. Often she will be so crushed that she will not dare to make an attempt to leave, and therefore they both will continue to believe that what he says is true. But if she musters up enough courage to declare that she will leave him, something quite unexpected to both of them may happen: he will become desperate, break down, and beg her not to leave him; he will say he cannot live without her, and will declare how much he loves her and so on. Usually, being afraid of asserting herself anyhow, she will be prone to believe him, change her decision and stay. At this point the play starts again. He resumes his old behavior, she finds it increasingly difficult to stay with him, explodes again, he breaks down again, she stays, and so on and on many times.

There are thousands upon thousands of marriages and other personal relationships in which this cycle is repeated again and again, and the magic circle is never broken through. Did he lie when he said he loved her so much that he could not live without her? As far as love is concerned, it all depends on what one means by love. As far as his assertion goes that he could not live without her, it is—of course not taking it literally—perfectly true. He cannot live without her—or at least without someone else whom he feels to be the helpless instrument in his hands. While in such a case feelings of love appear only when the relationship threatens to be dissolved, in other cases the sadistic person quite manifestly "loves" those over whom he feels power. Whether it is his wife, his child, an assistant, a waiter, or a beggar on the street, there is a feeling of "love" and even gratitude for those objects of his domination. He may think that he wishes to dominate their lives because he loves them so much. *He actually "loves" them because he dominates them.* He bribes them with material things, with praise, assurances of love, the display of wit and brilliance, or by showing concern. He may give them everything—everything except one thing: the right to be free and independent. This constellation is often to be found particularly in the relationship of parents and children. There, the attitude of domination—and ownership—is often covered by what seems to be the "natural" concern or feeling of protectiveness for a child. The child is put into a golden cage, it can have everything provided it does not want to leave the cage. The result of this is often a profound fear of love on the part of the child when he grows up, as "love" to him implies being caught and blocked in his own quest for freedom.

Sadism to many observers seemed less of a puzzle than masochism. That one wished to hurt others or to dominate them seemed, though not necessarily "good," quite natural. Hobbes assumed as a "general inclination of all mankind" the existence of "a perpetual and restless desire of power after power that ceaseth only in Death."[2] For him the wish for power has no diabolical quality but is a perfectly rational result of man's desire for pleasure and security. From Hobbes to Hitler, who explains the wish for domination as the logical result of the biologically conditioned struggle for survival of the fittest, the lust for power has been explained as a part of human nature which does not warrant any explanation beyond the obvious. Masochistic strivings, however, tendencies directed against one's own self, seem to be a riddle. How should one understand the fact that people not only want to belittle and weaken and hurt themselves, but even enjoy doing so? Does not the phenomenon of masochism contradict our whole picture of the human psyche as directed toward pleasure and self-preservation? How can one explain that some men are attracted by and tend to incur what we all seem to go to such length to avoid: pain and suffering?

There is a phenomenon, however, which proves that suffering and weakness can be the aim of human striving: the masochistic perversion. Here we find that people quite consciously want to suffer in one way or another and enjoy it. In the masochistic perversion, a person feels sexual

[2] Hobbes, Leviathan, London, 1651. p. 47.

excitement when experiencing pain inflicted upon them by another person. But this is not the only form of masochistic perversion. Frequently it is not the actual suffering of pain that is sought for, but the excitement and satisfaction aroused by being physically bound, made helpless and weak. Often all that is wanted in the masochistic perversion is to be made weak "morally," by being treated or spoken to like a little child, or by being scolded or humiliated in different ways. In the sadistic perversion, we find the satisfaction derived from corresponding devices, that is, from hurting other persons physically, from tying them with ropes or chains, or from humiliating them by actions or words.

The masochistic perversion with its conscious and intentional enjoyment of pain or humiliation caught the eye of psychologists and writers earlier than the masochistic character (or moral masochism). More and more, however, one recognized how closely the masochistic tendencies of the kind we described first are akin to the sexual perversion, and that both types of masochism are essentially one and the same phenomenon.

Certain psychologists assumed that since there are people who want to submit and to suffer, there must be an "instinct" which has this very aim. Sociologists, like Vierkand, came to the same conclusion. The first one to attempt a more thorough theoretical explanation was Freud. He originally thought that sado-masochism was essentially a sexual phenomenon. Observing sado-masochistic practices in little children, he assumed that sado-masochism was a "partial drive" which regularly appears in the development of the sexual instinct. He believed that sado-masochistic tendencies in adults are due to a fixation of a person's psychosexual development on an early level or to a later regression to it. Later on Freud became increasingly aware of the importance of those phenomena which he called moral masochism, a tendency to suffer not physically, but mentally. He stressed also the fact that masochistic and sadistic tendencies were always to be found together in spite of their seeming contradiction. However, he changed his theoretical explanation of masochistic phenomena. Assuming that there is a biologically given tendency to destroy which can be directed either against others or against oneself, Freud suggested that masochism is essentially the product of this so-called death-instinct. He further suggested that this death-instinct, which we cannot observe directly, amalgamates itself with the sexual instinct and in the amalgamation appears as masochism if directed against one's own person, and as sadism if directed against others. He assumed that this very mixture with the sexual instinct protects man from the dangerous effect the unmixed death-instinct would have. In short, according to Freud man has only the choice of either destroying himself or destroying others, if he fails to amalgamate destructiveness with sex. This theory is basically different from Freud's original assumption about sado-masochism. There, sado-masochism was essentially a sexual phenomenon, but in the newer theory it is essentially a nonsexual phenomenon, the sexual factor in it being only due to the amalgamation of the death-instinct with the sexual instinct.

Although Freud has for many years paid little attention to the phenomenon of nonsexual aggression, Alfred Adler has put the tendencies we are discussing here in the center of his system. But he deals with them not as sado-masochism, but as "inferiority feelings" and the "wish for power." Adler sees only the rational side of these phenomena. While we are speaking of an irrational tendency to belittle oneself and make oneself small, he thinks of inferiority feelings as adequate reaction to actual inferiorities, such as organic inferiorities or the general helplessness of a child. And while we think of the wish for power as an expression of an irrational impulse to rule over others, Adler looks at it entirely from the rational side and speaks of the wish for power as an adequate reaction which has the function of protecting a person against the dangers springing from his insecurity and inferiority. Adler, here, as always, cannot see beyond purposeful and rational determinations of human behavior; and though he has contributed valuable insights into the intricacies of motivation, he remains always on the surface and never descends into the abyss of irrational impulses as Freud has done.

In psychoanalytic literature a viewpoint different from Freud's has been presented by Wilhelm Reich,[3] Karen Horney,[4] and myself.[5]

Although Reich's views are based on the original concept of Freud's libido theory, he points out that the masochistic person ultimately seeks pleasure and that the pain incurred is a by-product, not an aim in itself. Horney was the first one to recognize the fundamental role of

[3] *Charakteranalyse*, Wien, 1933.
[4] *The Neurotic Personality of Our Time*, W. W. Norton & Company, New York, 1936.
[5] *Psychologie der Autorität in Autorität und Familie*, ed. Max Horkheimer, Alcan, Paris, 1936.

masochistic strivings in the neurotic personality, to give a full and detailed description of the masochistic character traits, and to account for them theoretically as the outcome of the whole character structure. In her writings, as well as in my own, instead of the masochistic character traits being thought of as rooted in the sexual perversion, the latter is understood to be the sexual expression of psychic tendencies that are anchored in a particular kind of character structure.

I come now to the main question: What is the root of both the masochistic perversion and masochistic character traits respectively? Furthermore, what is the common root of both the masochistic and the sadistic strivings?

The direction in which the answer lies has already been suggested in the beginning of this chapter. Both the masochistic and sadistic strivings tend to help the individual to escape his unbearable feeling of aloneness and powerlessness. Psychoanalytic and other empirical observations of masochistic persons give ample evidence (which I cannot quote here without transcending the scope of this book) that they are filled with a terror of aloneness and insignificance. Frequently this feeling is not conscious; often it is covered by compensatory feelings of eminence and perfection. However, if one only penetrates deeply enough into the unconscious dynamics of such a person, one finds these feelings without fail. The individual finds himself "free" in the negative sense, that is, alone with his self and confronting an alienated, hostile world. In this situation, to quote a telling description of Dostoevski, in *The Brothers Karamasov*, he has "no more pressing need than the one to find somebody to whom he can surrender, as quickly as possible, that gift of freedom which he, the unfortunate creature, was born with." The frightened individual seeks for somebody or something to tie his self to; he cannot bear to be his own individual self any longer, and he tries frantically to get rid of it and to feel security again by the elimination of this burden: the self.

Masochism is one way toward this goal. The different forms which the masochistic strivings assume have one aim: *to get rid of the individual self, to lose oneself;* in other words, *to get rid of the burden of freedom.* This aim is obvious in those masochistic strivings in which the individual seeks to submit to a person or power which he feels as being overwhelmingly strong. (Incidentally, the conviction of superior strength of another person is always to be understood in relative terms. It can be based either upon the actual strength of the other person, or upon a conviction of one's own utter insignificance and powerlessness. In the latter event a mouse or a leaf can assume threatening features.) In other forms of masochistic strivings the essential aim is the same. In the masochistic feeling of smallness we find a tendency which serves to increase the original feeling of insignificance. How is this to be understood? Can we assume that by making a fear worse one is trying to remedy it? Indeed, this is what the masochistic person does. As long as I struggle between my desire to be independent and strong and my feeling of insignificance or powerlessness I am caught in a tormenting conflict. If I succeed in reducing my individual self to nothing, if I can overcome the awareness of my separateness as an individual, I may save myself from this conflict. To feel utterly small and helpless is one way toward this aim; to be over-

whelmed by pain and agony another; to be overcome by
the effects of intoxication still another. The phantasy of
suicide is the last hope if all other means have not succeeded in bringing relief from the burden of aloneness.

Under certain conditions these masochistic strivings are
relatively successful. If the individual finds cultural patterns that satisfy these masochistic strivings (like the submission under the "leader" in Fascist ideology), he gains
some security by finding himself united with millions of
others who share these feelings. Yet even in these cases, the
masochistic "solution" is no more of a solution than neurotic manifestations ever are: the individual succeeds in
eliminating the conspicuous suffering but not in removing
the underlying conflict and the silent unhappiness. When
the masochistic striving does not find a cultural pattern or
when it quantitatively exceeds the average amount of
masochism in the individual's social group, the masochistic
solution does not even solve anything in relative terms. It
springs from an unbearable situation, tends to overcome it,
and leaves the individual caught in new suffering. If human
behavior were always rational and purposeful, masochism
would be as inexplicable as neurotic manifestations in general are. This, however, is what the study of emotional and
mental disturbances has taught us: that human behavior
can be motivated by strivings which are caused by anxiety
or some other unbearable state of mind, that these strivings
tend to overcome this emotional state and yet merely cover
up its most visible manifestations, or not even these. Neurotic manifestations resemble the irrational behavior in a
panic. Thus a man, trapped in a fire, stands at the window
of his room and shouts for help, forgetting entirely that no

one can hear him and that he could still escape by the staircase which will also be aflame in a few minutes. He shouts because he wants to be saved, and for the moment this behavior appears to be a step on the way to being saved—and yet it will end in complete catastrophe. In the same way the masochistic strivings are caused by the desire to get rid of the individual self with all its shortcomings, conflicts, risks, doubts, and unbearable aloneness, but they only succeed in removing the most noticeable pain or they even lead to greater suffering. The irrationality of masochism, as of all other neurotic manifestations, consists in the ultimate futility of the means adopted to solve an untenable emotional situation.

These considerations refer to an important difference between neurotic and rational activity. In the latter the *result* corresponds to the *motivation* of an activity—one acts in order to attain a certain result. In neurotic strivings one acts from a compulsion which has essentially a negative character: to escape an unbearable situation. The strivings tend in a direction which only fictitiously is a solution. Actually the result is contradictory to what the person wants to attain; the compulsion to get rid of an unbearable feeling was so strong that the person was unable to choose a line of action that could be a solution in any other but a fictitious sense.

The implication of this for masochism is that the individual is driven by an unbearable feeling of aloneness and insignificance. He then attempts to overcome it by getting rid of his self (as a psychological, not as a physiological entity) ; his way to achieve this is to belittle himself, to suffer, to make himself utterly insignificant. But pain and suffering are not what he wants; pain and suffering are the price he pays for an aim which he compulsively tries to attain. The price is dear. He has to pay more and more and, like a peon, he only gets into greater debts without ever getting what he has paid for: inner peace and tranquillity.

I have spoken of the masochistic perversion because it proves beyond doubt that suffering can be something sought for. However, in the masochistic perversion as little as in moral masochism suffering is not the real aim; in both cases it is the means to an aim: forgetting one's self. The difference between the perversion and masochistic character traits lies essentially in the following: In the perversion the trend to get rid of one's self is expressed through the medium of the body and linked up with sexual feelings. While in moral masochism, the masochistic trends get hold of the whole person and tend to destroy all the aims which the ego consciously tries to achieve, in the perversion the masochistic strivings are more or less restricted to the physical realm; moreover by their amalgamation with sex they participate in the release of tension occurring in the sexual sphere and thus find some direct release.

The annihilation of the individual self and the attempt to overcome thereby the unbearable feeling of powerlessness are only one side of the masochistic strivings. The other side is the attempt to become a part of a bigger and more powerful whole outside of oneself, to submerge and participate in it. This power can be a person, an institution, God, the nation, conscience, or a psychic compulsion. By becoming part of a power which is felt as unshakably strong, eternal, and glamorous, one participates in its strength and glory. One surrenders one's own self and re-nounces all strength and pride connected with it, one loses one's integrity as an individual and surrenders freedom; but one gains a new security and a new pride in the participation in the power in which one submerges. One gains also security against the torture of doubt. The masochistic person, whether his master is an authority outside of himself or whether he has internalized the master as conscience or a psychic compulsion, is saved from making decisions, saved from the final responsibility for the fate of his self, and thereby saved from the doubt of what decision to make. He is also saved from the doubt of what the meaning of his life is or who "he" is. These questions are answered by the relationship to the power to which he has attached himself. The meaning of his life and the identity of his self are determined by the greater whole into which the self has submerged.

The masochistic bonds are fundamentally different from the primary bonds. The latter are those that exist before the process of individuation has reached its completion. The individual is still part of "his" natural and social world, he has not yet completely emerged from his surroundings. The primary bonds give him genuine security and the knowledge of where he belongs. The masochistic bonds are escape. The individual self has emerged, but it is unable to realize his freedom; it is overwhelmed by anxiety, doubt, and a feeling of powerlessness. The self attempts to find security in "secondary bonds," as we might call the masochistic bonds, but this attempt can never be successful. The emergence of the individual self cannot be reversed; consciously the individual can feel secure and as if he "belonged," but basically he remains a powerless atom who suffers under the submergence of his self. He and the power to which he clings never become one, a basic antagonism remains and with it an impulse, even if it is not conscious at all, to overcome the masochistic dependence and to become free.

What is the essence of the sadistic drives? Again, the wish to inflict pain on others is not the essence. All the different forms of sadism which we can observe go back to one essential impulse, namely, to have complete mastery over another person, to make of him a helpless object of our will, to become the absolute ruler over him, to become his God, to do with him as one pleases. To humiliate him, to enslave him, are means to this end and the most radical aim is to make him suffer, since there is no greater power over another person than that of inflicting pain on him, to force him to undergo suffering without his being able to defend himself. The pleasure in the complete domination over another person (or other animate objects) is the very essence of the sadistic drive.[6]

It seems that this tendency to make oneself the absolute

[6] Marquis de Sade held the view that the quality of domination is the essence of sadism in this passage from *Juliette II* (quoted from *Marquis de Sade*, by G. Gorer, Liveright Publishing Corporation, New York, 1934): "It is not pleasure which you want to make your partner feel but impression you want to produce; that of pain is far stronger than that of pleasure . . . one realizes that; one uses it and is satisfied." Gorer in his analysis of de Sade's work defines sadism "as the pleasure felt from the observed modifications on the external world produced by the observer." This definition comes nearer to my own view of sadism than that of other psychologists. I think, however, that Gorer is wrong in identifying sadism with the pleasure in mastery or productivity. The sadistic mastery is characterized by the fact that it wants to make the object a will-less instrument in the sadist's hands, while the nonsadistic joy in influencing others respects the integrity of the other person and is based on a feeling of equality. In Gorer's definition sadism loses its specific quality and becomes identical with any kind of productivity.

master over another person is the opposite of the masochistic tendency, and it is puzzling that these two tendencies
should be so closely knitted together. No doubt with regard
to its practical consequences the wish to be dependent or
to suffer is the opposite of the wish to dominate and to
make others suffer. Psychologically, however, both tendencies are the outcomes of one basic need, springing from
the inability to bear the isolation and weakness of one's
own self. I suggest calling the aim which is at the basis of
both sadism and masochism: symbiosis. Symbiosis, in this
psychological sense, means the union of one individual self
with another self (or any other power outside of the own
self) in such a way as to make each lose the integrity of its
own self and to make them completely dependent on each
other. The sadistic person needs his object just as much as
the masochistic needs his. Only instead of seeking security
by being swallowed, he gains it by swallowing somebody
else. In both cases the integrity of the individual self is
lost. In one case I dissolve myself in an outside power; I
lose myself. In the other case I enlarge myself by making
another being part of myself and thereby I gain the
strength I lack as an independent self. It is always the
inability to stand the aloneness of one's individual self that
leads to the drive to enter into a symbiotic relationship
with someone else. It is evident from this why masochistic
and sadistic trends are always blended with each other.
Although on the surface they seem contradictions, they are
essentially rooted in the same basic need. People are not
sadistic or masochistic, but there is a constant oscillation
between the active and the passive side of the symbiotic
complex, so that it is often difficult to determine which side

of it is operating at a given moment. In both cases individuality and freedom are lost.

If we think of sadism, we usually think of the destructiveness and hostility which is so blatantly connected with it. To be sure, a greater or lesser amount of destructiveness is always to be found linked up with sadistic tendencies. But this is also true of masochism. Every analysis of masochistic traits shows this hostility. The main difference seems to be that in sadism the hostility is usually more conscious and directly expressed in action, while in masochism the hostility is mostly unconscious and finds an indirect expression. I shall try to show later on that destructiveness is the result of the thwarting of the individual's sensuous, emotional, and intellectual expansiveness; it is therefore to be expected as an outcome of the same conditions that make for the symbiotic need. The point I wish to emphasize here is that sadism is not identical with destructiveness, although it is to a great extent blended with it. The destructive person wants to destroy the object, that is, to do away with it and to get rid of it. The sadist wants to dominate his object and therefore suffers a loss if his object disappears.

Sadism, as we have used the word, can also be relatively free from destructiveness and blended with a friendly attitude towards its object. This kind of "loving" sadism has found classical expression in Balzac's *Lost Illusions*, a description which also conveys the particular quality of what we mean by the need for symbiosis. In this passage Balzac describes the relationship between young Lucien and the Bagno prisoner who poses as an Abbé. Shortly after he makes the acquaintance of the young man who has just tried to commit suicide the Abbé says: ". . . This young man has nothing in common with the poet who died just now. I have picked you up, I have given life to you, and you belong to me as the creature belongs to the creator, as—in the Orient's fairy tales—the Ifrit belongs to the spirit, as the body belongs to the soul. With powerful hands I will keep you straight on the road to power; I promise you, nevertheless, a life of pleasures, of honors, of everlasting feasts. You will never lack money, you will sparkle, you will be brilliant; whereas I, stooped down in the filth of promoting, shall secure the brilliant edifice of your success. I love power for the sake of power! I shall always enjoy your pleasures although I shall have to renounce them. Shortly: I shall be one and the same person with you. . . . I will love my creature, I will mold him, will shape him to my services, in order to love him as a father loves his child. I shall drive at your side in your Tilbury, my dear boy, I shall delight in your successes with women. I shall say: I am this handsome young man. I have created this Marquis de Rubempré and have placed him among the aristocracy; his success is my product. He is silent and he talks with my voice, he follows my advice in everything."

Frequently, and not only in the popular usage, sadomasochism is confounded with love. Masochistic phenomena, especially, are looked upon as expressions of love. An attitude of complete self-denial for the sake of another person and the surrender of one's own rights and claims to another person have been praised as examples of "great love." It seems that there is no better proof for "love" than sacrifice and the readiness to give oneself up for the sake of the beloved person. Actually, in these cases, "love" is essentially a masochistic yearning and rooted in the symbiotic need of the person involved. If we mean by love the passionate affirmation and active relatedness to the essence of a particular person, if we mean by it the union with another person on the basis of the independence and integrity of the two persons involved, then masochism and love are opposites. Love is based on equality and freedom. If it is based on subordination and loss of integrity of one partner, it is masochistic dependence, regardless of how the relationship is rationalized. Sadism also appears frequently under the disguise of love. To rule over another person, if one can claim that to rule him is for that person's own sake, frequently appears as an expression of love, but the essential factor is the enjoyment of domination.

At this point a question will have arisen in the mind of many a reader: Is not sadism, as we have described it here, identical with the craving for power? The answer to this question is that although the more destructive forms of sadism, in which the aim is to hurt and torture another person, are not identical with the wish for power, the latter is the most significant expression of sadism. The problem has gained added significance in the present day. Since Hobbes, one has seen in power the basic motive of human behavior; the following centuries, however, gave increased weight to legal and moral factors which tended to curb power. With the rise of Fascism, the lust for power and the conviction of its right has reached new heights. Millions are impressed by the victories of power and take it for the sign of strength. To be sure, power over people is an expression of superior strength in a purely material sense.

If I have the power over another person to kill him, I am "stronger" than he is. But in a psychological sense, *the lust for power is not rooted in strength but in weakness*. It is the expression of the inability of the individual self to stand alone and live. It is the desperate attempt to gain secondary strength where genuine strength is lacking.

The word "power" has a twofold meaning. One is the possession of power over somebody, the ability to dominate him; the other meaning is the possession of power to do something, to be able, to be potent. The latter meaning has nothing to do with domination; it expresses mastery in the sense of ability. If we speak of powerlessness we have this meaning in mind; we do not think of a person who is not able to dominate others, but of a person who is not able to do what he wants. Thus power can mean one of two things, *domination* or *potency*. Far from being identical, these two qualities are mutually exclusive. Impotence, using the term not only with regard to the sexual sphere but to all spheres of human potentialities, results in the sadistic striving for domination; to the extent to which an individual is potent, that is, able to realize his potentialities on the basis of freedom and integrity of his self, he does not need to dominate and is lacking the lust for power. Power, in the sense of domination, is the perversion of potency, just as sexual sadism is the perversion of sexual love.

Sadistic and masochistic traits are probably to be found in everybody. At one extreme there are individuals whose whole personality is dominated by these traits, and at the other there are those for whom these sado-masochistic traits are not characteristic. Only in discussing the former can we speak of a sado-masochistic character. The term "character" is used here in the dynamic sense in which Freud speaks of character. In this sense it refers not to the sum total of behavior patterns characteristic for one person, but to the dominant drives that motivate behavior. Since Freud assumed that the basic motivating forces are sexual ones, he arrived at concepts like "oral," "anal," or "genital" characters. If one does not share this assumption, one is forced to devise different character types. But the dynamic concept remains the same. The driving forces are not necessarily conscious as such to a person whose character is dominated by them. A person can be entirely dominated by his sadistic strivings and consciously believe that he is motivated only by his sense of duty. He may not even commit any overt sadistic acts but suppress his sadistic drives sufficiently to make him appear on the surface as a person who is not sadistic. Nevertheless, any close analysis of his behavior, his phantasies, dreams, and gestures, would show the sadistic impulses operating in deeper layers of his personality.

Although the character of persons in whom sado-masochistic drives are dominant can be characterized as sado-masochistic, such persons are not necessarily neurotic. It depends to a large extent on the particular tasks people have to fulfill in their social situation and what patterns of feelings and behavior are present in their culture whether or not a particular kind of character structure is "neurotic" or "normal." As a matter of fact, for great parts of the lower middle class in Germany and other European countries, the sado-masochistic character is typical, and, as will be shown later, it is this kind of character structure to which Nazi ideology had its strongest appeal. Since the term "sado-masochistic" is associated with ideas of perversion and neurosis, I prefer to speak of the sado-masochistic character, especially when not the neurotic but the normal person is meant, as the *"authoritarian character."* This terminology is justifiable because the sado-masochistic person is always characterized by his attitude toward authority. He admires authority and tends to submit to it, but at the same time he wants to be an authority himself and have others submit to him. There is an additional reason for choosing this term. The Fascist system call themselves authoritarian because of the dominant role of authority in their social and political structure. By the term "authoritarian character," we imply that it represents the personality structure which is the human basis of Fascism.

Before going on with the discussion of the authoritarian character, the term "authority" needs some clarification. Authority is not a quality one person "has," in the sense that he has property or physical qualities. Authority refers to an interpersonal relation in which one person looks upon another as somebody superior to him. But there is a fundamental difference between a kind of superiority-inferiority relation which can be called rational authority and one which may be described as inhibiting authority.

An example will show what I have in mind. The relationship between teacher and student and that between slave owner and slave are both based on the superiority of the one over the other. The interests of teacher and pupil lie in the same direction. The teacher is satisfied if he succeeds in furthering the pupil; if he has failed to do so, the failure is his and the pupil's. The slave owner, on the other hand,

wants to exploit the slave as much as possible; the more he
gets out of him, the more he is satisfied. At the same time,
the slave seeks to defend as best he can his claims for a
minimum of happiness. These interests are definitely antagonistic, as what is of advantage to the one is detrimental
to the other. The superiority has a different function in
both cases: in the first, it is the condition for the helping
of the person subjected to the authority; in the second, it is
the condition for his exploitation.

The dynamics of authority in these two types are different too: the more the student learns, the less wide is the
gap between him and the teacher. He becomes more and
more like the teacher himself. In other words, the authority
relationship tends to dissolve itself. But when the superiority serves as a basis for exploitation, the distance becomes
intensified through its long duration.

The psychological situation is different in each of these
authority situations. In the first, elements of love, admiration, or gratitude are prevalent. The authority is at the
same time an example with which one wants to identify
one's self partially or totally. In the second situation, resentment or hostility will arise against the exploiter, subordination to whom is against one's own interests. But often,
as in the case of a slave, this hatred would only lead to conflicts which would subject the slave to suffering without a
chance of winning. Therefore, the tendency will usually
be to repress the feeling of hatred and sometimes even to
replace it by a feeling of blind admiration. This has two
functions: (1) to remove the painful and dangerous feeling of hatred, and (2) to soften the feeling of humiliation.
If the person who rules over me is so wonderful or perfect,

then I should not be ashamed of obeying him. I cannot be his equal because he is so much stronger, wiser, better, and so on, than I am. As a result, in the inhibiting kind of authority, the element either of hatred or of irrational over-estimation and admiration of the authority will tend to increase. In the rational kind of authority, it will tend to decrease in direct proportion to the degree in which the person subjected to the authority becomes stronger and thereby more similar to the authority.

The difference between rational and inhibiting authority is only a relative one. Even in the relationship between slave and master there are elements of advantage for the slave. He gets a minimum of food and protection which at least enables him to work for his master. On the other hand, it is only in an ideal relationship between teacher and student that we find a complete lack of antagonism of interests. There are many gradations between these two extreme cases, as in the relationship of a factory worker with his boss, or a farmer's son with his father, or a hausfrau with her husband. Nevertheless, although in reality two types of authority are blended, they are essentially differ-ent, and an analysis of a concrete authority situation must always determine the specific weight of each kind of authority.

Authority does not have to be a person or institution which says: you have to do this, or you are not allowed to do that. While this kind of authority may be called external authority, authority can appear as internal author-ity, under the name of duty, conscience, or superego. As a matter of fact, the development of modern thinking from Protestantism to Kant's philosophy, can be characterized as the substitution of internalized authority for an external one. With the political victories of the rising middle class, external authority lost prestige and man's own conscience assumed the place which external authority once had held. This change appeared to many as the victory of freedom. To submit to orders from the outside (at least in spiritual matters) appeared to be unworthy of a free man; but the conquest of his natural inclinations, and the establishment of the domination of one part of the individual, his nature, by another, his reason, will or conscience, seemed to be the very essence of freedom. Analysis shows that conscience rules with a harshness as great as external authorities, and furthermore that frequently the contents of the orders issued by man's conscience are ultimately not governed by demands of the individual self but by social demands which have assumed the dignity of ethical norms. The rulership of conscience can be even harsher than that of external authorities, since the individual feels its orders to be his own; how can he rebel against himself?

In recent decades "conscience" has lost much of its significance. It seems as though neither external nor internal authorities play any prominent role in the individual's life. Everybody is completely "free," if only he does not interfere with other people's legitimate claims. But what we find is rather that instead of disappearing, authority has made itself invisible. Instead of overt authority, "anonymous" authority reigns. It is disguised as common sense, science, psychic health, normality, public opinion. It does not demand anything except the self-evident. It seems to use no pressure but only mild persuasion. Whether a mother says to her daughter, "I know you will not like to go out with that boy," or an advertisement suggests, "Smoke this brand of cigarettes—you will like their coolness," it is the same atmosphere of subtle suggestion which actually pervades our whole social life. Anonymous authority is more effective than overt authority, since one never suspects that there is any order which one is expected to follow. In external authority it is clear that there is an order and who gives it; one can fight against the authority, and in this fight personal independence and moral courage can develop. But whereas in internalized authority the command, though an internal one, remains visible, in anonymous authority both command and commander have become invisible. It is like being fired at by an invisible enemy. There is nobody and nothing to fight back against.

Returning now to the discussion of the authoritarian character, the most important feature to be mentioned is its attitude towards power. For the authoritarian character there exist, so to speak, two sexes: the powerful ones and the powerless ones. His love, admiration and readiness for submission are automatically aroused by power, whether of a person or of an institution. Power fascinates him not for any values for which a specific power may stand, but just because it is power. Just as his "love" is automatically aroused by power, so powerless people or institutions automatically arouse his contempt. The very sight of a powerless person makes him want to attack, dominate, humiliate him. Whereas a different kind of character is appalled by the idea of attacking one who is helpless, the authoritarian character feels the more aroused the more helpless his object has become.

There is one feature of the authoritarian character which

has misled many observers: a tendency to defy authority and to resent any kind of influence from "above." Sometimes this defiance overshadows the whole picture and the submissive tendencies are in the background. This type of person will constantly rebel against any kind of authority, even one that actually furthers his interests and has no elements of suppression. Sometimes the attitude toward authority is divided. Such persons might fight against one set of authorities, especially if they are disappointed by its lack of power, and at the same time or later on submit to another set of authorities which through greater power or greater promises seems to fulfill their masochistic longings. Finally, there is a type in which the rebellious tendencies are completely repressed and come to the surface only when conscious control is weakened; or they can be recognized ex posteriori, in the hatred that arises against an authority when its power is weakened and when it begins to totter. In persons of the first type in whom the rebellious attitude is in the center of the picture, one is easily led to believe that their character structure is just the opposite to that of the submissive masochistic type. It appears as if they are persons who oppose every authority on the basis of an extreme degree of independence. They look like persons who, on the basis of their inner strength and integrity, fight those forces that block their freedom and independence. However, the authoritarian character's fight against authority is essentially defiance. It is an attempt to assert himself and to overcome his own feeling of powerlessness by fighting authority, although the longing for submission remains present, whether consciously or unconsciously. The authoritarian character is never a "revolutionary"; I should like to call him a "rebel." There are many individuals and political movements that are puzzling to the superficial observer because of what seems to be an inexplicable change from "radicalism" to extreme authoritarianism. Psychologically, those people are the typical "rebels."

The attitude of the authoritarian character toward life, his whole philosophy, is determined by his emotional strivings. The authoritarian character loves those conditions that limit human freedom, he loves being submitted to fate. It depends on his social position what "fate" means to him. For a soldier it may mean the will or whim of his superior, to which he gladly submits. For the small businessman the economic laws are his fate. Crisis and prosperity to him are not social phenomena which might be changed by human activity, but the expression of a higher power to which one has to submit. For those on the top of the pyramid it is basically not different. The difference lies only in the size and generality of the power to which one submits, not in the feeling of dependence as such.

Not only the forces that determine one's own life directly but also those that seem to determine life in general are felt as unchangeable fate. It is fate that there are wars and that one part of mankind has to be ruled by another. It is fate that the amount of suffering can never be less than it always has been. Fate may be rationalized philosophically as "natural law" or as "destiny of man," religiously as the "will of the Lord," ethically as "duty"—for the authoritarian character it is always a higher power outside of the individual, toward which the individual can do nothing but submit. The authoritarian character worships the past. What has been, will eternally be. To wish or to work for something that has not yet been before is crime or madness. The miracle of creation—and creation is always a miracle—is outside of his range of emotional experience.

Schleiermacher's definition of religious experience as experience of absolute dependence is the definition of the masochistic experience in general; a special role in this feeling of dependence is played by sin. The concept of original sin, which weighs upon all future generations, is characteristic of the authoritarian experience. Moral like any other kind of human failure becomes a fate which man can never escape. Whoever has once sinned is chained eternally to his sin with iron shackles. Man's own doing becomes the power that rules over him and never lets him free. The consequences of guilt can be softened by atonement, but atonement can never do away with the guilt.[7] Isaiah's words, "Though your sins be as scarlet, they shall be as white as snow," express the very opposite of authoritarian philosophy.

The feature common to all authoritarian thinking is the conviction that life is determined by forces outside of man's own self, his interest, his wishes. The only possible happiness lies in the submission to these forces. The powerlessness of man is the leitmotif of masochistic philosophy. One of the ideological fathers of Nazism, Moeller van der Bruck, expressed this feeling very clearly. He writes: "The conservative believes rather in catastrophe, in the powerlessness of man to avoid it, in its necessity, and in the

---

[7] Victor Hugo gave a most telling expression to the idea of inescapability of guilt in the character of Javert in *Les Misérables*.

terrible disappointment of the seduced optimist."[8] In Hitler's writing we shall see more illustrations of the same spirit.

The authoritarian character does not lack activity, courage, or belief. But these qualities for him mean something entirely different from what they mean for the person who does not long for submission. For the authoritarian character activity is rooted in a basic feeling of powerlessness which it tends to overcome. Activity in this sense means to act in the name of something higher than one's own self. It is possible in the name of God, the past, nature, or duty, but never in the name of the future, of the unborn, of what has no power, or of life as such. The authoritarian character wins his strength to act through his leaning on superior power. This power is never assailable or changeable. For him lack of power is always an unmistakable sign of guilt and inferiority, and if the authority in which he believes shows signs of weakness, his love and respect change into contempt and hatred. He lacks an "offensive potency" which can attack established power without first feeling subservient to another and stronger power.

The courage of the authoritarian character is essentially a courage to suffer what fate or its personal representative or "leader" may have destined him for. To suffer without complaining is his highest virtue—not the courage of trying to end suffering or at least to diminish it. Not to change fate, but to submit to it, is the heroism of the authoritarian character.

He has belief in authority as long as it is strong and com-

[8] Moeller van der Bruck, *Das Dritte Reich*, Hanseatische Verlag-anstalt, Hamburg. 1931. pp. 223, 224

manding. His belief is rooted ultimately in his doubts and constitutes an attempt to compensate them. But he has no faith, if we mean by faith the secure confidence in the realization of what now exists only as a potentiality. Authoritarian philosophy is essentially relativistic and nihilistic, in spite of the fact that it often claims so violently to have conquered relativism and in spite of its show of activity. It is rooted in extreme desperation, in the complete lack of faith, and it leads to nihilism, to the denial of life.[9]

In authoritarian philosophy the concept of equality does not exist. The authoritarian character may sometimes use the word equality either conventially or because it suits his purposes. But it has no real meaning or weight for him, since it concerns something outside the reach of his emotional experience. For him the world is composed of people with power and those without it, of superior ones and inferior ones. On the basis of his sado-masochistic strivings, he experiences only domination or submission, but never solidarity. Differences, whether of sex or race, to him are necessarily signs of superiority or inferiority. A difference which does not have this connotation is unthinkable to him.

The description of the sado-masochistic strivings and the authoritarian character refers to the more extreme forms of helplessness and the corespondingly more extreme forms of escaping it by the symbiotic relationship to the object of worship or domination.

Although these sado-masochistic strivings are common, we can consider only certain individuals and social groups

[9] Rauschning has given a good description of the nihilistic character of Fascism in The Revolution of Nihilism, Alliance Book Corporation, Longmans, Green & Co., New York, 1939.

as typically sado-masochistic. There is, however, a milder form of dependency which is so general in our culture that only in exceptional cases does it seem to be lacking. This dependency does not have the dangerous and passionate qualities of sado-masochism, but it is important enough not to be omitted from our discussion here.

I am referring to the kind of persons whose whole life is in a subtle way related to some power outside themselves.[10] There is nothing they do, feel, or think which is not somehow related to this power. They expect protection from "him," wish to be taken care of by "him," make "him" also responsible for whatever may be the outcome of their own actions. Often the fact of his dependence is something the person is not aware of at all. Even if there is a dim awareness of some dependency, the person or power on whom he is dependent often remains nebulous. There is no definite image linked up with that power. Its essential quality is to represent a certain function, namely to protect, help, and develop the individual, to be with him and never leave him alone. The "X" which has these qualities may be called the *magic helper*. Frequently, of course, the "magic helper" is personified: he is conceived of as God, as a principle, or as real persons such as one's parent, husband, wife, or superior. It is important to recognize that when real persons assume the role of the magic helper they are endowed with magic qualities, and the significance they have results from their being the personification of the magic helper. This process of personification of the magic helper is to be observed frequently in what is called "falling

[10] In this connection, cf. Karen Horney, *New Ways in Psychoanalysis*, W. W. Norton & Company, New York, 1939.

in love." A person with that kind of relatedness to the magic helper seeks to find him in flesh and blood. For some reason or other—often supported by sexual desires—a certain other person assumes for him those magic qualities, and he makes that person into the being to whom and on whom his whole life becomes related and dependent. The fact that the other person frequently does the same with the first one does not alter the picture. It only helps to strengthen the impression that this relationship is one of "real love."

This need for the magic helper can be studied under experiment-like conditions in the psychoanalytic procedure. Often the person who is analyzed forms a deep attachment to the psychoanalyst and his or her whole life, all actions, thoughts, and feeling are related to the analyst. Consciously or unconsciously the analysand asks himself: would he (the analyst) be pleased with this, displeased with that, agree to this, scold me for that? In love relationships the fact that one chooses this or that person as a partner serves as a proof that this particular person is loved just because he is "he"; but in the psychoanalytic situation this illusion cannot be upheld. The most different kinds of persons develop the same feelings toward the most different kinds of psychoanalysts. The relationship looks like love; it is often accompanied by sexual desires; yet it is essentially a relationship to the personified magic helper, a role which obviously a psychoanalyst, like certain other persons who have some authority (physicians, ministers, teachers), is able to play satisfactorily for the person who is seeking the personified magic helper.

The reasons why a person is bound to a magic helper

are, in principle, the same that we have found at the root of the symbiotic drives: an inability to stand alone and to fully express his own individual potentialities. In the sado-masochistic strivings this inability leads to a tendency to get rid of one's individual self through dependency on the magic helper—in the milder form of dependency I am discussing now it only leads to a wish for guidance and protection. The intensity of the relatedness to the magic helper is in reverse proportion to the ability to express spontaneously one's own intellectual, emotional, and sensuous potentialities. In other words, one hopes to get everything one expects from life, from the magic helper, instead of by one's own actions. The more this is the case, the more is the center of life shifted from one's own person to the magic helper and his personifications. The question is then no longer how to live oneself, but how to manipulate "him" in order not to lose him and how to make him do what one wants, even to make him responsible for what one is responsible oneself.

In the more extreme cases, a person's whole life consists almost entirely in the attempt to manipulate "him"; people differ in the means which they use; for some obedience, for some "goodness," for others suffering is the main means of manipulation. We see, then, that there is no feeling, thought, or emotion that is not at least colored by the need to manipulate "him"; in other words, that no psychic act is really spontaneous or free. This dependency, springing from and at the same time leading to a blockage of spontaneity, not only gives a certain amount of security but also results in a feeling of weakness and bondage. As far as this is the case, the very person who is dependent on the magic helper also feels, although often unconsciously, enslaved by "him" and, to a greater or lesser degree, rebels against "him." This rebelliousness against the very person on whom one has put one's hopes for security and happiness, creates new conflicts. It has to be suppressed if one is not to lose "him," but the underlying antagonism constantly threatens the security sought for in the relationship.

If the magic helper is personified in an actual person, the disappointment that follows when he falls short of what one is expecting from this person—and since the expectation is an illusory one, any actual person is inevitably disappointing—in addition to the resentment resulting from one's own enslavement to that person, leads to continuous conflicts. These sometimes end only with separation, which is usually followed by the choice of another object who is expected to fulfill all hopes connected with the magic helper. If this relationship proves to be a failure too, it may be broken up again or the person involved may decide that this is just "life," and resign. What he does not recognize is the fact that his failure is not essentially the result of his not having chosen the right magic person; it is the direct result of having tried to obtain by the manipulation of a magic force that which only the individual can achieve himself by his own spontaneous activity.

The phenomenon of life-long dependency on an object outside of oneself has been seen by Freud. He has interpreted it as the continuation of the early, essentially sexual, bonds with the parents throughout life. As a matter of fact, the phenomenon has impressed him so much that he has asserted that the Oedipus complex is the nucleus of all neuroses, and in the successful overcoming of the Oedipus complex he has seen the main problem of normal development.

In seeing the Oedipus complex as the central phenomenon of psychology Freud has made one of the most important discoveries in psychology. But he has failed in its adequate interpretation; for although the phenomenon of sexual attraction between parents and children does exist and although conflicts arising from it sometimes constitute part of the neurotic development, neither the sexual attraction nor the resulting conflicts are the essential in the fixation of children on their parents. As long as the infant is small it is quite naturally dependent on the parents, but this dependence does not necessarily imply a restriction of the child's own spontaneity. However, when the parents, acting as the agents of society, start to suppress the child's spontaneity and independence, the growing child feels more and more unable to stand on its own feet; it therefore seeks for the magic helper and often makes the parents the personification of "him." Later on, the individual transfers these feelings to somebody else, for instance, to a teacher, a husband, or a psychoanalyst. Again, the need for being related to such a symbol of authority is not caused by the continuation of the original sexual attraction to one of the parents but by the thwarting of the child's expansiveness and spontaneity and by the consequent anxiety.

What we can observe at the kernel of every neurosis, as well as of normal development, is the struggle for freedom and independence. For many normal persons this struggle has ended in a complete giving up of their individual selves, so that they are thus well adapted and considered to be normal. The neurotic person is the one who has not given up fighting against complete submission, but who, at the same time, has remained bound to the figure of the magic helper, whatever form or shape "he" may have assumed. His neurosis is always to be understood as an attempt, and essentially an unsuccessful one, to solve the conflict between that basic dependency and the quest for freedom.

2. DESTRUCTIVENESS

We have already mentioned that the sado-masochistic strivings have to be differentiated from destructiveness, although they are mostly blended with each other. Destructiveness is different since it aims not at active or passive symbiosis but at elimination of its object. But it, too, is rooted in the unbearableness of individual powerlessness and isolation. I can escape the feeling of my own powerlessness in comparison with the world outside of myself by destroying it. To be sure, if I succeed in removing it, I remain alone and isolated, but mine is a splendid isolation in which I cannot be crushed by the overwhelming power of the objects outside of myself. The destruction of the world is the last, almost desperate attempt to save myself from being crushed by it. Sadism aims at incorporation of the object; destructiveness at its removal. Sadism tends to strengthen the atomized individual by the domination over others; destructiveness by the absence of any threat from the outside.

Any observer of personal relations in our social scene cannot fail to be impressed with the amount of destructiveness to be found everywhere. For the most part it is not conscious as such but is rationalized in various ways. As a matter of fact, there is virtually nothing that is not used as a rationalization for destructiveness. Love, duty, conscience, patriotism have been and are being used as disguises to destroy others or oneself. However, we must differentiate between two different kinds of destructive tendencies. There are destructive tendencies which result from a specific situation; as reaction to attacks on one's own or others' life and integrity, or on ideas which one is identified with. This kind of destructiveness is the natural and necessary concomitant of one's affirmation of life.

The destructiveness here under discussion, however, is not this rational—or as one might call it "reactive"—hostility, but a constantly lingering tendency within a person which so to speak waits only for an opportunity to be expressed. If there is no objective "reason" for the expression of destructiveness, we call the person mentally or emotionally sick (although the person himself will usually build up some sort of a rationalization). In most cases the destructive impulses, however, are rationalized in such a way that at least a few other people or a whole social group share in the rationalization and thus make it appear to be "realistic" to the member of such a group. But the objects of irrational destructiveness and the particular reasons for their being chosen are only of secondary importance; the destructive impulses are a passion within a person, and they always succeed in finding some object. If for any reason other persons cannot become the object of an individual's destructiveness, his own self easily becomes the object. When this happens in a marked degree, physical illness is often the result and even suicide may be attempted.

We have assumed that destructiveness is an escape from
the unbearable feeling of powerlessness, since it aims at the
removal of all objects with which the individual has to
compare himself. But in view of the tremendous role that
destructive tendencies play in human behavior, this interpretation does not seem to be a sufficient explanation; the
very conditions of isolation and powerlessness are responsible for two other sources of destructiveness: anxiety and
the thwarting of life. Concerning the role of anxiety not
much needs to be said. Any threat against vital (material
and emotional) interests creates anxiety,[11] and destructive
tendencies are the most common reaction to such anxiety.
The threat can be circumscribed in a particular situation by
particular persons. In such a case, the destructiveness is
aroused towards these persons. It can also be a constant
—though not necessarily conscious—anxiety springing from
an equally constant feeling of being threatened by the
world outside. This kind of constant anxiety results from
the position of the isolated and powerless individual and
is one other source of the reservoir of destructiveness that
develops in him.

Another important outcome of the same basic situation
is what I have just called the thwarting of life. The isolated and powerless individual is blocked in realizing his
sensuous, emotional, and intellectual potentialities. He is
lacking the inner security and spontaneity that are the conditions of such realization. This inner blockage is increased
by cultural taboos on pleasure and happiness, like those
that have run through the religion and mores of the middle

---

[11] Cf. the discussion of this point in Karen Horney's *New Ways in Psychoanalysis*, W W Norton & Company, New York, 1938

class since the period of the Reformation. Nowadays, the external taboo has virtually vanished, but the inner blockage has remained strong in spite of the conscious approval of sensous pleasure.

This problem of the relation between the thwarting of life and destructiveness has been touched upon by Freud, and in discussing his theory we shall be able to express some suggestions of our own.

Freud realized that he had neglected the weight and importance of destructive impulses in his original assumption that the sexual drive and the drive for self-preservation were the two basic motivations of human behavior. Believing, later, that destructive tendencies are as important as the sexual ones, he proceeded to the assumption that there are two basic strivings to be found in man: a drive that is directed toward life and is more or less identical with sexual libido, and a death-instinct whose aim is the very destruction of life. He assumed that the latter can be blended with the sexual energy and then be directed either against one's own self or against objects outside of oneself. He furthermore assumed that the death-instinct is rooted in a biological quality inherent in all living organisms and therefore a necessary and unalterable part of life.

The assumption of the death-instinct is satisfactory inasmuch as it takes into consideration the full weight of destructive tendencies, which had been neglected in Freud's earlier theories. But it is not satisfactory inasmuch as it resorts to a biological explanation that fails to take account sufficiently of the fact that the amount of destructiveness varies enormously among individuals and social groups. If Freud's assumptions were correct, we would have to assume that the amount of destructiveness either against others or oneself is more or less constant. But what we do observe is to the contrary. Not only does the weight of destructiveness among individuals in our culture vary a great deal, but also destructiveness is of unequal weight among different social groups. Thus, for instance, the weight of destructiveness in the character of the members of the lower middle class in Europe is definitely much greater than among the working class and the upper classes. Anthropological studies have acquainted us with peoples in whom a particularly great amount of destructiveness is characteristic, whereas others show an equally marked lack of destructiveness, whether in the form of hostility against others or against oneself.

It seems that any attempt to understand the roots of destructiveness must start with the observation of these very differences and proceed to the question of what other differentiating factors can be observed and whether these factors may not account for the differences in the amount of destructiveness.

This problem offers such difficulties that it requires a detailed treatment of its own which we cannot attempt here. However, I should like to suggest in what direction the answer seems to lie. It would seem that the amount of destructiveness to be found in individuals is proportionate to the amount to which expansiveness of life is curtailed. By this we do not refer to individual frustrations of this or that instinctive desire but to the thwarting of the whole of life, the blockage of spontaneity of the growth and expression of man's sensuous, emotional, and intellectual capacities. Life has an inner dynamism of its own; it tends to grow, to be expressed, to be lived. It seems that if this tendency is thwarted the energy directed toward life undergoes a process of decomposition and changes into energies directed toward destruction. In other words: the drive for life and the drive for destruction are not mutually independent factors but are in a reversed interdependence. The more the drive toward life is thwarted, the stronger is the drive toward destruction; the more life is realized, the less is the strength of destructiveness. *Destructiveness is the outcome of unlived life.* Those individual and social conditions that make for suppression of life produce the passion for destruction that forms, so to speak, the reservoir from which the particular hostile tendencies—either against others or against oneself—are nourished.

It goes without saying how important it is not only to realize the dynamic role of destructiveness in the social process but also to understand what the specific conditions for its intensity are. We have already noted the hostility which pervaded the middle class in the age of the Reformation and which found its expression in certain religious concepts of Protestantism, especially in its ascetic spirit, and in Calvin's picture of a merciless God to whom it had been pleasing to sentence part of mankind to eternal damnation for no fault of their own. Then, as later, the middle class expressed its hostility mainly disguised as moral indignation, which rationalized an intense envy against those who had the means to enjoy life. In our contemporary scene the destructiveness of the lower middle class has been an important factor in the rise of Nazism which appealed to these destructive strivings and used them in the battle against its enemies. The root of destructiveness in the lower middle class is easily recognizable as the one which has been assumed in this discussion: the isolation of the individual and the suppression of individual expansiveness, both of which were true to a higher degree for the lower middle class than for the classes above and below.

3. AUTOMATON CONFORMITY

In the mechanisms we have been discussing, the individual overcomes the feeling of insignificance in comparison with the overwhelming power of the world outside of himself either by renouncing his individual integrity, or by destroying others so that the world ceases to be threatening.

Other mechanisms of escape are the withdrawal from the world so completely that it loses its threat (the picture we find in certain psychotic states[12]), and the inflation of oneself psychologically to such an extent that the world outside becomes small in comparison. Although these mechanisms of escape are important for individual psychology, they are only of minor relevance culturally. I shall not, therefore, discuss them further here, but instead will turn to another mechanism of escape which is of the greatest social significance.

This particular mechanism is the solution that the majority of normal individuals find in modern society. To put it briefly, the individual ceases to be himself; he adopts entirely the kind of personality offered to him by cultural

---

[12] Cf. H. S. Sullivan, op. cit., p. 68 ff., and his Research in Schizophrenia, American Journal of Psychiatry, Vol. IX, No. 3; also Frieda Fromm Reichmann, Transference Problems in Schizophrenia, The Psychoanalytic Quarterly, Vol. VIII, No. 4.

patterns; and he therefore becomes exactly as all others are and as they expect him to be. The discrepancy between "I" and the world disappears and with it the conscious fear of aloneness and powerlessness. This mechanism can be compared with the protective coloring some animals assume. They look so similar to their surroundings that they are hardly distinguishable from them. The person who gives up his individual self and becomes an automaton, identical with millions of other automatons around him, need not feel alone and anxious any more. But the price he pays, however, is high; it is the loss of his self.

The assumption that the "normal" way of overcoming aloneness is to become an automaton contradicts one of the most widespread ideas concerning man in our culture. The majority of us are supposed to be individuals who are free to think, feel, act as they please. To be sure this is not only the general opinion on the subject of modern individualism, but also each individual sincerely believes that he is "he" and that his thoughts, feelings, wishes are "his." Yet, although there are true individuals among us, this belief is an illusion in most cases and a dangerous one for that matter, as it blocks the removal of those conditions that are responsible for this state of affairs.

We are dealing here with one of the most fundamental problems of psychology which can most quickly be opened up by a series of questions. What is the self? What is the nature of those acts that give only the illusion of being the person's own acts? What is spontaneity? What is an original mental act? Finally, what has all this to do with freedom? In this chapter we shall try to show how feelings and thoughts can be induced from the outside and yet be subjectively experienced as one's own, and how one's own feelings and thoughts can be repressed and thus cease to be part of one's self. We shall continue the discussion of the questions raised here in the chapter on "Freedom and Democracy."

Let us start the discussion by analyzing the meaning of the experience which if put into words is, "I feel," "I think," "I will." When we say "I think," this seems to be a clear and unambiguous statement. The only question seems to be whether what I think is right or wrong, not whether or not *I* think it. Yet, one concrete experimental situation shows at once that the answer to this question is not necessarily what we suppose it to be. Let us attend an hypnotic experiment.[13] Here is the subject A whom the hypnotist B puts into hypnotic sleep and suggests to him that after awaking from the hypnotic sleep he will want to read a manuscript which he will believe he has brought with him, that he will seek it and not find it, that he will then believe that another person, C, has stolen it, that he will get very angry at C. He is also told that he will forget that all this was a suggestion given him during the hypnotic sleep. It must be added that C is a person toward whom the subject has never felt any anger and according to the circumstances has no reason to feel angry; furthermore, that he actually has not brought any manuscript with him.

What happens? A awakes and, after a short conversation about some topic, says, "Incidentally, this reminds me of something I have written in my manuscript. I shall read

[13] Regarding the problems of hypnosis cf. list of publications by M. H. Erickson, *Psychiatry*, 1939, Vol. 2, No. 3, p. 472.

it to you." He looks around, does not find it, and then turns to C, suggesting that he may have taken it; getting more and more excited when C repudiates the suggestion, he eventually bursts into open anger and directly accuses C of having stolen the manuscript. He goes even further. He puts forward reasons which should make it plausible that C is the thief. He has heard from others, he says, that C needs the manuscript very badly, that he had a good opportunity to take it, and so on. We hear him not only accusing C, but making up numerous "rationalizations" which should make his accusation appear plausible. (None of these, of course, are true and A would never have thought of them before.)

Let us assume that another person enters the room at this point. He would not have any doubt that A says what he thinks and feels; the only question in his mind would be whether or not his accusation is right, that is, whether or not the contents of A's thoughts conform to the real facts We, however, who have witnessed the whole procedure from the start, do not care to ask whether the accusation is true. We know that this is not the problem, since we are certain that what A feels and thinks now are not *his* thoughts and feelings but are alien elements put into his head by another person.

The conclusion to which the person entering in the middle of the experiment comes might be something like this. "Here is A, who clearly indicates that he has all these thoughts. He is the one to know best what he thinks and there is no better proof than his own statement about what he feels. There are those other persons who say that his thoughts are superimposed upon him and are alien

elements which come from without. In all fairness, I cannot decide who is right; any one of them may be mistaken.
Perhaps, since there are two against one, the greater chance
is that the majority is right." We, however, who have
witnessed the whole experiment would not be doubtful,
nor would the newcomer be if he attended other hypnotic
experiments. He would then see that this type of experiment can be repeated innumerable times with different
persons and different contents. The hypnotist can suggest
that a raw potato is a delicious pineapple, and the subject
will eat the potato with all the gusto associated with eating
a pineapple. Or that the subject cannot see anything, and
the subject will be blind. Or again, that he thinks that the
world is flat and not round, and the subject will argue
heatedly that the world is flat.

What does the hypnotic—and especially the posthyp-
notic—experiment prove? It proves that we can have
thoughts, feelings, wishes, and even sensual sensations
which we subjectively feel to be ours, and yet that, although we experience these thoughts and feelings, they
have been put into us from the outside, are basically alien,
and are not what we think, feel, and so on.

What does the specific hypnotic experiment with which
we started show? (1) The subject *wills* something, namely,
to read his manuscript, (2) he *thinks* something, namely,
that C has taken it, and (3) he *feels* something, namely,
anger against C We have seen that all three mental acts
—his will impulse, his thought, his feeling—are not his own
in the sense of being the result of his own mental activity;
that they have not originated in him, but are put into him
from the outside and are subjectively felt *as if* they were

his own. He gives expression to a number of thoughts which have not been put into him during the hypnosis, namely, those "rationalizations" by which he "explains" his assumption that C has stolen the manuscript. But nevertheless these thoughts are his own only in a formal sense. Although they appear to explain the suspicion, we know that the suspicion is there first and that the rationalizing thoughts are only invented to make the feeling plausible; they are not really explanatory but come *post factum*.

We started with the hypnotic experiment because it shows in the most unmistakable manner that, although one may be convinced of the spontaneity of one's mental acts, they actually result from the influence of a person other than oneself under the conditions of a particular situation. The phenomenon, however, is by no means to be found only in the hypnotic situation. The fact that the contents of our thinking, feeling, willing, are induced from the outside and are not genuine, exists to an extent that gives the impression that these pseudo acts are the rule, while the genuine or indigenous mental acts are the exceptions.

The pseudo character which *thinking* can assume is better known than the same phenomenon in the sphere of willing and feeling. It is best, therefore, to start with the discussion of the difference between genuine thinking and pseudo thinking. Let us suppose we are on an island where there are fishermen and summer guests from the city. We want to know what kind of weather we are to expect and ask a fisherman and two of the city people, who we know have all listened to the weather forecast on the radio. The fisherman, with his long experience and concern with this problem of weather, will start thinking, assuming that he had not as yet made up his mind before we asked him. Knowing what the direction of the wind, temperature, humidity, and so on mean as a basis for weather forecast, he will weigh the different factors according to their respective significance and come to a more or less definite judgment. He will probably remember the radio forecast and quote it as supporting or contradicting his own opinion; if it is contradictory, he may be particularly careful in weighing the reasons for his opinion; but, and this is the essential point, it is *his* opinion, the result of *his* thinking, which he tells us.

The first of the two city summer guests is a man who, when we ask him his opinion, knows that he does not understand much about the weather nor does he feel any compulsion to understand anything about it. He merely replies, "I cannot judge. All I know is that the radio forecast is thus and thus." The other man whom we ask is of a different type. He believes that he knows a great deal about the weather, although actually he knows little about it. He is the kind of person who feels that he must be able to answer every question. He thinks for a minute and then tells us "his" opinion, which in fact is identical with the radio forecast. We ask him for his reasons and he tells us that on account of wind direction, temperature, and so on, he has come to his conclusion.

This man's behavior as seen from the outside is the same as the fisherman's. Yet, if we analyze it more closely, it becomes evident that he has heard the radio forecast and has accepted it. Feeling compelled, however, to have his *own* opinion about it, he forgets that he is simply repeating somebody else's authoritative opinion, and believes that this opinion is one that he arrived at through his own thinking. He imagines that the reasons he gives us preceded his opinion, but if we examine these reasons we see that they could not possibly have led him to any conclusion about the weather if he had not formed an opinion beforehand. They are actually only pseudo reasons which have the function of making his opinion appear to be the result of his own thinking. He has the illusion of having arrived at an opinion of his own, but in reality he has merely adopted an authority's opinion without being aware of this process. It could very well be that he is right about the weather and the fisherman wrong, but in that event it would not be "his" opinion which would be right, although the fisherman would be really mistaken in "his own" opinion.

The same phenomenon can be observed if we study people's opinions about certain subjects, for instance, politics. Ask an average newspaper reader what he thinks about a certain political question. He will give you as "his" opinion a more or less exact account of what he has read, and yet—and this is the essential point—he believes that what he is saying is the result of his own thinking. If he lives in a small community where political opinions are handed down from father to son, "his own" opinion may be governed far more than he would for a moment believe by the lingering authority of a strict parent. Another reader's opinion may be the outcome of a moment's embarrassment, the fear of being thought uninformed, and hence the "thought" is essentially a front and not the result of a natural combination of experience, desire, and knowledge. The same phenomenon is to be found in aesthetic judgments. The average person who goes to a museum and looks at a picture by a famous painter, say Rembrandt, judges it to be a beautiful and impressive picture. If we analyze his judgment, we find that he does not have any particular inner response to the picture but thinks it is beautiful because he knows that he is supposed to think it is beautiful. The same phenomenon is evident with regard to people's judgment of music and also with regard to the act of perception itself. Many persons looking at a famous bit of scenery actually reproduce the pictures they have seen of it numerous times, say on postal cards, and while believing "they" see the scenery, they have these pictures before their eyes. Or, in experiencing an accident which occurs in their presence, they see or hear the situation in terms of the newspaper report they anticipate. As a matter of fact, for many people an experience which they have had, an artistic performance or a political meeting they have attended, becomes real to them only after they have read about it in the newspaper.

The suppression of critical thinking usually starts early. A five-year-old girl, for instance, may recognize the insincerity of her mother, either by subtly realizing that, while the mother is always talking of love and friendliness, she is actually cold and egotistical, or in a cruder way by noticing that her mother is having an affair with another man while constantly emphasizing her high moral standards. The child feels the discrepancy. Her sense of justice and truth is hurt, and yet, being dependent on the mother who would not allow any kind of criticism and, let us say, having a weak father on whom she cannot rely, the child is forced to suppress her critical insight. Very soon

she will no longer notice the mother's insincerity or un-
faithfulness. She will lose the ability to think critically since
it seems to be both hopeless and dangerous to keep it alive.
On the other hand, the child is impressed by the pattern
of having to believe that her mother is sincere and decent
and that the marriage of the parents is a happy one, and
she will be ready to accept this idea as if it where her own.

In all these illustrations of pseudo thinking, the problem
is whether the thought is the result of one's own thinking,
that is, of one's own activity; the problem is not whether or
not the contents of the thought are right. As has been already
suggested in the case of the fisherman making a weather
forecast, "his" thought may even be wrong, and that of the
man who only repeats the thought put into him may be
right. The pseudo thinking may also be perfectly logical
and rational. Its pseudo character does not necessarily appear in illogical elements. This can be studied in rationalizations which tend to explain an action or a feeling on
rational and realistic grounds, although it is actually
determined by irrational and subjective factors. The
rationalization may be in contradiction to facts or to the
rules of logical thinking. But frequently it will be logical
and rational in itself; then its irrationality lies only in the
fact that is not the real motive of the action which it pre-
tends to have caused.

An example of irrational rationalization is brought forward in a well-known joke. A person who had borrowed a
glass jar from a neighbor had broken it and, on being
asked to return it, answered, "In the first place, I have
already returned it to you; in the second place, I never
borrowed it from you; and in the third place, it was already

broken when you gave it to me." We have an example of "rational" rationalization when a person, A, who finds himself in a situation of economic distress, asks a relative of his, B, to lend him a sum of money. B declines and says that he does so because by lending money he could only support A's inclinations to be irresponsible and to lean on others for support. Now this reasoning may be perfectly sound, but it would nevertheless be a rationalization because B had not wanted to let A have the money in any event, and although he believes himself to be motivated by concern for A's welfare he is actually motivated by his own stinginess.

We cannot learn, therefore, whether we are dealing with a rationalization merely by determining the logicality of a person's statement as such, but we must also take into account the psychological motivations operating in a person. The decisive point is not *what* is thought but *how* it is thought. The thought that is the result of active thinking is always new and original; original, not necessarily in the sense that others have not thought it before, but always in the sense that the person who thinks, has used thinking as a tool to discover something new in the world outside or inside of himself. Rationalizations are essentially lacking this quality of discovering and uncovering; they only confirm the emotional prejudice existing in oneself. Rationalizing is not a tool for penetration of reality but a post-factum attempt to harmonize one's own wishes with existing reality.

With feeling as with thinking, one must distinguish between a genuine feeling, which originates in ourselves, and a pseudo feeling, which is really not our own although we believe it to be. Let us choose an example from every-day life which is typical of the pseudo character of our feelings in contact with others. We observe a man who is attending a party. He is gay, he laughs, makes friendly conversation, and all in all seems to be quite happy and contented. On taking his leave, he has a friendly smile while saying how much he enjoyed the evening. The door closes behind him—and this is the moment when we watch him carefully. A sudden change is noticed in his face. The smile has disappeared; of course, that is to be expected since he is now alone and has nothing or nobody with him to evoke a smile. But the change I am speaking of is more than just the disappearance of the smile. There appears on his face an expression of deep sadness, almost of desper-ation. This expression probably stays only for a few sec-onds, and then the face assumes the usual masklike expres-sion; the man gets into his car, thinks about the evening, wonders whether or not he made a good impression, and feels that he did. But was "he" happy and gay during the party? Was the brief expression of sadness and desperation we observed on his face only a momentary reaction of no great significance? It is almost impossible to decide the question without knowing more of this man. There is one incident, however, which may provide the clue for under-standing what his gayety meant.

That night he dreams that he is back with the A.E.F. in the war. He has received orders to get through the opposite lines into enemy headquarters. He dons an of-ficer's uniform, which seems to be German, and suddenly finds himself among a group of German officers. He is surprised that the headquarters are so comfortable and that everyone is so friendly to him, but he gets more and more frightened that they will find out that he is a spy. One of the younger officers for whom he feels a particular liking approaches him and says "I know who you are. There is only one way for you to escape. Start telling jokes, laugh and make them laugh so much that they are diverted by your jokes from paying any attention to you." He is very grateful for this advice and starts making jokes and laughing. Eventually his joking increases to such an extent that the other officers get suspicious, and the greater their suspicions the more forced his jokes appear to be. At last such a feeling of terror fills him that he cannot bear to stay any longer; he suddenly jumps up from his chair and they all run after him. Then the scene changes, and he is sitting in a streetcar which stops just in front of his house. He wears a business suit and has a feeling of relief at the thought that the war is over.

Let us assume that we are in a position to ask him the next day what occurs to him in connection with the individual elements of the dream. We record here only a few associations which are particularly significant for understanding the main point we are interested in. The German uniform reminds him that there was one guest at the party on the previous evening who spoke with a heavy German accent. He remembered having been annoyed by this man because he had not paid much attention to him, although he (our dreamer) had gone out of his way to make a good impression. While rambling along with these thoughts he recalls that for a moment at the party he had had the feeling that this man with the German accent had actually made fun of him and smiled impertinently at some statement he had made. Thinking about the comfortable room in which the head-quarters were, it occurs to him that it looked like the room in which he had sat during the party last night, but that the windows looked like the windows of a room in which he had once failed in an examination. Surprised at this association, he went on to recall that before going to the party he was somewhat concerned about the impression he would make, partly because one of the guests was the brother of a girl whose interest he wanted to win, and partly because the host had much influence with a superior on whose opinion about him much depended for his professional success. Speaking about this superior he says how much he dislikes him, how humiliated he feels in having to show a friendly front toward him, and that he had felt some dislike for his host too, although he was almost not aware of it at all. Another of his associations is that he had told a funny incident about a bald man and then was slightly appre-hensive lest he might have hurt his host who happened to be almost bald too. The streetcar struck him as strange since there did not seem to be any tracks. While talking about it, he remembers the streetcar he was riding on as a boy on his way to school, and a further detail occurs to him, namely, that he had taken the place of the streetcar driver and had thought that driving a streetcar was astonishingly little different from driving an automobile. It is evident that the streetcar stands for his own car in which he had driven home, and that his returning home reminded him of going home from school.

To anyone accustomed to understand the meaning of dreams, the implication of the dream and the accompanying associations will be clear by now, although only part of his associations have been mentioned and practically nothing has been said about the personality structure, the past and the present situation of the man. The dream reveals what his real feeling was at the previous night's party. He was anxious, afraid of failing to make the impression he wanted to make, angry at several persons by whom he felt ridiculed and not sufficiently liked. The dream shows that his gaiety was a means of concealing his anxiety and his anger, and at the same time of pacifying those at whom he was angry. All his gaiety was a mask; it did not originate in himself, but covered what "he" really felt: fear and anger. This also made his whole position insecure, so that he felt like a spy in an enemy camp who might be found out any moment. The fleeting expression of sadness and desperation we noticed on him just when he was leaving, now finds its affirmation and also its explanation: at that moment his face expressed what "he" really felt, although it was something "he" was not really aware of feeling. In the dream, the feeling is described in a dramatic and explicit way, although it does not overtly refer to the people toward whom his feelings were directed.

This man is not neurotic, nor was he under a hypnotic spell; he is a rather normal individual with the same anxiety and need for approval as are customary in modern man. He was not aware of the fact that his gaiety was not "his," since he is so accustomed to feel what he is supposed to feel in a particular situation, that it would be the exception rather than the rule which would make him aware of anything being "strange."

What holds true of thinking and feeling holds also true

of willing. Most people are convinced that as long as they are not overtly forced to do something by an outside power, their decisions are theirs, and that if they want something, it is they who want it. But this is one of the great illusions we have about ourselves. A great number of our decisions are not really our own but are suggested to us from the outside; we have succeeded in persuading ourselves that it is we who have made the decision, whereas we have actually conformed with expectations of others, driven by the fear of isolation and by more direct threats to our life, freedom, and comfort.

When children are asked whether they want to go to school every day, and their answer is, "Of course, I do," is the answer true? In many cases certainly not. The child may want to go to school quite frequently, yet very often would like to play or do something else instead. If he feels, "I want to go to school every day," he may repress his disinclination for the regularity of schoolwork. He feels that he is expected to want to go to school every day, and this pressure is strong enough to submerge the feeling that he goes so often only because he has to. The child might feel happier if he could be aware of the fact that sometimes he wants to go and sometimes he only goes because he has to go. Yet the pressure of the sense of duty is great enough to give him the feeling that "he" wants what he is supposed to want.

It is a general assumption that most men marry voluntarily. Certainly there are those cases of men consciously marrying on the basis of a feeling of duty or obligation. There are cases in which a man marries because "he" really wants to. But there are also not a few cases in which a man (or a woman for that matter) consciously believes that he *wants* to marry a certain person while actually he finds himself caught in a sequence of events which leads to marriage and seems to block every escape. All the months leading up to his marriage he is firmly convinced that "he" wants to marry, and the first and rather belated indication that this may not be so is the fact that on the day of his marriage he suddenly gets panicky and feels an impulse to run away. If he is "sensible" this feeling lasts only for a few minutes, and he will answer the question whether it is his intention to marry with the unshakable conviction that it is.

We could go on quoting many more instances in daily life in which people seem to make decisions, seem to want something, but actually follow the internal or external pressure of "having" to want the thing they are going to do. As a matter of fact, in watching the phenomenon of human decisions, one is struck by the extent to which people are mistaken in taking as "their" decision what in effect is submission to convention, duty, or simple pressure. It almost seems that "original" decision is a comparatively rare phenomenon in a society which supposedly makes individual decision the cornerstone of its existence.

I wish to add one detailed example of a case of pseudo willing which can frequently be observed in the analysis of people who do not have any neurotic symptoms. One reason for doing so is the fact that, although this individual case has little to do with the broad cultural issues with which we are mainly concerned in this book, it gives the reader who is not familiar with the operation of unconscious forces an additional opportunity to become acquainted with this phenomenon. Moreover, this example stresses one point which, though being implicitly made already, should be brought forward explicitly: the connection of repression with the problem of pseudo acts. Although one looks at repression mostly from the standpoint of the operation of the repressed forces in neurotic behavior, dreams, and so on, it seems important to stress the fact that every repression eliminates parts of one's real self and enforces the substitution of a pseudo feeling for the one which has been repressed.

The case I want to present now is one of a twenty-two-year-old medical student. He is interested in his work and gets along with people pretty normally. He is not particularly unhappy, although he often feels slightly tired and has no particular zest for life. The reason why he wants to be analyzed is a theoretical one since he wants to become a psychiatrist. His only complaint is some sort of blockage in his medical work. He frequently cannot remember things he has read, gets inordinately tired during lectures, and makes a comparatively poor showing in examinations. He is puzzled by this since in other subjects he seems to have a much better memory. He has no doubts about wanting to study medicine, but often has very strong doubts as to whether he has the ability to do it.

After a few weeks of analysis he relates a dream in which he is on the top floor of a skyscraper he had built and looks out over the other buildings with a slight feeling of triumph. Suddenly the skyscraper collapses and he finds himself buried under the ruins. He is aware of efforts being made to remove the debris in order to free him, and can hear someone say that he is badly injured and that the doctor will come very soon. But he has to wait what seems to be an endless length of time before the doctor arrives. When he eventually gets there the doctor discovers that he has forgotten to bring his instruments and can therefore do nothing to help him. An intense rage wells up in him against the doctor and he suddenly finds himself standing up, realizing that he is not hurt at all. He sneers at the doctor, and at that moment he awakes.

He does not have many associations in connection with the dream, but these are some of the more relevant ones. Thinking of the skyscraper he has built, he mentions in a casual way how much he was always interested in architecture. As a child his favorite pastime for many years consisted of playing with construction blocks, and when he was seventeen, he had considered becoming an architect. When he mentioned this to his father, the latter had responded in a friendly fashion that of course he was free to choose his career, but that he (the father) was sure that the idea was a residue of his childish wishes, that he really preferred to study medicine. The young man thought that his father was right and since then had never mentioned the problem to his father again, but had started to study medicine as a matter of course. His associations about the doctor being late and then forgetting his instruments were rather vague and scant. However, while talking about this part of the dream, it occurred to him that his analytic hour had been changed from its regular time and that while he had agreed to the change without any objection he had really felt quite angry. He can feel his anger rising now while he is talking. He accuses the analyst of being arbitrary and eventually says, "Well, after all, I cannot do what I want anyway."

He is quite surprised at his anger and at this sentence, because so far he had never felt any antagonism toward the analyst or the analytic work.

Some time afterwards he has another dream of which he only remembers a fragment: his father is wounded in an automobile accident. He himself is a doctor and is supposed to take care of the father. While he is trying to examine him, he feels completely paralyzed and cannot do anything. He is terror-stricken and wakes up.

In his associations he reluctantly mentions that in the last few years he has had thoughts that his father might die suddenly, and these thoughts have frightened him. Sometimes he had even thought of the estate which would be left to him and of what he would do with the money. He had not proceeded very far with these phantasies, as he suppressed them as soon as they began to appear. In comparing this dream with the one mentioned before, it strikes him that in both cases the doctor is unable to render any efficient help. He realizes more clearly than ever before that he feels that he can never be of any use as a doctor. When it is pointed out to him that in the first dream there is a definite feeling of anger and derision at the impotence of the doctor, he remembers that often when he hears or reads about cases in which a doctor has been unable to help the patient, he has a certain feeling of triumph of which he was not aware at the time.

In the further course of the analysis other material which had been repressed comes up. He discovers to his own surprise a strong feeling of rage against his father, and furthermore that his feeling of impotence as a doctor is part of a more general feeling of powerlessness which pervades his whole life. Although on the surface he thought that he had arranged his life according to his own plans, he can feel now that deeper down he was filled with a sense of resignation. He realizes that he was convinced that he could not do what he wanted but had to conform with what was expected of him. He sees more and more clearly that he had never really wanted to become a physician and that the things which had impressed him as a lack of ability were nothing but the expression of passive resistance.

This case is a typical example of the repression of a person's real wishes and the adoption of expectations of others in a way that makes them appear to be his own wishes. We might say that the original wish is replaced by a pseudo wish.

This substitution of pseudo acts for original acts of thinking, feeling, and willing, leads eventually to the replacement of the original self by a pseudo self. The original self is the self which is the originator of mental activities. The pseudo self is only an agent who actually represents the role a person is supposed to play but who does so under the name of the self. It is true that a person can play many roles and subjectively be convinced that he is "he" in each role. Actually he is in all these roles what he believes he is expected to be, and for many people, if not most, the original self is completely suffocated by the pseudo self. Sometimes in a dream, in phantasies, or when a person is drunk, some of the original self may appear, feelings and thoughts which the person has not experienced for years. Often they are bad ones which he has repressed because he is afraid or ashamed of them. Sometimes, however, they are the very best things in him, which he has repressed because of his fear of being ridiculed or attacked for having such feelings.[14]

The loss of the self and its substitution by a pseudo self leave the individual in an intense state of insecurity. He is obsessed by doubt since, being essentially a reflex of other people's expectation of him, he has in a measure lost his identity. In order to overcome the panic resulting from such loss of identity, he is compelled to conform, to seek his identity by continuous approval and recognition by others. Since he does not know who he is, at least the others will know—if he acts according to their expectation; if they know, he will know too, if he only takes their word for it.

The automatization of the individual in modern society has increased the helplessness and insecurity of the average individual. Thus, he is ready to submit to new authorities which offer him security and relief from doubt. The following chapter will discuss the special conditions that were necessary to make this offer accepted in Germany; it will show that for the nucleus—the lower middle class—of the Nazi movement, the authoritarian mechanism was most characteristic. In the last chapter of this book we shall continue the discussion of the automaton with regard to the cultural scene in our own democracy.

[14] The psychoanalytic procedure is essentially a process in which a person tries to uncover this original self. "Free association" means to express one's original feelings and thoughts, telling the truth; but truth in this sense does not refer to the fact that one says what one thinks, but the thinking itself is original and not an adaptation to an expected thought. Freud has emphasized the repression of "bad" things; it seems that he has not sufficiently seen the extent to which the "good" things are subjected to repression also.

CHAPTER VI

Psychology of Nazism

I N the last chapter our attention was focused on two psychological types: the authoritarian character and the automaton. I hope that the detailed discussion of these types will help in the understanding of the problems which this and the next chapter offer: the psychology of Nazism on the one hand, modern democracy on the other.

In discussing the psychology of Nazism we have first to consider a preliminary question—the relevance of psychological factors in the understanding of Nazism. In the scientific and still more so in the popular discussion of Nazism, two opposite views are frequently presented: the first, that psychology offers no explanation of an economic and political phenomenon like Fascism, the second, that Fascism is wholly a psychological problem.

The first view looks upon Nazism either as the outcome of an exclusively economic dynamism—of the expansive tendencies of German imperialism, or as an essentially political phenomenon—the conquest of the state by one political party backed by industrialists and Junkers; in short, the victory of Nazism is looked upon as the result of a minority's trickery and coercion of the majority of the population.

The second view, on the other hand, maintains that Nazism can be explained only in terms of psychology, or

207

rather in those of psychopathology. Hitler is looked upon as a madman or as a "neurotic," and his followers as equally mad and mentally unbalanced. According to this explanation, as expounded by L. Mumford, the true sources of Fascism are to be found "in the human soul, *not in economics.*" He goes on: "In overwhelming pride, delight in cruelty, neurotic disintegration—in this and not in the Treaty of Versailles or in the incompetence of the German Republic lies the explanation of Fascism."[1]

In our opinion none of these explanations which emphasize political and economic factors to the exclusion of psychological ones—or vice versa—is correct. Nazism is a psychological problem, but the psychological factors themselves have to be understood as being molded by socioeconomic factors; Nazism is an economic and political problem, but the hold it has over a whole people has to be understood on psychological grounds. What we are concerned with in this chapter is this psychological aspect of Nazism, its human basis. This suggests two problems: the character structure of those people to whom it appealed, and the psychological characteristics of the ideology that made it such an effective instrument with regard to those very people.

In considering the psychological basis for the success of Nazism this differentiation has to be made at the outset: one part of the population bowed to the Nazi regime without any strong resistance, but also without becoming admirers of the Nazi ideology and political practice. Another part was deeply attracted to the new ideology

[1] L. Mumford, *Faith for Living*, Harcourt, Brace & Co., New York, 1940. p. 118.

and fanatically attached to those who proclaimed it. The first group consisted mainly of the working class and the liberal and Catholic bourgeoisie. In spite of an excellent organization, especially among the working class, these groups, although continuously hostile to Nazism from its beginning up to 1933, did not show the inner resistance one might have expected as the outcome of their political convictions. Their will to resist collapsed quickly and since then they have caused little difficulty for the regime (excepting, of course, the small minority which has fought heroically against Nazism during all these years). Psychologically, this readiness to submit to the Nazi regime seems to be due mainly to a state of inner tiredness and resignation, which, as will be indicated in the next chapter, is characteristic of the individual in the present era even in democratic countries. In Germany one additional condition was present as far as the working class was concerned: the defeat it suffered after the first victories in the revolution of 1918. The working class had entered the postwar period with strong hopes for the realization of socialism or at least for a definite rise in its political, economic, and social position; but, whatever the reasons, it had witnessed an unbroken succession of defeats, which brought about the complete disappointments of all its hopes. By the beginning of 1930 the fruits of its initial victories were almost completely destroyed and the result was a deep feeling of resignation, of disbelief in their leaders, of doubt about the value of any kind of political organization and political activity. They still remained members of their respective parties and, consciously, continued to believe in their political doctrines; but deep within themselves many had given up any hope in the effectiveness of political action.

An additional incentive for the loyalty of the majority of the population to the Nazi government became effective after Hitler came into power. For millions of people Hitler's government then became identical with "Germany." Once he held the power of government, fighting him implied shutting oneself out of the community of Germans; when other political parties were abolished and the Nazi party "was" Germany, opposition to it meant opposition to Germany. It seems that nothing is more difficult for the average man to bear than the feeling of not being identified with a larger group. However much a German citizen may be opposed to the principles of Nazism, if he has to choose between being alone and feeling that he belongs to Germany, most persons will choose the latter. It can be observed in many instances that persons who are not Nazis nevertheless defend Nazism against criticism of foreigners because they feel that an attack on Nazism is an attack on Germany. The fear of isolation and the relative weakness of moral principles help any party to win the loyalty of a large sector of the population once that party has captured the power of the state.

This consideration results in an axiom which is important for the problems of political propaganda: any attack on Germany as such, any defamatory propaganda concerning "the Germans" (such as the "Hun" symbol of the last war), only increases the loyalty of those who are not wholly identified with the Nazi system. This problem, however, cannot be solved basically by skillful propaganda but only by the victory in all countries of one fundamental truth:

that ethical principles stand above the existence of the nation and that by adhering to these principles an individual belongs to the community of all those who share, who have shared, and who will share this belief.

In contrast to the negative or resigned attitude of the working class and of the liberal and Catholic bourgeoisie, the Nazi ideology was ardently greeted by the lower strata of the middle class, composed of small shopkeepers, artisans, and white-collar workers.[2]

Members of the older generation among this class formed the more passive mass basis; their sons and daughters were the more active fighters. For them the Nazi ideology—its spirit of blind obedience to a leader and of hatred against racial and political minorities, its craving for conquest and domination, its exaltation of the German people and the "Nordic Race"—had a tremendous emotional appeal, and it was this appeal which won them over and made them into ardent believers in and fighters for the Nazi cause. The answer to the question why the Nazi ideology was so appealing to the lower middle class has to be sought for in the social character of the lower middle class. Their social character was markedly different from that of the working class, of the higher strata of the middle class, and of the nobility before the war of 1914. As a matter of fact, certain features were characteristic for this part of the middle class throughout its history: their love of the strong, hatred of the weak, their pettiness, hostility, thrifti-

---

[2] Cf. to this whole chapter and specifically to the role of the lower middle class, Harold D. Lasswell's illuminating paper on "The Psychology of Hitlerism" in *The Political Quarterly*, Vol. IV, 1933, MacMillan & Co., London, p. 374, and F. L. Schuman's *The Nazi Dictatorship*, Alfred A. Knopf, New York, 1939.

ness with feelings as well as with money, and essentially their asceticism. Their outlook on life was narrow, they suspected and hated the stranger, and they were curious and envious of their acquaintances, rationalizing their envy as moral indignation; their whole life was based on the principle of scarcity—economically as well as psychologically.

To say that the social character of the lower middle class differed from that of the working class does not imply that this character structure was not present in the working class also. But it was *typical* for the lower middle class, while only a minority of the working class exhibited the same character structure in a similarly clear-cut fashion; the one or the other trait, however, in a less intense form, like enhanced respect of authority or thrift, was to be found in most members of the working class too. On the other hand it seems that a great part of the white-collar workers —probably the majority—more closely resembled the character structure of the manual workers (especially those in big factories) than that of the "old middle class," which did not participate in the rise of monopolistic capitalism but was essentially threatened by it.[8]

Although it is true that the social character of the lower middle class had been the same long before the war of 1914, it is also true that the events after the war intensified

[8] The view presented here is based on the results of an unpublished study of the "Character of German Workers and Employees in 1929/30," undertaken by A. Hartoch, E. Herzog, H. Schachtel, and myself (with an historical introduction by F. Neumann), under the auspices of the International Institute of Social Research, Columbia University. Analysis of the responses of six hundred persons to a detailed questionnaire showed that a minority of the respondents exhibited the authoritarian character, that with about the same number the quest for freedom and independence was prevalent, while the great majority exhibited a less clear-cut mixture of different traits.

the very traits to which the Nazi ideology had its strong appeal: its craving for submission and its lust for power.

In the period before the German Revolution of 1918, the economic position of the lower strata of the old middle class, the small independent businessman and artisan, was already on the decline; but it was not desperate and there were a number of factors which made for its stability.

The authority of the monarchy was undisputed, and by leaning on it and identifying with it the member of the lower middle class acquired a feeling of security and narcissistic pride. Also, the authority of religion and traditional morality was still firmly rooted. The family was still unshaken and a safe refuge in a hostile world. The individual felt that he belonged to a stable social and cultural system in which he had his definite place. His submission and loyalty to existing authorities were a satisfactory solution of his masochistic strivings; yet he did not go to the extreme of self-surrender and he retained a sense of the importance of his own personality. What he was lacking in security and aggressiveness as an individual, he was compensated for by the strength of the authorities to whom he submitted himself. In brief his economic position was still solid enough to give him a feeling of self-pride and of relative security, and the authorities on whom he leaned were strong enough to give him the additional security which his own individual position could not provide.

The postwar period changed this situation considerably. In the first place, the economic decline of the old middle class went at a faster pace; this decline was accelerated by the inflation, culminating in 1923, which wiped out almost completely the savings of many years' work.

While the years between 1924 and 1928 brought economic improvement and new hopes to the lower middle class, these gains were wiped out by the depression after 1929. As in the period of inflation, the middle class, squeezed in between the workers and the upper classes, was the most defenseless group and therefore the hardest hit.[4]

But besides these economic factors there were psychological considerations that aggravated the situation. The defeat in the war and the downfall of the monarchy was one. While the monarchy and the state had been the solid rock on which, psychologically speaking, the petty bourgeois had built his existence, their failure and defeat shattered the basis of his own life. If the Kaiser could be publicly ridiculed, if officers could be attacked, if the state had to change its form and to accept "red agitators" as cabinet ministers and a saddlemaker as president, what could the little man put his trust in? He had identified himself in his subaltern manner with all these institutions; now, since they had gone, where was he to go?

The inflation, too, played both an economic and a psychological role. It was a deadly blow against the principle of thrift as well as against the authority of the state. If the savings of many years, for which one had sacrificed so many little pleasures, could be lost through no fault of one's own, what was the point in saving anyway? If the state could break its promises printed on its bank notes and loans, whose promises could one trust any longer?

It was not only the economic position of the lower middle class that declined more rapidly after the war, but

‘ Schuman, *op. cit.*, p. 104.

its social prestige as well. Before the war one could feel himself as something better than a worker. After the revolution the social prestige of the working class rose considerably and in consequence the prestige of the lower middle class fell in relative terms. There was nobody to look down upon any more, a privilege that had always been one of the strongest assets in the life of small shopkeepers and their like.

In addition to these factors the last stronghold of middle-class security had been shattered too: the family. The postwar development, in Germany perhaps more than in other countries, had shaken the authority of the father and the old middle-class morality. The younger generation acted as they pleased and cared no longer whether their actions were approved by their parents or not.

The reasons for this development are too manifold and complex to discuss here in detail. I shall mention only a few. The decline of the old social symbols of authority like monarchy and state affected the role of the individual authorities, the parents. If these authorities, which the younger generation had been taught by the parents to respect, proved to be weak, then the parents lost prestige and authority too. Another factor was that, under the changed conditions, especially the inflation, the older generation was bewildered and puzzled and much less adapted to the new conditions than the smarter, younger generation. Thus the younger generation felt superior to their elders and could not take them, and their teachings, quite seriously any more. Furthermore, the economic decline of the middle class deprived the parents of their economic role as backers of the economic future of their children.

The older generation of the lower middle class grew more bitter and resentful, but in a passive way; the younger generation was driving for action. Its economic position was aggravated by the fact that the basis for an independent economic existence, such as their parents had had, was lost; the professional market was saturated, and the chances of making a living as a physician or lawyer were slight. Those who had fought in the war felt that they had a claim for a better deal than they were actually getting. Especially the many young officers, who for years had been accustomed to command and to exercise power quite naturally, could not reconcile themselves to becoming clerks or traveling salesmen.

The increasing social frustration led to a projection which became an important source for National Socialism: instead of being aware of the economic and social fate of the old middle class, its members consciously thought of their fate in terms of the nation. The national defeat and the Treaty of Versailles became the symbols to which the actual frustration—the social one—was shifted.

It has often been said that the treatment of Germany by the victors in 1918 was one of the chief reasons for the rise of Nazism. This statement needs qualification. The majority of Germans felt that the peace treaty was unjust; but while the middle class reacted with intense bitterness, there was much less bitterness at the Versailles Treaty among the working class. They had been opposed to the old regime and the loss of the war for them meant defeat of that regime. They felt that they had fought bravely and that they had no reason to be ashamed of themselves. On the other hand the victory of the revolution which had only been possible by the defeat of the monarchy had brought them economic, political, and human gains. The resentment against Versailles had its basis in the lower middle class; the nationalistic resentment was a rationalization, projecting social inferiority to national inferiority.

This projection is quite apparent in Hitler's personal development. He was the typical representative of the lower middle class, a nobody with no chances or future. He felt very intensely the role of being an outcast. He often speaks in *Mein Kampf* of himself as the "nobody," the "unknown man" he was in his youth. But although this was due essentially to his own social position, he could rationalize it in national symbols. Being born outside of the Reich he felt excluded not so much socially as nationally, and the great German Reich to which all her sons could return became for him the symbol of social prestige and security.[5]

The old middle class's feeling of powerlessness, anxiety, and isolation from the social whole and the destructiveness springing from this situation was not the only psychological source of Nazism. The peasants felt resentful against the urban creditors to whom they were in debt, while the workers felt deeply disappointed and discouraged by the constant political retreat after their first victories in 1918 under a leadership which had lost all strategic initiative. The vast majority of the population was seized with the feeling of individual insignificance and powerlessness which we have described as typical for monopolistic capitalism in general.

Those psychological conditions were not the "cause"

[5] Adolph Hitler, *Mein Kampf*, Reynal & Hitchcock, New York, 1940, p. 3.

of Nazism. They constituted its human basis without which it could not have developed, but any analysis of the whole phenomenon of the rise and victory of Nazism must deal with the strictly economic and political, as well as with the psychological, conditions. In view both of the literature dealing with this aspect and of the specific aims of this book, there is no need to enter into a discussion of these economic and political questions. The reader may be reminded, however, of the role which the representatives of big industry and the half-bankrupt Junkers played in the establishment of Nazism. Without their support Hitler could never have won, and their support was rooted in their understanding of their economic interests much more than in psychological factors.

This property-owning class was confronted with a parliament in which 40 per cent of the deputies were Socialists and Communists representing groups which were dissatisfied with the existing social system, and in which were an increasing number of Nazi deputies who also represented a class that was in bitter opposition to the most powerful representatives of German capitalism. A parliament which thus in its majority represented tendencies directed against their economic interest deemed them dangerous. They said democracy did not work. Actually one might say democracy worked too well. The parliament was a rather adequate representation of the respective interests of the different classes of the German population, and for this very reason the parliamentary system could not any longer be reconciled with the need to preserve the privileges of big industry and half-feudal landowners. The representatives of these privileged groups expected that Nazism would shift the emotional resentment which threatened them into other channels and at the same time harness the nation into the service of their own economic interests. On the whole they were not disappointed. To be sure, in minor details they were mistaken. Hitler and his bureaucracy were not tools to be ordered around by the Thyssens and Krupps, who had to share their power with the Nazi bureaucracy and often to submit to them. But although Nazism proved to be economically detrimental to all other classes, it fostered the interests of the most powerful groups of German industry. The Nazi system is the "streamlined" version of German prewar imperialism and it continued where the monarchy had failed. (The Republic, however, did not really interrupt the development of German monopolistic capitalism but furthered it with the means at her disposal.)

There is one question that many a reader will have in mind at this point: How can one reconcile the statement that the psychological basis of Nazism was the old middle class with the statement that Nazism functions in the interests of German imperialism? The answer to this question is in principle the same as that which was given to the question concerning the role of the urban middle class during the period of the rise of capitalism. In the postwar period it was the middle class, particularly the lower middle class, that was threatened by monopolistic capitalism. Its anxiety and thereby its hatred were aroused; it moved into a state of panic and was filled with a craving for submission to as well as for domination over those who were powerless. These feelings were used by an entirely different class for a regime which was to work for their own interests. Hitler proved to be such an efficient tool because he combined the characteristics of a resentful, hating, petty bourgeois, with whom the lower middle class could identify themselves emotionally and socially, with those of an opportunist who was ready to serve the interests of the German industrialists and Junkers. Originally he posed as the Messiah of the old middle class, promised the destruction of department stores, the breaking of the domination of banking capital, and so on. The record is clear enough. These promises were never fulfilled. However, that did not matter. Nazism never had any genuine political or economic principles. It is essential to understand that the very principle of Nazism is its radical opportunism. What mattered was that hundreds of thousands of petty bourgeois, who in the normal course of development had little chance to gain money or power, as members of the Nazi bureaucracy now got a large slice of the wealth and prestige they forced the upper classes to share with them. Others who were not members of the Nazi machine were given the jobs taken away from Jews and political enemies; and as for the rest, although they did not get more bread, they got "circuses." The emotional satisfaction afforded by these sadistic spectacles and by an ideology which gave them a feeling of superiority over the rest of mankind was able to compensate them—for a time at least— for the fact that their lives had been impoverished, economically and culturally.

We have seen, then, that certain socioeconomic changes, notably the decline of the middle class and the rising power of monopolistic capital, had a deep psychological effect. These effects were increased or systematized by a political ideology—as by religious ideologies in the sixteenth century —and the psychic forces thus aroused became effective in a direction that was opposite to the original economic interests of that class. Nazism resurrected the lower middle class psychologically while participating in the destruction of its old socioeconomic position. It mobilized its emotional energies to become an important force in the struggle for the economic and political aims of German imperialism.

In the following pages we shall try to show that Hitler's personality, his teachings, and the Nazi system express an extreme form of the character structure which we have called "authoritarian" and that by this very fact he made a powerful appeal to those parts of the population which were—more or less—of the same character structure.

Hitler's autobiography is as good an illustration of the authoritarian character as any, and since in addition to that it is the most representative document of Nazi literature I shall use it as the main source for analyzing the psychology of Nazism.

The essence of the authoritarian character has been described as the simultaneous presence of sadistic and masochistic drives. Sadism was understood as aiming at unrestricted power over another person more or less mixed with destructiveness; masochism as aiming at dissolving oneself in an overwhelmingly strong power and participating in its strength and glory. Both the sadistic and the masochistic trends are caused by the inability of the isolated individual to stand alone and his need for a symbiotic relationship that overcomes this aloneness.

The *sadistic craving for power* finds manifold expressions

in *Mein Kampf*. It is characteristic of Hitler's relationship
to the German masses whom he despises and "loves" in
the typically sadistic manner, as well as to his political
enemies towards whom he evidences those destructive elements that are an important component of his sadism. He
speaks of the satisfaction the masses have in domination.
"What they want is the victory of the stronger and the
annihilation or the unconditional surrender of the
weaker."⁶ "Like a woman, . . . who will submit to the
strong man rather than dominate the weakling, thus the
masses love the ruler rather than the suppliant, and in-
wardly they are far more satisfied by a doctrine which
tolerates no rival than by the grant of liberal freedom;
they often feel at a loss what to do with it, and even easily
feel themselves deserted. They neither realize the im-
pudence with which they are spiritually terrorized, nor
the outrageous curtailment of their human liberties for
in no way does the delusion of this doctrine dawn on
them."⁷

He describes the breaking of the will of the audience by
the superior strength of the speaker as the essential factor
in propaganda. He does not even hesitate to admit that
physical tiredness of his audience is a most welcome condition for their suggestibility. Discussing the question which
hour of the day is most suited for political mass meetings
he says: "It seems that in the morning and even during
the day men's will power revolts with highest energy
against an attempt at being forced under another's will and
another's opinion. In the evening, however, they succumb

⁶ op. cit., p. 469.
⁷ op. cit., p. 56.

more easily to the dominating force of a stronger will. For truly every such meeting presents a wrestling match between two opposed forces. The superior oratorical talent of a domineering apostolic nature will now succeed more easily in winning for the new will people who themselves have in turn experienced a weakening of their force of resistance in the most natural way, than people who still have full command of the energies of their minds and their will power."[8]

Hitler himself is very much aware of the conditions which make for the longing for submission and gives an excellent description of the situation of the individual attending a mass meeting.

"The mass meeting is necessary if only for the reason that in it the individual, who in becoming an adherent of a new movement feels lonely and is easily seized with the fear of being alone, receives for the first time the pictures of a greater community, something that has a strengthening and encouraging effect on most people. . . . If he steps for the first time out of his small workshop or out of the big enterprise, in which he feels very small, into the mass meeting and is now surrounded by thousands and thousands of people with the same conviction . . . he himself succumbs to the magic influence of what we call mass suggestion."[9]

Goebbels describes the masses in the same vein. "People want nothing at all, except to be governed decently," he writes in his novel Michael.[10] They are for him, "nothing

[8] op. cit., p. 710 ff.
[9] op. cit., pp. 715, 716.
[10] Joseph Goebbels, Michael, F. Eher, München, 1936. p. 57.

more than the stone is for the sculptor. Leader and masses is as little a problem as painter and color."[11]

In another book Goebbels gives an accurate description of the dependence of the sadistic person on his objects; how weak and empty he feels unless he has power over somebody and how this power gives him new strength. This is Goebbels' account of what is going on in himself: "Sometimes one is gripped by a deep depression. One can only overcome it, if one is in front of the masses again. The people are the fountain of our power."[12]

A telling account of that particular kind of power over people which the Nazis call leadership is given by the leader of the German labor front, Ley. In discussing the qualities required in a Nazi leader and the aims of education of leaders, he writes: "We want to know whether these men have the will to lead, to be masters, in one word, to rule . . . We want to rule and enjoy it . . . We shall teach these men to ride horseback . . . in order to give them the feeling of absolute domination over a living being."[13]

The same emphasis on power is also present in Hitler's formulation of the aims of education. He says that the pupil's "entire education and development has to be directed at giving him the conviction of being absolutely superior to the others."[14]

The fact that somewhere else he declares that a boy

<hr/>

[11] op. cit., p. 21.

[12] Goebbels, Vom Kaiserhof zur Reichskanzlei, F. Eher, München, 1934. p. 120.

[13] Ley, Der Weg zur Ordensburg, Sonderdruck des Reichsorganisations-leiters der NSDAP für das Führercorps der Partei; quoted from Konrad Heiden, Ein Mann gegen Europa, Zürich, 1937.

[14] Hitler, Mein Kampf, p. 618.

should be taught to suffer injustice without rebelling will no longer strike the reader—or so I hope—as strange. This contradiction is the typical one for the sado-masochistic ambivalence between the craving for power and for submission.

The wish for power over the masses is what drives the member of the "elite," the Nazi leaders. As the quotations above show, this wish for power is sometimes revealed with an almost astonishing frankness. Sometimes it is put in less offensive forms by emphasizing that to be ruled is just what the masses wish. Sometimes the necessity to flatter the masses and therefore to hide the cynical contempt for them leads to tricks like the following: In speaking of the instinct of self-preservation, which for Hitler as we shall see later is more or less identical with the drive for power, he says that with the Aryan the instinct for self-preservation has reached the most noble form "because he willingly subjects his own ego to the life of the community and, if the hour should require it, he also sacrifices it."[15]

While the "leaders" are the ones to enjoy power in the first place, the masses are by no means deprived of sadistic satisfaction. Racial and political minorities within Germany and eventually other nations which are described as weak or decaying are the objects of sadism upon which the masses are fed. While Hitler and his bureaucracy enjoy the power over the German masses, these masses themselves are taught to enjoy power over other nations and to be driven by the passion for domination of the world.

Hitler does not hesitate to express the wish for world domination as his or his party's aim. Making fun of

[15] op. cit., p. 408.

pacifism, he says: "Indeed, the pacifist-humane idea is perhaps quite good whenever the man of the highest standard has previously conquered and subjected the world to a degree that makes him the only master of this globe."[16]

Again he says: "A state which in the epoch of race poisoning dedicates itself to the cherishing of its best racial elements, must some day be master of the world."[17]

Usually Hitler tries to rationalize and justify his wish for power. The main justifications are the following: his domination of other peoples is for their own good and for the good of the culture of the world; the wish for power is rooted in the eternal laws of nature and he recognizes and follows only these laws; he himself acts under the command of a higher power—God, Fate, History, Nature; his attempts for domination are only a defense against the attempts of others to dominate him and the German people. He wants only peace and freedom.

An example of the first kind of rationalization is the following paragraph from *Mein Kampf*:

"If, in its historical development, the German people had possessed this group unity as it was enjoyed by other peoples, then the German Reich would today probably be the mistress of this globe." German domination of the world could lead, Hitler assumes, to a "peace, supported not by the palm branches of tearful pacifist professional female mourners, but founded by the victorious sword of a people of overlords which puts the world into the service of a higher culture."[18]

In recent years his assurances that his aim is not only

[16] *op. cit.*, p. 394 f.   [17] *op. cit.*, p. 994.   [18] *op. cit.*, p. 598 ff.

the welfare of Germany but that his actions serve the best interests of civilization in general have become well-known to every newspaper reader.

The second rationalization, that his wish for power is rooted in the laws of nature, is more than a mere rationalization; it also springs from the wish for submission to a power outside of oneself, as expressed particularly in Hitler's crude popularization of Darwinism. In "the instinct of preserving the species," Hitler sees "the first cause of the formation of human communities."[19]

This instinct of self-preservation leads to the fight of the stronger for the domination of the weaker and economically, eventually, to the survival of the fittest. The identification of the instinct of self-preservation with power over others finds a particularly striking expression in Hitler's assumption that "the first culture of mankind certainly depended less on the tamed animal, but rather on the use of inferior people."[20] He projects his own sadism upon Nature who is "the cruel Queen of all Wisdom,"[21] and her law of preservation is "bound to the brazen law of necessity and of the right of the victory of the best and the the strongest in this world."[22]

It is interesting to observe that in connection with this crude Darwinism the "socialist" Hitler champions the liberal principles of unrestricted competition. In a polemic against co-operation between different nationalistic groups he says: "By such a combination the free play of energies is tied up, the struggle for choosing the best is stopped, and accordingly the necessary and final victory of the

[19] op. cit., p. 197.   [20] op. cit., p. 405.   [21] op. cit., p. 170.
[22] op. cit., p. 396

healthier and stronger man is prevented forever."[23] Else-where he speaks of the free play of energies as the wisdom of life.

To be sure, Darwin's theory as such was not an expression of the feelings of a sado-masochistic character. On the contrary, for many of its adherents it appealed to the hope of a further evolution of mankind to higher stages of culture. For Hitler, however, it was an expression of and simultaneously a justification for his own sadism. He reveals quite naïvely the psychological significance which the Darwinian theory had for him. When he lived in Munich, still an unknown man, he used to awake at 5 o'clock in the morning. He had "gotten into the habit of throwing pieces of bread or hard crusts to the little mice which spent their time in the small room, and then of watching these droll little animals romp and scuffle for these few delicacies."[24] This "game" was the Darwinian "struggle for life" on a small scale. For Hitler it was the petty bourgeois substitute for the circuses of the Roman Caesars, and a preliminary for the historical circuses he was to produce.

The last rationalization for his sadism, his justification of it as a defense against attacks of others, finds manifold expressions in Hitlers writings. He and the German people are always the ones who are innocent and the enemies are sadistic brutes. A great deal of this propaganda consists of deliberate, conscious lies. Partly, however, it has the same emotional "sincerity" which paranoid accusations have. These accusations always have the function of a defense

[23] op. cit., p. 761.
[24] op. cit., p. 295.

against being found out with regard to one's own sadism or destructiveness. They run according to the formula: It is you who have sadistic intention. Therefore I am innocent. With Hitler this defensive mechanism is irrational to the extreme, since he accuses his enemies of the very things he quite frankly admits to be his own aims. Thus he accuses the Jews, the Communists, and the French of the very things that he says are the most legitimate aims of his own actions. He scarcely bothers to cover this contradiction by rationalizations. He accuses the Jews of bringing the French African troops to the Rhine with the intention to destroy, by the bastardization which would necessarily set in, the white race and thus "in turn to rise personally to the position of master."[25] Hitler must have detected the contradiction of condemning others for that which he claims to be the most noble aim of his race, and he tries to rationalize the contradiction by saying of the Jews that their instinct for self-preservation lacks the idealistic character which is to be found in the Aryan drive for mastery.[26]

The same accusations are used against the French. He accuses them of wanting to strangle Germany and to rob it of its strength. While this accusation is used as an argument for the necessity of destroying "the French drive for European hegemony,"[27] he confesses that he would have acted like Clemenceau had he been in his place.[28]

The Communists are accused of brutality and the success of Marxism is attributed to its political will and activistic brutality. At the same time, however, Hitler declares:

[25] op. cit., p. 448 ff.   [26] Cf. op. cit., p. 414.   [27] op. cit., p. 966.
[28] Cf. op. cit., p. 978.

"What Germany was lacking was a close co-operation of brutal power and ingenious political intention."[29]

The Czech crisis in 1938 and this present war brought many examples of the same kind. There was no act of Nazi oppression which was not explained as a defense against oppression by others. One can assume that these accusations were mere falsifications and have not the paranoid "sincerity" which those against the Jews and the French might have been colored by. They still have a definite propaganda value, and part of the population, in particular the lower middle class which is receptive to these paranoid accusations on account of its own character structure, believed them.

Hitler's contempt for the powerless ones becomes particularly apparent when he speaks of people whose political aims—the fight for national freedom—were similar to those which he himself professed to have. Perhaps nowhere is the insincerity of Hitler's interest in national freedom more blatant than in his scorn for powerless revolutionaries. Thus he speaks in an ironical and contemptuous manner of the little group of National Socialists he had originally joined in Munich. This was his impression of the first meeting he went to: "Terrible, terrible; this was club-making of the worst kind and manner. And this club I now was to join? Then the new memberships were discussed, that means, my being caught."[30]

He calls them "a ridiculous small foundation," the only advantage of which was to offer "the chance for real personal activity."[31] Hitler says that he would never have

[29] op. cit., p. 783.   [30] op. cit., p. 298.   [31] op. cit., p. 300.

joined one of the existing big parties and this attitude is very characteristic of him. He had to start in a group which he felt to be inferior and weak. His initiative and courage would not have been stimulated in a constellation where he had to fight existing power or to compete with his equals.

He shows the same contempt for the powerless ones in what he writes about Indian revolutionaries. The same man who has used the slogan of national freedom for his own purposes more than anybody else has nothing but contempt for such revolutionists who had no power and who dared to attack the powerful British Empire. He remembers, Hitler says, "some Asiatic fakir or other, perhaps, for all I care, some real Indian 'fighters for freedom,' who were then running around Europe, contrived to stuff even otherwise quite intelligent people with the fixed idea that the British Empire, whose keystone is in India, was on the verge of collapse right there. . . . Indian rebels will, however, never achieve this . . . It is simply an impossibility for a coalition of cripples to storm a powerful State . . . I may not, simply because of my knowledge of their racial inferiority, link my own nation's fate with that of these so-called 'oppressed nations.' "[32]

The love for the powerful and the hatred for the powerless which is so typical for the sado-masochistic character explains a great deal of Hitler's and his followers' political actions. While the Republican government thought they could "appease" the Nazis by treating them leniently, they not only failed to appease them but aroused their hatred

[32] op. cit., p. 955 ff.

by the very lack of power and firmness they showed. Hitler hated the Weimar Republic *because* it was weak and he admired the industrial and military leaders because they had power. He never fought against established strong power but always against groups which he thought to be essentially powerless. Hitler's—and for that matter, Mussolini's—"revolution" happened under protection of existing power and their favorite objects were those who could not defend themselves. One might even venture to assume that Hitler's attitude toward Great Britain was determined, among other factors, by this psychological complex. As long as he felt Britain to be powerful, he loved and admired her. His book gives expression to this love for Britain. When he recognized the weakness of the British position before and after Munich his love changed into hatred and the wish to destroy it. From this viewpoint "appeasement" was a policy which for a personality like Hitler was bound to arouse hatred, not friendship.

So far we have spoken of the *sadistic* side in Hitler's ideology. However, as we have seen in the discussion of the authoritarian character, there is the *masochistic* side as well as the sadistic one. There is the wish to submit to an overwhelmingly strong power, to annihilate the self, besides the wish to have power over helpless beings. This masochistic side of the Nazi ideology and practice is most obvious with respect to the masses. They are told again and again: the individual is nothing and does not count. The individual should accept this personal insignificance, dissolve himself in a higher power, and then feel proud in participating in the strength and glory of this higher power.

Hitler expresses this idea clearly in his definition of idealism: "Idealism alone leads men to voluntary acknowledg-
ment of the privilege of force and strength and thus makes
them become a dust particle of that order which forms and
shapes the entire universe."[33]

Goebbels gives a similar definition of what he calls
Socialism: "To be a socialist," he writes, "is to submit the
I to the thou; socialism is sacrificing the individual to the
whole."[34]

Sacrificing the individual and reducing it to a bit of
dust, to an atom, implies, according to Hitler, the renunciation of the right to assert one's individual opinion, interests, and happiness. This renunciation is the essence of a
political organization in which "the individual renounces
representing his personal opinion and his interests. . ."[35]
He praises "unselfishness" and teaches that "in the hunt
for their own happiness people fall all the more out of
heaven into hell."[36] It is the aim of education to teach the
individual not to assert his self. Already the boy in school
must learn "to be silent, not only when he is blamed
justly but he has also to learn, if necessary, to bear injustice
in silence."[37] Concerning his ultimate goal he writes: "In
the folkish State the folkish view of life has finally to succeed in bringing about that nobler era when men see their
care no longer in the better breeding of dogs, horses and
cats, but rather in the uplifting of mankind itself, an era
in which the one knowingly and silently renounces, and
the other gladly gives and sacrifices."[38]

[33] op. cit., p. 411.
[35] op. cit., p. 408.
[37] op. cit., p. 620 ff.
[34] Goebbels, Michael, p. 25.
[36] op. cit., p. 412.
[38] op. cit., p. 610.

This sentence is somewhat surprising. One would expect that after the description of the one type of individual, who "knowingly and silently renounces," an opposite type would be described, perhaps the one who leads, takes responsibility, or something similar. But instead of that Hitler defines that "other" type also by his ability to sacrifice. It is difficult to understand the difference between "silently renounces," and "gladly sacrifices." If I may venture a guess, I believe that Hitler really intended in his mind to differentiate between the masses who should resign and the ruler who should rule. But while sometimes he quite overtly admits his and the "elite's" wish for power, he often denies it. In this sentence he apparently did not want to be so frank and therefore substituted for the wish to rule, the wish to "gladly give and sacrifice."

Hitler recognizes clearly that his philosophy of self-denial and sacrifice is meant for those whose economic situation does not allow them any happiness. He does not want to bring about a social order which would make personal happiness possible for every individual; he wants to exploit the very poverty of the masses in order to make them believe in his evangelism of self-annihilation. Quite frankly he declares: "We turn to the great army of those who are so poor that their personal lives could not mean the highest fortune of the world . . ."[39]

This whole preaching of self-sacrifice has an obvious purpose: The masses have to resign themselves and submit if the wish for power on the side of the leader and the "elite" is to be realized. But this masochistic longing is also to be found in Hitler himself. For him the superior

[39] op. cit., p. 610.

power to which he submits is God, Fate, Necessity, History, Nature. Actually all these terms have about the same meaning to him, that of symbols of an overwhelmingly strong power. He starts his autobiography with the remark that to him it was a "good fortune that *Fate* designated Braunau on the Inn as the place of my birth."[40] He then goes on to say that the whole German people must be united in one state because only then, when this state would be too small for them all, *necessity* would give them "the moral right to acquire soil and territory."[41]

The defeat in the war of 1914–1918 to him is "a deserved punishment by *eternal retribution*."[42] Nations that mix themselves with other races "sin against the will of eternal *Providence*"[43] or, as he puts it another time, "against the will of the Eternal *Creator*."[44] Germany's mission is ordered by "the Creator of the universe."[45] *Heaven* is superior to people, for luckily one can fool people but "Heaven could not be bribed."[46]

The power which impresses Hitler probably more than God, Providence, and Fate, is *Nature*. While it was the trend of the historical development of the last four hundred years to replace the domination over men by the domination over Nature, Hitler insists that one can and should rule over men but that one cannot rule over Nature. I have already quoted his saying that the history of mankind probably did not start with the domestication of animals but with the domination over inferior people. He ridicules the idea that man could conquer Nature and

---

[40] *op. cit.*, p. 1.
[43] *op. cit.*, p. 309.
[44] *op. cit.*, p. 392.
[46] *op. cit.*, p. 972.

[41] *op. cit.*, p. 3.
[42] *op. cit.*, p. 452.
[45] *op. cit.*, p. 289

makes fun of those who believe to become conquerors of Nature "whereas they have no other weapon at their disposal but an 'idea.'" He says that man "does not dominate Nature, but that, based on the knowledge of a few laws and secrets of Nature, he has risen to the position of master of those other living beings lacking this knowledge."[47] There again we find the same idea: Nature is the great power we have to submit to, but living beings are the ones we should dominate.

I have tried to show in Hitler's writings the two trends that we have already described as fundamental for the authoritarian character: the craving for power over men and the longing for submission to an overwhelmingly strong outside power. Hitler's ideas are more or less identical with the ideology of the Nazi party. The ideas expressed in his book are those which he expressed in the countless speeches by which he won mass following for his party. This ideology results from his personality which, with its inferiority feeling, hatred against life, asceticism, and envy of those who enjoy life, is the soil of sado-masochistic strivings; it was addressed to people who, on account of their similar character structure, felt attracted and excited by these teachings and became ardent followers of the man who expressed what they felt. But it was not only the Nazi ideology that satisfied the lower middle class; the political practice realized what the ideology promised. A hierarchy was created in which everyone has somebody above him to submit to and somebody beneath him to feel power over; the man at the top, the leader, has Fate, History, Nature above him as the power in which

" op cit., p. 393 ff.

to submerge himself. Thus the Nazi ideology and practice satisfies the desires springing from the character structure of one part of the population and gives direction and orientation to those who, though not enjoying domination and submission, were resigned and had given up faith in life, in their own decisions, in everything.

Do these considerations give any clue for a prognosis with regard to the stability of Nazism in the future? I do not feel qualified to make any predictions. Yet a few points —such as those that follow from the psychological premises we have been discussing—would seem to be worth raising. Given the psychological conditions, does Nazism not fulfill the emotional needs of the population, and is this psychological function not one factor that makes for its growing stability?

From all that has been said so far, it is evident that the answer to this question is in the negative. The fact of human individuation, of the destruction of all "primary bonds," cannot be reversed. The process of the destruction of the medieval world has taken four hundred years and is being completed in our era. Unless the whole industrial system, the whole mode of production, should be destroyed and changed to the preindustrial level, man will remain an individual who has completely emerged from the world surrounding him. We have seen that man cannot endure this negative freedom; that he tries to escape into new bondage which is to be a substitute for the primary bonds which he has given up. But these new bonds do not constitute real union with the world. He pays for the new security by giving up the integrity of his self. The factual dichotomy between him and these authorities does not disappear. They thwart and cripple his life even though consciously he may submit voluntarily. At the same time he lives in a world in which he has not only developed into being an "atom" but which also provides him with every potentiality for becoming an individual. The modern industrial system has virtually a capacity to produce not only the means for an economically secure life for everybody but also to create the material basis for the full expression of man's intellectual, sensuous, and emotional potentialities, while at the same time reducing considerably the hours of work.

The function of an authoritarian ideology and practice can be compared to the function of neurotic symptoms. Such symptoms result from unbearable psychological conditions and at the same time offer a solution that makes life possible. Yet they are not a solution that leads to happiness or growth of personality. They leave unchanged the conditions that necessitate the neurotic solution. The dynamism of man's nature is an important factor that tends to seek for more satisfying solutions if there is a possibility of attaining them. The aloneness and powerlessness of the individual, his quest for the realization of potentialities which developed in him, the objective fact of the increasing productive capacity of modern industry, are dynamic factors, which constitute the basis for a growing quest for freedom and happiness. The escape into symbiosis can alleviate the suffering for a time but it does not eliminate it. The history of mankind is the history of growing individuation, but it is also the history of growing freedom. The quest for freedom is not a metaphysical force and cannot be explained by natural law; it is the necessary result of the process of individuation and of the growth of culture. The authoritarian systems cannot do away with the basic conditions that make for the quest for freedom; neither can they exterminate the quest for freedom that springs from these conditions.

CHAPTER VII

Freedom and Democracy

1. THE ILLUSION OF INDIVIDUALITY

IN the previous chapters I have tried to show that certain factors in the modern industrial system in general and in its monopolistic phase in particular make for the development of a personality which feels powerless and alone, anxious and insecure. I have discussed the specific conditions in Germany which make part of her population fertile soil for an ideology and political practice that appeal to what I have described as the authoritarian character.

But what about ourselves? Is our own democracy threatened only by Fascism beyond the Atlantic or by the "fifth column" in our own ranks? If that were the case, the situation would be serious but not critical. But although foreign and internal threats of Fascism must be taken seriously, there is no greater mistake and no graver danger than not to see that in our own society we are faced with the same phenomenon that is fertile soil for the rise of Fascism anywhere: the insignificance and powerlessness of the individual.

This statement challenges the conventional belief that by freeing the individual from all external restraints modern democracy has achieved true individualism. We are proud that we are not subject to any external authority, that we are free to express our thoughts and feelings, and we take it for granted that this freedom almost automatically guarantees our individuality. *The right to express our thoughts,* however, *means something only if we are able to have thoughts of our own;* freedom from external authority is a lasting gain only if the inner psychological conditions are such that we are able to establish our own individuality. Have we achieved that aim, or are we at least approaching it? This book deals with the human factor; its task, therefore, is to analyze this very question critically. In doing so we take up threads that were dropped in earlier chapters. In discussing the two aspects of freedom for modern man, we have pointed out the economic conditions that make for increasing isolation and powerlessness of the individual in our era; in discussing the psychological results we have shown that this powerlessness leads either to the kind of escape that we find in the authoritarian character, or else to a compulsive conforming in the process of which the isolated individual becomes an automaton, loses his self, and yet at the same time consciously conceives of himself as free and subject only to himself.

It is important to consider how our culture fosters this tendency to conform, even though there is space for only a few outstanding examples. The suppression of spontaneous feelings, and thereby of the development of genuine individuality, starts very early, as a matter of fact with the earliest training of a child.[1] This is not to say that

[1] According to a communication by Anna Hartoch (from a forthcoming book on case studies of Sarah Lawrence Nursery School children, jointly by M. Gay, A. Hartoch, L. B. Murphy) Rorschach tests of three to five

training must inevitably lead to suppression of spontaneity if the real aim of education is to further the inner independence and individuality of the child, its growth and integrity. The restrictions which such a kind of education may have to impose upon the growing child are only transitory measures that really support the process of growth and expansion. In our culture, however, education too often results in the elimination of spontaneity and in the substitution of original psychic acts by superimposed feelings, thoughts, and wishes. (By original I do not mean, let me repeat, that an idea has not been thought before by someone else, but that it originates in the individual, that it is the result of his own activity and in this sense is *his* thought.) To choose one illustration somewhat arbitrarily, one of the earliest suppressions of *feelings* concerns hostility and dislike. To start with, most children have a certain measure of hostility and rebelliousness as a result of their conflicts with a surrounding world that tends to block their expansiveness and to which, as the weaker opponent, they usually have to yield. It is one of the essential aims of the educational process to eliminate this antagonistic reaction. The methods are different; they vary from threats and punishments, which frighten the child, to the subtler methods of bribery or "explanations," which confuse the child and make him give up his hostility. The child starts with giving up the expression of his feeling and eventually gives up the very feeling itself. Together with that, he is taught to suppress the awareness of hostility and insin-

---

year old children have shown that the attempt to preserve their spontaneity gives rise to the chief conflict between the children and the authorative adults.

cerity in others; sometimes this is not entirely easy, since children have a capacity for noticing such negative qualities in others without being so easily deceived by words as adults usually are. They still dislike somebody "for no good reason"—except the very good one that they feel the hostility, or insincerity, radiating from that person. This reaction is soon discouraged; it does not take long for the child to reach the "maturity" of the average adult and to lose the sense of discrimination between a decent person and a scoundrel, as long as the latter has not committed some flagrant act.

On the other hand, early in his education, the child is taught to have feelings that are not at all "his"; particularly is he taught to like people, to be uncritically friendly to them, and to smile. What education may not have accomplished is usually done by social pressure in later life. If you do not smile you are judged lacking in a "pleasing personality"—and you need to have a pleasing personality if you want to sell your services, whether as a waitress, a salesman, or a physician. Only those at the bottom of the social pyramid, who sell nothing but their physical labor, and those at the very top do not need to be particularly "pleasant." Friendliness, cheerfulness, and everything that a smile is supposed to express, become automatic responses which one turns on and off like an electric switch.[2]

[2] As one telling illustration of the commercialization of friendliness I should like to cite Fortune's report on "The Howard Johnson Restaurants." (Fortune, September, 1940. p. 96.) Johnson employs a force of "shoppers" who go from restaurant to restaurant to watch for lapses. "Since everything is cooked on the premises according to standard recipes and measurements issued by the home office, the inspector knows how large a portion of steak he should receive and how the vegetable should taste. He also knows how long it should take for the dinner to be served and he knows the exact degree of friendliness that should be shown by the hostess and the waitress."

To be sure, in many instances the person is aware of merely making a gesture; in most cases, however, he loses that awareness and thereby the ability to discriminate between the pseudo feeling and spontaneous friendliness.

It is not only hostility that is directly suppressed and friendliness that is killed by superimposing its counterfeit. A wide range of spontaneous emotions are suppressed and replaced by pseudo feelings. Freud has taken one such suppression and put it in the center of his whole system, namely the suppression of sex. Although I believe that the discouragement of sexual joy is not the only important suppression of spontaneous reactions but one of many, certainly its importance is not to be underrated. Its results are obvious in cases of sexual inhibitions and also in those where sex assumes a compulsive quality and is consumed like liquor or a drug, which has no particular taste but makes you forget yourself. Regardless of the one or the other effect, their suppression, because of the intensity of sexual desires, not only affects the sexual sphere but also weakens the person's courage for spontaneous expression in all other spheres.

In our society emotions in general are discouraged. While there can be no doubt that any creative thinking—as well as any other creative activity—is inseparably linked with emotion, it has become an ideal to think and to live without emotions. To be "emotional" has become synonymous with being unsound or unbalanced. By the acceptance of this standard the individual has become greatly weakened; his thinking is impoverished and flattened. On the other hand, since emotions cannot be completely killed, they must have their existence totally apart from the intellectual side of the personality; the result is the cheap and insincere sentimentality with which movies and popular songs feed millions of emotion-starved customers.

There is one tabooed emotion that I want to mention in particular, because its suppression touches deeply on the roots of personality: the sense of tragedy. As we saw in an earlier chapter, the awareness of death and of the tragic aspect of life, whether dim or clear, is one of the basic characteristics of man. Each culture has its own way of coping with the problem of death. For those societies in which the process of individuation has progressed but little, the end of individual existence is less of a problem since the experience of individual existence itself is less developed. Death is not yet conceived as being basically different from life. Cultures in which we find a higher development of individuation have treated death according to their social and psychological structure. The Greeks put all emphasis on life and pictured death as nothing but a shadowy and dreary continuation of life. The Egyptians based their hopes on a belief in the indestructibility of the human body, at least of those whose power during life was indestructible. The Jews admitted the fact of death realistically and were able to reconcile themselves with the idea of the destruction of individual life by the vision of a state of happiness and justice ultimately to be reached by mankind in this world. Christianity has made death unreal and tried to comfort the unhappy individual by promises of a life after death. Our own era simply denies death and with it one fundamental aspect of life. Instead of allowing the awareness of death and suffering to become one of the strongest incentives for life, the basis for human solidarity, and an experience without which joy and enthusiasm lack intensity and depth, the individual is forced to repress it. But, as is always the case with repression, by being removed from sight the repressed elements do not cease to exist. Thus the fear of death lives an illegitimate existence among us. It remains alive in spite of the attempt to deny it, but being repressed it remains sterile. It is one source of the flatness of other experiences, of the restlessness pervading life, and it explains, I would venture to say, the exorbitant amount of money this nation pays for its funerals.

In the process of tabooing emotions modern psychiatry plays an ambiguous role. On the one hand its greatest representative, Freud, has broken through the fiction of the rational, purposeful character of the human mind and opened a path which allows a view into the abyss of human passions. On the other hand psychiatry, enriched by these very achievements of Freud, has made itself an instrument of the general trends in the manipulation of personality. Many psychiatrists, including psychoanalysts, have painted the picture of a "normal" personality which is never too sad, too angry, or too excited. They use words like "infantile" or "neurotic" to denounce traits or types of personalities that do not conform with the conventional pattern of a "normal" individual. This kind of influence is in a way more dangerous than the older and franker forms of namecalling. Then the individual knew at least that there was some person or some doctrine which criticized him and he could fight back. But who can fight back at "science"?

The same distortion happens to original *thinking* as happens to feelings and emotions. From the very start of education original thinking is discouraged and ready-made thoughts are put into people's heads. How this is done with young children is easy enough to see. They are filled with curiosity about the world, they want to grasp it physically as well as intellectually. They want to know the truth, since that is the safest way to orient themselves in a strange and powerful world. Instead, they are not taken seriously, and it does not matter whether this attitude takes the form of open disrespect or of the subtle condescension which is usual towards all who have no power (such as children, aged or sick people). Although this treatment by itself offers strong discouragement to independent thinking, there is a worse handicap: the insincerity—often unintentional—which is typical of the average adult's behavior toward a child. This insincerity consists partly in the fictitious picture of the world which the child is given. It is about as useful as instructions concerning life in the Arctic would be to someone who has asked how to prepare for an expedition to the Sahara Desert. Besides this general misrepresentation of the world there are the many specific lies that tend to conceal facts which, for various personal reasons, adults do not want children to know. From a bad temper, which is rationalized as justified dissatisfaction with the child's behavior, to concealment of the parents' sexual activities and their quarrels, the child is "not supposed to know" and his inquiries meet with hostile or polite discouragement.

The child thus prepared enters school and perhaps college. I want to mention briefly some of the educational methods used today which in effect further discourage original thinking. One is the emphasis on knowledge of facts, or I should rather say on information. The pathetic superstition prevails that by knowing more and more facts one arrives at knowledge of reality. Hundreds of scattered and unrelated facts are dumped into the heads of students; their time and energy are taken up by learning more and more facts so that there is little left for thinking. To be sure, thinking without a knowledge of facts remains empty and fictitious; but "information" alone can be just as much of an obstacle to thinking as the lack of it.

Another closely related way of discouraging original thinking is to regard all truth as relative.[3] Truth is made out to be a metaphysical concept, and if anyone speaks about wanting to discover the truth he is thought backward by the "progressive" thinkers of our age. Truth is declared to be an entirely subjective matter, almost a matter of taste. Scientific endeavor must be detached from subjective factors, and its aim is to look at the world without passion and interest. The scientist has to approach facts with sterilized hands as a surgeon approaches his patient. The result of this relativism, which often presents itself by the name of empiricism or positivism or which recommends itself by its concern for the correct usage of words, is that thinking loses its essential stimulus—the wishes and interests of the person who thinks; instead it becomes a machine to register "facts." Actually, just as thinking in general has developed out of the need for mastery of material life, so the quest for truth is rooted in the interests and needs of individuals and social groups.

[3] Cf. to this whole problem Robert S. Lynd's *Knowledge for What?* Princeton University Press, Princeton, 1939. For its philosophical aspects cf. M. Horkheimer's *Zum Rationalismusstreit in der Gegenwärtigen Philosophie.* Zeitschrift für Sozialforschung, Vol. 3, 1934. Alcan, Paris.

Without such interest the stimulus for seeking the truth would be lacking. There are always groups whose interest is furthered by truth, and their representatives have been the pioneers of human thought; there are other groups whose interests are furthered by concealing truth. Only in the latter case does interest prove harmful to the cause of truth. The problem, therefore, is not that there is an interest at stake, but *which kind* of interest is at stake. I might say that inasmuch as there is some longing for the truth in every human being, it is because every human being has some need for it.

This holds true in the first place with regard to a person's orientation in the outer world, and it holds especially true for the child. As a child, every human being passes through a state of powerlessness, and truth is one of the strongest weapons of those who have no power. But the truth is in the individual's interest not only with regard to his orientation in the outer world; his own strength depends to a great extent on his knowing the truth about himself. Illusions about onself can become crutches useful to those who are not able to walk alone; but they increase a person's weakness. The individual's greatest strength is based on the maximum of integration of his personality, and that means also on the maximum of transparence to himself. "Know thyself" is one of the fundamental commands that aim at human strength and happiness.

In addition to the factors just mentioned there are others which actively tend to confuse whatever is left of the capacity for original thinking in the average adult. With regard to all basic questions of individual and social life, with regard to psychological, economic, political, and moral problems, a great sector of our culture has just one function—to befog the issues. One kind of smokescreen is the assertion that the problems are too complicated for the average individual to grasp. On the contrary it would seem that many of the basic issues of individual and social life are very simple, so simple, in fact, that everyone should be expected to understand them. To let them appear to be so enormously complicated that only a "specialist" can understand them, and he only in his own limited field, actually—and often intentionally—tends to discourage people from trusting their own capacity to think about those problems that really matter. The individual feels helplessly caught in a chaotic mass of data and with pathetic patience waits until the specialists have found out what to do and where to go.

The result of this kind of influence is a twofold one: one is a scepticism and cynicism towards everything which is said or printed, while the other is a childish belief in anything that a person is told with authority. This combination of cynicism and naïveté is very typical of the modern individual. Its essential result is to discourage him from doing his own thinking and deciding.

Another way of paralyzing the ability to think critically is the destruction of any kind of structuralized picture of the world. Facts lose the specific quality which they can have only as parts of a structuralized whole and retain merely an abstract, quantitative meaning; each fact is just another fact and all that matters is whether we know more or less. Radio, moving pictures, and newspapers have a devastating effect on this score. The announcement of the bombing of a city and the death of hundreds of people is shamelessly followed or interrupted by an advertisement for soap or wine. The same speaker with the same suggestive, ingratiating, and authoritative voice, which he has just used to impress you with the seriousness of the political situation, impresses now upon his audience the merits of the particular brand of soap which pays for the news broadcast. Newsreels let pictures of torpedoed ships be followed by those of a fashion show. Newspapers tell us the trite thoughts or breakfast habits of a debutante with the same space and seriousness they use for reporting events of scientific or artistic importance. Because of all this we cease to be genuinely related to what we hear. We cease to be excited, our emotions and our critical judgment become hampered, and eventually our attitude to what is going on in the world assumes a quality of flatness and indifference. In the name of "freedom" life loses all structure; it is composed of many little pieces, each separate from the other and lacking any sense as a whole. The individual is left alone with these pieces like a child with a puzzle; the difference, however, is that the child knows what a house is and therefore can recognize the parts of the house in the little pieces he is playing with, whereas the adult does not see the meaning of the "whole," the pieces of which come into his hands. He is bewildered and afraid and just goes on gazing at his little meaningless pieces.

What has been said about the lack of "originality" in feeling and thinking holds true also of the act of *willing*. To recognize this is particularly difficult; modern man seems, if anything, to have too many wishes and his only problem seems to be that, although he knows what he wants, he cannot have it. All our energy is spent for the purpose of getting what we want, and most people never question the premise of this activity: that they know their true wants. They do not stop to think whether the aims they are pursuing are something they themselves want. In school they want to have good marks, as adults they want to be more and more successful, to make more money, to have more prestige, to buy a better car, to go places, and so on. Yet when they do stop to think in the midst of all this frantic activity, this question may come to their minds: "If I do get this new job, if I get this better car, if I can take this trip—what then? What is the use of it all? Is it really I who wants all this? Am I not running after some goal which is supposed to make me happy and which eludes me as soon as I have reached it?" These questions, when they arise, are frightening, for they question the very oasis on which man's whole activity is built, his knowledge of what he wants. People tend, therefore, to get rid as soon as possible of these disturbing thoughts. They feel that they have been bothered by these questions because they were tired or depressed—and they go on in the pursuit of the aims which they believe are their own.

Yet all this bespeaks a dim realization of the truth—the truth that modern man lives under the illusion that he knows what he wants, while he actually wants what he is *supposed* to want. In order to accept this it is necessary to realize that to know what one really wants is not comparatively easy, as most people think, but one of the most difficult problems any human being has to solve. It is a task we frantically try to avoid by accepting ready-made goals as though they were our own. Modern man is ready to take great risks when he tries to achieve the aims which are supposed to be "his"; but he is deeply afraid of taking the risk and the responsibility of giving himself his own aims. Intense activity is often mistaken for evidence of self-determined action, although we know that it may well be no more spontaneous than the behavior of an actor or a person hypnotized. When the general plot of the play is handed out, each actor can act vigorously the role he is assigned and even make up his lines and certain details of the action by himself. Yet he is only playing a role that has been handed over to him.

The particular difficulty in recognizing to what extent our wishes—and our thoughts and feelings as well—are not really our own but put into us from the outside, is closely linked up with the problem of authority and freedom. In the course of modern history the authority of the Church has been replaced by that of the State, that of the State by that of conscience, and in our era, the latter has been replaced by the anonymous authority of common sense and public opinion as instruments of conformity. Because we have freed ourselves of the older overt forms of authority, we do not see that we have become the prey of a new kind of authority. We have become automatons who live under the illusion of being self-willing individuals This illusion helps the individual to remain unaware of his insecurity, but this is all the help such an illusion can give. Basically the self of the individual is weakened, so that he feels powerless and extremely insecure. He lives in a world to which he has lost genuine relatedness and in which everybody and everything has become instrumentalized, where he has become a part of the machine that his hands have built. He thinks, feels, and wills what he believes he is supposed to think, feel, and will; in this very process he loses his self upon which all genuine security of a free individual must be built.

The loss of the self has increased the necessity to conform, for it results in a profound doubt of one's own identity. If I am nothing but what I believe I am supposed to be—who am "I"? We have seen how the doubt about one's own self started with the breakdown of the medieval order in which the individual had had an unquestionable place in a fixed order. The identity of the individual has been a major problem of modern philosophy since Descartes. Today we take for granted that we are we. Yet the doubt about ourselves still exists, or has even grown. In his plays Pirandello has given expression to this feeling of modern man. He starts with the question: Who am I? What proof have I for my own identity other than the continuation of my physical self? His answer is not like Descartes'—the affirmation of the individual self—but its denial: I have no identity, there is no self excepting the one which is the reflex of what others expect me to be: I am "as you desire me."

This loss of identity then makes it still more imperative to conform; it means that one can be sure of oneself only if one lives up to the expectations of others. If we do not live up to this picture we not only risk disapproval and increased isolation, but we risk losing the identity of our personality, which means jeopardizing sanity.

By conforming with the expectations of others, by not being different, these doubts about one's own identity are silenced and a certain security is gained. However, the price paid is high. Giving up spontaneity and individuality results in a thwarting of life. Psychologically the automaton, while being alive biologically, is dead emotionally and mentally. While he goes through the motions of living, his life runs through his hands like sand. Behind a front of satisfaction and optimism modern man is deeply unhappy; as a matter of fact, he is on the verge of desperation. He desperately clings to the notion of individuality; he wants to be "different," and he has no greater recommendation of anything than that "it is different." We are informed of the individual name of the railroad clerk we buy our tickets from; handbags, playing cards, and portable radios are "personalized," by having the initials of the owner put on them. All this indicates the hunger for "difference" and yet these are almost the last vestiges of individuality that are left. Modern man is starved for life. But since, being an automaton, he cannot experience life in the sense of spontaneous activity he takes as surrogate any kind of excitement and thrill: the thrill of drinking, of sports, of vicariously living the excitements of fictitious persons on the screen.

What then is the meaning of freedom for modern man?

He has become free from the external bonds that would prevent him from doing and thinking as he sees fit. He would be free to act according to his own will, if he knew what he wanted, thought, and felt. But he does not know. He conforms to anonymous authorities and adopts a self which is not his. The more he does this, the more powerless he feels, the more is he forced to conform. In spite of a veneer of optimism and initiative, modern man is overcome by a profound feeling of powerlessness which makes him gaze toward approaching catastrophes as though he were paralyzed.

Looked at superficially, people appear to function well enough in economic and social life; yet it would be dangerous to overlook the deep-seated unhappiness behind that comforting veneer. If life loses its meaning because it is not lived, man becomes desperate. People do not die quietly from physical starvation; they do not die quietly from psychic starvation either. If we look only at the economic needs as far as the "normal" person is concerned, if we do not see the unconscious suffering of the average automatized person, then we fail to see the danger that threatens our culture from its human basis: the readiness to accept any ideology and any leader, if only he promises excitement and offers a political structure and symbols which allegedly give meaning and order to an individual's life. The despair of the human automaton is fertile soil for the political purposes of Fascism.

2. FREEDOM AND SPONTANEITY

So far this book has dealt with one aspect of freedom: the powerlessness and insecurity of the isolated individual in modern society who has become free from all bonds that once gave meaning and security to life. We have seen that the individual cannot bear this isolation; as an isolated being he is utterly helpless in comparison with the world outside and therefore deeply afraid of it; and because of his isolation, the unity of the world has broken down for him and he has lost any point of orientation. He is therefore overcome by doubts concerning himself, the meaning of life, and eventually any principle according to which he can direct his actions. Both helplessness and doubt paralyze life, and in order to live man tries to escape from freedom, negative freedom. He is driven into new bondage. This bondage is different from the primary bonds, from which, though dominated by authorities or the social group, he was not entirely separated. The escape does not restore his lost security, but only helps him to forget his self as a separate entity. He finds new and fragile security at the expense of sacrificing the integrity of his individual self. He chooses to lose his self since he cannot bear to be alone. Thus freedom—as freedom from— leads into new bondage.

Does our analysis lend itself to the conclusion that there is an inevitable circle that leads from freedom into new dependence? Does freedom from all primary ties make the individual so alone and isolated that inevitably he must escape into new bondage? Are *independence* and freedom identical with *isolation* and fear? Or is there a state of positive freedom in which the individual exists as an independent self and yet is not isolated but united with the world, with other men, and nature?

We believe that there is a positive answer, that the process of growing freedom does not constitute a vicious circle, and that man can be free and yet not alone, critical and yet not filled with doubts, independent and yet an integral part of mankind. This freedom man can attain by the realization of his self, by being himself. What is realization of the self? Idealistic philosophers have believed that self-realization can be achieved by intellectual insight alone. They have insisted upon splitting human personality, so that man's nature may be suppressed and guarded by his reason. The result of this split, however, has been that not only the emotional life of man but also his intellectual faculties have been crippled. Reason, by becoming a guard set to watch its prisoner, nature, has become a prisoner itself; and thus both sides of human personality, reason and emotion, were crippled. We believe that the realization of the self is accomplished not only by an act of thinking but also by the realization of man's total personality, by the active expression of his emotional and intellectual potentialities. These potentialities are present in everybody; they become real only to the extent to which they are expressed. In other words, *positive freedom consists in the spontaneous activity of the total, integrated personality.*

We approach here one of the most difficult problems of psychology: the problem of spontaneity. An attempt to discuss this problem adequately would require another volume. However, on the basis of what we have said so far, it is possible to arrive at an understanding of the essential quality of spontaneous activity by means of contrast. Spontaneous activity is not compulsive activity, to which the individual is driven by his isolation and powerlessness; it is not the activity of the automaton, which is the uncritical adoption of patterns suggested from the outside. Spontaneous activity is free activity of the self and implies, psychologically, what the Latin root of the word, *sponte*, means literally: of one's free will. By activity we do not mean "doing something," but the quality of creative activity that can operate in one's emotional, intellectual, and sensuous experiences and in one's will as well. One premise for this spontaneity is the acceptance of the total per-

sonality and the elimination of the split between "reason"
and "nature"; for only if man does not repress essential
parts of his self, only if he has become transparent to himself, and only if the different spheres of life have reached
a fundamental integration, is spontaneous activity possible.

While spontaneity is a relatively rare phenomenon in
our culture, we are not entirely devoid of it. In order to
help in the understanding of this point, I should like to
remind the reader of some instances where we all catch a
glimpse of spontaneity.

In the first place, we know of individuals who are—or
have been—spontaneous, whose thinking, feeling, and acting were the expression of their selves and not of an automaton. These individuals are mostly known to us as artists.
As a matter of fact, the artist can be defined as an individual who can express himself spontaneously. If this were
the definition of an artist—Balzac defined him just in that
way—then certain philosophers and scientists have to be
called artists too, while others are as different from them
as an old-fashioned photographer from a creative painter.
There are other individuals who, though lacking the ability—or perhaps merely the training—for expressing themselves in an objective medium as the artist does, possess the
same spontaneity. The position of the artist is vulnerable,
though, for it is really only the successful artist whose individuality or spontaneity is respected; if he does not succeed in selling his art, he remains to his contemporaries a
crank, a "neurotic." The artist in this matter is in a similar
position to that of the revolutionary throughout history.
The successful revolutionary is a statesman, the unsuccessful one a criminal.

Small children offer another instance of spontaneity. They have an ability to feel and think that which is really *theirs;* this spontaneity shows in what they say and think, in the feelings that are expressed in their faces. If one asks what makes for the attraction small children have for most people I believe that, aside from sentimental and conventional reasons, the answer must be that it is this very quality of spontaneity. It appeals profoundly to everyone who is not so dead himself that he has lost the ability to perceive it. As a matter of fact, there is nothing more attractive and convincing than spontaneity whether it is to be found in a child, in an artist, or in those individuals who cannot thus be grouped according to age or profession.

Most of us can observe at least moments of our own spontaneity which are at the same time moments of genuine happiness. Whether it be the fresh and spontaneous perception of a landscape, or the dawning of some truth as the result of our thinking, or a sensuous pleasure that is not stereotyped, or the welling up of love for another person—in these moments we all know what a spontaneous act is and may have some vision of what human life could be if these experiences were not such rare and uncultivated occurrences.

Why is spontaneous activity the answer to the problem of freedom? We have said that negative freedom by itself makes the individual an isolated being, whose relationship to the world is distant and distrustful and whose self is weak and constantly threatened. Spontaneous activity is the one way in which man can overcome the terror of aloneness without sacrificing the integrity of his self; for

in the spontaneous realization of the self man unites himself anew with the world—with man, nature, and himself. Love is the foremost component of such spontaneity;
not love as the dissolution of the self in another person,
not love as the possession of another person, but love as
spontaneous affirmation of others, as the union of the individual with others on the basis of the preservation of the
individual self. The dynamic quality of love lies in this
very polarity: that it springs from the need of overcoming
separateness, that it leads to oneness—and yet that individuality is not eliminated. Work is the other component;
not work as a compulsive activity in order to escape aloneness, not work as a relationship to nature which is partly
one of dominating her, partly one of worship of and enslavement by the very products of man's hands, but work
as creation in which man becomes one with nature in
the act of creation. What holds true of love and work holds
true of all spontaneous action, whether it be the realization of sensuous pleasure or participation in the political
life of the community. It affirms the individuality of the
self and at the same time it unites the self with man and
nature. The basic dichotomy that is inherent in freedom—
the birth of individuality and the pain of aloneness—is dissolved on a higher plane by man's spontaneous action.

In all spontaneous activity the individual embraces the
world. Not only does his individual self remain intact; it
becomes stronger and more solidified. *For the self is as
strong as it is active.* There is no genuine strength in possession as such, neither of material property nor of mental
qualities like emotions or thoughts. There is also no
strength in use and manipulation of objects; what we use

is not ours simply because we use it. Ours is only that to which we are genuinely related by our creative activity, be it a person or an inanimate object. Only those qualities that result from our spontaneous activity give strength to the self and thereby form the basis of its integrity. The inability to act spontaneously, to express what one genuinely feels and thinks, and the resulting necessity to present a pseudo self to others and oneself, are the root of the feeling of inferiority and weakness. Whether or not we are aware of it, there is nothing of which we are more ashamed than of not being ourselves, and there is nothing that gives us greater pride and happiness than to think, to feel, and to say what is ours.

This implies that what matters is the activity as such, the process and not the result. In our culture the emphasis is just the reverse. We produce not for a concrete satisfaction but for the abstract purpose of selling our commodity; we feel that we can acquire everything material or immaterial by buying it, and thus things become ours independently of any creative effort of our own in relation to them. In the same way we regard our personal qualities and the result of our efforts as commodities that can be sold for money, prestige, and power. The emphasis thus shifts from the present satisfaction of creative activity to the value of the finished product. Thereby man misses the only satisfaction that can give him real happiness—the experience of the activity of the present moment—and chases after a phantom that leaves him disappointed as soon as he believes he has caught it—the illusory happiness called success.

If the individual realizes his self by spontaneous activity

and thus relates himself to the world, he ceases to be an isolated atom; he and the world become part of one structuralized whole; he has his rightful place, and thereby his doubt concerning himself and the meaning of life disappears. This doubt sprang from his separateness and from the thwarting of life; when he can live, neither compulsively nor automatically but spontaneously, the doubt disappears. He is aware of himself as an active and creative individual and recognizes that there is only one meaning of life: the act of living itself.

If the individual overcomes the basic doubt concerning himself and his place in life, if he is related to the world by embracing it in the act of spontaneous living, he gains strength as an individual and he gains security. This security, however, differs from the security that characterizes the preindividualist state in the same way in which the new relatedness to the world differs from that of the primary ties. The new security is not rooted in the protection which the individual has from a higher power outside of himself; neither is it a security in which the tragic quality of life is eliminated. The new security is dynamic; it is not based on protection, but on man's spontaneous activity. It is the security acquired each moment by man's spontaneous activity. It is the security that only freedom can give, that needs no illusions because it has eliminated those conditions that necessitate illusions.

Positive freedom as the realization of the self implies the full affirmation of the uniqueness of the individual. Men are born equal but they are also born different. The basis of this difference is the inherited equipment, physiological and mental, with which they start life, to which is added the particular constellation of circumstances and experiences that they meet with. This individual basis of the personality is as little identical with any other as two organisms are ever identical physically. The genuine growth of the self is always a growth on this particular basis; it is an organic growth, the unfolding of a nucleus that is peculiar for this one person and only for him. The development of the automaton, in contrast, is not an organic growth. The growth of the basis of the self is blocked and a pseudo self is superimposed upon this self, which is— as we have seen—essentially the incorporation of extraneous patterns of thinking and feeling. Organic growth is possible only under the condition of supreme respect for the peculiarity of the self of other persons as well as of our own self. This respect for and cultivation of the uniqueness of the self is the most valuable achievement of human culture and it is this very achievement that is in danger today.

The uniqueness of the self in no way contradicts the principle of equality. The thesis that men are born equal implies that they all share the same fundamental human qualities, that they share the basic fate of human beings, that they all have the same inalienable claim on freedom and happiness. It furthermore means that their relationship is one of solidarity, not one of domination-submission. What the concept of equality does not mean is that all men are alike. Such a concept of equality is derived from the role that the individual plays in his economic activities today. In the relation between the man who buys and the one who sells, the concrete differences of personality are eliminated. In this situation only one thing matters, that the one has something to sell and the other has money to buy it. In economic life one man is not different from another; as real persons they are, and the cultivation of their uniqueness is the essence of individuality.

Positive freedom also implies the principle that there is no higher power than this unique individual self, that man is the center and purpose of his life; that the growth and realization of man's individuality is an end that can never be subordinated to purposes which are supposed to have greater dignity. This interpretation may arouse serious objections. Does it not postulate unbridled egotism? Is it not the negation of the idea of sacrifice for an ideal? Would its acceptance not lead to anarchy? These questions have actually already been answered, partly explicitly, partly implicitly, during our previous discussion. However, they are too important for us not to make another attempt to clarify the answers and to avoid misunderstanding.

To say that man should not be subject to anything higher than himself does not deny the dignity of ideals. On the contrary, it is the strongest affirmation of ideals. It forces us, however, to a critical analysis of what an ideal is. One is generally apt today to assume that an ideal is any aim whose achievement does not imply material gain, anything for which a person is ready to sacrifice egotistical ends. This is a purely psychological—and for that matter relativistic—concept of an ideal. From this subjectivist viewpoint a Fascist, who is driven by the desire to subordinate himself to a higher power and at the same time to overpower other people, has an ideal just as much as the man who fights for human equality and freedom. On this basis the problem of ideals can never be solved.

We must recognize the difference between genuine and fictitious ideals, which is just as fundamental a difference as that between truth and falsehood. All genuine ideals have one thing in common: they express the desire for something which is not yet accomplished but which is desirable for the purposes of the growth and happiness of the individual.[4] We may not always know what serves this end, we may disagree about the function of this or that ideal in terms of human development, but this is no reason for a relativism which says that we cannot know what furthers life or what blocks it. We are not always sure which food is healthy and which is not, yet we do not conclude that we have no way whatsoever of recognizing poison. In the same way we can know, if we want to, what is poisonous for mental life. We know that poverty, intimidation, isolation, are directed *against* life; that everything that serves freedom and furthers the courage and strength to be oneself is *for* life. What is good or bad for man is not a metaphysical question, but an empirical one that can be answered on the basis of an analysis of man's nature and the effect which certain conditions have on him.

But what about "ideals" like those of the Fascists which are definitely directed against life? How can we understand the fact that men are following these false ideals as fervently as others are following true ideals? The answer to this question is provided by certain psychological considerations. The phenomenon of masochism shows us that men can be drawn to the experiencing of suffering or sub-

[4] Cf. Max Otto, *The Human Enterprise*, T. S. Croft, New York, 1940. Chaps. IV and V.

mission. There is no doubt that suffering, submission, or suicide is the antithesis of positive aims of living. Yet these aims can be subjectively experienced as gratifying and attractive. This attraction to what is harmful in life is the phenomenon which more than any other deserves the name of a pathological perversion. Many psychologists have assumed that the experience of pleasure and the avoidance of pain is the only legitimate principle guiding human action; but dynamic psychology can show that the subjective experience of pleasure is not a sufficient criterion for the value of certain behavior in terms of human happiness. The analysis of masochistic phenomena is a case in point. Such analysis shows that the sensation of pleasure can be the result of a pathological perversion and proves as little about the objective meaning of the experience as the sweet taste of a poison would prove about its function for the organism.[5] We thus come to define a genuine ideal as any aim which furthers the growth, freedom, and happiness of the self, and to define as fictitious ideals those compulsive and irrational aims which subjectively are attractive experiences (like the drive for submission), but which actually are harmful to life. Once we accept this definition, it follows that a genuine ideal is not some veiled force superior to the individual, but that

---

[5] The question discussed here leads to a point of great significance which I want at least to mention: that problems of ethics can be clarified by dynamic psychology. Psychologists will only be helpful in this direction when they can see the relevance of moral problems for the understanding of personality. Any psychology, including Freud's, which treats such problems in terms of the pleasure principle, fails to understand one important sector of personality and leaves the field to dogmatic and unempirical doctrines of morality. The analysis of self-love, masochistic sacrifice, and ideals as offered in this book provides illustrations for this field of psychology and ethics that warrant further development.

it is the articulate expression of utmost affirmation of the self. Any ideal which is in contrast to such affirmation proves by this very fact that it is not an ideal but a pathological aim.

From here we come to another question, that of sacrifice. Does our definition of freedom as nonsubmission to any *higher* power exclude sacrifices, including the sacrifice of one's life?

This is a particularly important question today, when Fascism proclaims self-sacrifice as the highest virtue and impresses many people with its idealistic character. The answer to this question follows logically from what has been said so far. There are two entirely different types of sacrifice. It is one of the tragic facts of life that the demands of our physical self and the aims of our mental self can conflict; that actually we may have to sacrifice our physical self in order to assert the integrity of our spiritual self. This sacrifice will never lose its tragic quality. Death is never sweet, not even if it is suffered for the highest ideal. It remains unspeakably bitter, and still it can be the utmost assertion of our individuality. Such sacrifice is fundamentally different from the "sacrifice" which Fascism preaches. There, sacrifice is not the highest price man may have to pay to assert his self, but it is an aim in itself. This masochistic sacrifice sees the fulfillment of life in its very negation, in the annihilation of the self. It is only the supreme expression of what Fascism aims at in all its ramifications—the annihilation of the individual self and its utter submission to a higher power. It is the perversion of true sacrifice as much as suicide is the utmost perversion of life. True sacrifice presupposes an uncompromising wish

for spiritual integrity. The sacrifice of those who have lost
it only covers up their moral bankruptcy.

One last objection is to be met: If individuals are allowed to act freely in the sense of spontaneity, if they
acknowledge no higher authority than themselves, will
anarchy be the inevitable result? In so far as the word
anarchy stands for heedless egotism and destructiveness,
the determining factor depends upon one's understanding
of human nature. I can only refer to what has been pointed
out in the chapter dealing with mechanisms of escape:
that man is neither good nor bad; that life has an inherent
tendency to grow, to expand, to express potentialities; that
if life is thwarted, if the individual is isolated and overcome
by doubt or a feeling of aloneness and powerlessness, then
he is driven to destructiveness and craving for power or
submission. If human freedom is established as *freedom to,*
if man can realize his self fully and uncompromisingly, the
fundamental cause for his asocial drives will have disappeared and only a sick and abnormal individual will be
dangerous. This freedom has never been realized in the
history of mankind, yet it has been an ideal to which mankind has stuck even if it was often expressed in abstruse
and irrational forms. There is no reason to wonder why the
record of history shows so much cruelty and destructiveness. If there is anything to be surprised at—and encour-
aged by—I believe it is the fact that the human race, in
spite of all that has happened to men, has retained—and
actually developed—such qualities of dignity, courage, de-
cency, and kindness as we find them throughout history
and in countless individuals today.

If by anarchy one means that the individual does not

acknowledge any kind of authority, the answer is to be found in what has been said about the difference between rational and irrational authority. Rational authority—like a genuine ideal—represents the aims of growth and expansion of the individual. It is, therefore, in principle never in conflict with the individual and his real, and not his pathological, aims.

It has been the thesis of this book that freedom has a twofold meaning for modern man: that he has been freed from traditional authorities and has become an "individual," but that at the same time he has become isolated, powerless, and an instrument of purposes outside of himself, alienated from himself and others; furthermore, that this state undermines his self, weakens and frightens him, and makes him ready for submission to new kinds of bondage. Positive freedom on the other hand is identical with the full realization of the individual's potentialities, together with his ability to live actively and spontaneously. Freedom has reached a critical point where, driven by the logic of its own dynamism, it threatens to change into its opposite. The future of democracy depends on the realization of the individualism that has been the ideological aim of modern thought since the Renaissance. The cultural and political crisis of our day is not due to the fact that there is too much individualism but that what we believe to be individualism has become an empty shell. The victory of freedom is possible only if democracy develops into a society in which the individual, his growth and happiness, is the aim and purpose of culture, in which life does not need any justification in success or anything else, and in which the individual is not subordinated to or manipulated by any power outside of himself, be it the State or the economic machine; finally, a society in which his conscience and ideals are not the internalization of external demands, but are really *his* and express the aims that result from the peculiarity of his self. These aims could not be fully realized in any previous period of modern history; they had to remain largely ideological aims, because the material basis for the development of genuine individualism was lacking. Capitalism has created this premise. The problem of production is solved—in principle at least—and we can visualize a future of abundance, in which the fight for economic privileges is no longer necessitated by economic scarcity. The problem we are confronted with today is that of the organization of social and economic forces, so that man—as a member of organized society—may become the master of these forces and cease to be their slave.

I have stressed the psychological side of freedom, but I have also tried to show that the psychological problem cannot be separated from the material basis of human existence, from the economic, social, and political structure of society. It follows from this premise that the realization of positive freedom and individualism is also bound up with economic and social changes that will permit the individual to become free in terms of the realization of his self. It is not the aim of this book to deal with the economic problems resulting from that premise or to give a picture of economic plans for the future. But I should not like to leave any doubt concerning the direction in which I believe the solution to lie.

In the first place this must be said: We cannot afford to lose any of the fundamental achievements of modern democracy—either the fundamental one of representative government, that is, government elected by the people and responsible to the people, or any of the rights which the Bill of Rights guarantees to every citizen. Nor can we compromise the newer democratic principle that no one shall be allowed to starve, that society is responsible for all its members, that no one shall be frightened into submission and lose his human pride through fear of unemployment and starvation. These basic achievements must not only be preserved; they must be fortified and expanded.

In spite of the fact that this measure of democracy has been realized—though far from completely—it is not enough. Progress for democracy lies in enhancing the actual freedom, initiative, and spontaneity of the individual, not only in certain private and spiritual matters, but above all in the activity fundamental to every man's existence, his work.

What are the general conditions for that? The irrational and planless character of society must be replaced by a planned economy that represents the planned and concerted effort of society as such. Society must master the social problem as rationally as it has mastered nature. One condition for this is the elimination of the secret rule of those who, though few in number, wield great economic power without any responsibility to those whose fate depends on their decisions. We may call this new order by the name of democratic socialism but the name does not matter; all that matters is that we establish a rational economic system serving the purposes of the people. Today the vast majority of the people not only have no control over the whole of the economic machine, but they have little chance to develop genuine initiative and spontaneity at the particular job they are doing. They are "employed," and nothing more is expected from them than that they do what they are told. Only in a planned economy in which the whole nation has rationally mastered the economic and social forces can the individual share responsibility and use creative intelligence in his work. All that matters is that the opportunity for genuine activity be restored to the individual; that the purposes of society and of his own become identical, not ideologically but in reality; and that he apply his effort and reason actively to the work he is doing, as something for which he can feel responsible because it has meaning and purpose in terms of his human ends. We must replace manipulation of men by active and intelligent co-operation, and expand the principle of government of the people, by the people, for the people, from the formal political to the economic sphere.

The question of whether an economic and political system furthers the cause of human freedom cannot be answered in political and economic terms alone. The only criterion for the realization of freedom is whether or not the individual actively participates in determining his life and that of society, and this not only by the formal act of voting but in his daily activity, in his work, and in his relations to others. Modern political democracy, if it restricts itself to the purely political sphere, cannot sufficiently counteract the results of the economic insignificance of the average individual. But purely economic concepts like socialization of the means of production are not sufficient either. I am not thinking here so much of the deceitful usage of the word socialism as it has been applied—for reasons of tactical expediency—in National Socialism. I have in mind Russia where socialism has become a deceptive word; for although socialization of the means of production has taken place, actually a powerful bureaucracy manipulates the vast mass of the population; this necessarily prevents the development of freedom and individualism, even if government control may be effective in the economic interest of the majority of the people.

Never have words been more misused in order to conceal the truth than today. Betrayal of allies is called appeasement, military aggression is camouflaged as defense against attack, the conquest of small nations goes by the name of a pact of friendship, and the brutal suppression of the whole population is perpetrated in the name of National Socialism. The words democracy, freedom, and individualism become objects of this abuse too. There is one way to define the real meaning of the difference between democracy and Fascism. Democracy is a system that creates the economic, political, and cultural conditions for the full development of the individual. Fascism is a system that, regardless under which name, makes the individual subordinate to extraneous purposes and weakens the development of genuine individuality.

Obviously, one of the greatest difficulties in the establishment of the conditions for the realization of democracy lies in the contradiction between a planned economy and the active co-operation of each individual. A planned economy of the scope of any big industrial system requires a great deal of centralization and, as a consequence, a bureaucracy to administer this centralized machine. On the other hand, the active control and co-operation by each individual and by the smallest units of the whole system requires a great amount of decentralization. Unless planning from the top is blended with active participation from below, unless the stream of social life continuously flows from below upwards, a planned economy will lead to renewed manipulation of the people. To solve this problem of combining centralization with decentralization is one of the major tasks of society. But it is certainly no less soluble than the technical problems we have already solved and which have brought us an almost complete mastery over nature. It is to be solved, however, only if we clearly recognize the necessity of doing so and if we have faith in the people, in their capacity to take care of their real interests as human beings.

In a way it is again the problem of individual initiative with which we are confronted. Individual initiative was one of the great stimuli both of the economic system and also of personal development under liberal capitalism. But there are two qualifications: it developed only selected qualities of man, his will and rationality, while leaving him otherwise subordinate to economic goals. It was a principle that functioned best in a highly individualized and competitive phase of capitalism which had room for countless independent economic units. Today this space has narrowed down. Only a small number can exercise individual initiative. If we want to realize this principle today and enlarge it so that the whole personality becomes free, it will be possible only on the basis of the rational and concerted effort of a society as a whole, and by an amount of decentralization which can guarantee real, genuine, active co-operation and control by the smallest units of the system.

Only if man masters society and subordinates the economic machine to the purposes of human happiness and only if he actively participates in the social process, can he overcome what now drives him into despair—his aloneness and his feeling of powerlessness. Man does not suffer so much from poverty today as he suffers from the fact that he has become a cog in a large machine, an automaton, that his life has become empty and lost its meaning. The victory over all kinds of authoritarian systems will be possible only if democracy does not retreat but takes the offensive and proceeds to realize what has been its aim in the minds of those who fought for freedom throughout the last centuries. It will triumph over the forces of nihilism only if it can imbue people with a faith that is the strongest the human mind is capable of, the faith in life and in truth, and in freedom as the active and spontaneous realization of the individual self.

APPENDIX

Character and the Social Process

THROUGHOUT this book we have dealt with the interrelation of socioeconomic, psychological, and ideological factors by analyzing certain historical periods like the
age of the Reformation and the contemporary era. For
those readers who are interested in the theoretical problems
involved in such analysis I shall try, in this appendix, to
discuss briefly the general theoretical basis on which the
concrete analysis is founded.

In studying the psychological reactions of a social
group we deal with the character structure of the members
of the group, that is, of individual persons; we are interested, however, not in the peculiarities by which these
persons differ from each other, but in that part of their
character structure that is common to most members of
the group. We can call this character the *social character*.
The social character necessarily is less specific than the individual character. In describing the latter we deal with the
whole of the traits which in their particular configuration
form the personality structure of this or that individual.
The social character comprises only a selection of traits,
*the essential nucleus of the character structure of most
members of a group which has developed as the result of
the basic experiences and mode of life common to that
group*. Although there will be always "deviants" with a

totally different character structure, the character structure of most members of the group are variations of this nucleus, brought about by the accidental factors of birth and life experience as they differ from one individual to another. If we want to understand one individual most fully, these differentiating elements are of the greatest importance. However, if we want to understand how human energy is channeled and operates as a productive force in a given social order, then the social character deserves our main interest.

The concept of social character is a key concept for the understanding of the social process. Character in the dynamic sense of analytic psychology is the specific form in which human energy is shaped by the dynamic adaptation of human needs to the particular mode of existence of a given society. Character in its turn determines the thinking, feeling, and acting of individuals. To see this is somewhat difficult with regard to our thoughts, since we all tend to share the conventional belief that thinking is an exclusively intellectual act and independent of the psychological structure of the personality. This is not so, however, and the less so the more our thoughts deal with ethical, philosophical, political, psychological or social problems rather than with the empirical manipulation of concrete objects. Such thoughts, aside from the purely logical elements that are involved in the act of thinking, are greatly determined by the personality structure of the person who thinks. This holds true for the whole of a doctrine or of a theoretical system as well as for a single concept, like love, justice, equality, sacrifice. Each such concept and each doctrine has an emotional matrix and this matrix is rooted in the character structure of the individual.

We have given many illustrations of this in the foregoing chapters. With regard to doctrines we have tried to show the emotional roots of early Protestantism and modern authoritarianism. With regard to single concepts we have shown that for the sado-masochistic character, for example, love means symbiotic dependence, not mutual affirmation and union on the basis of equality; sacrifice means the utmost subordination of the individual self to something higher, not assertion of one's mental and moral self; difference means difference in power, not the realization of individuality on the basis of equality; justice means that everybody should get what he deserves, not that the individual has an unconditional claim to the realization of inherent and inalienable rights; courage is the readiness to submit and to endure suffering, not the utmost assertion of individuality against power. Although the word which two people of different personality use when they speak of love, for instance, is the same, the meaning of the word is entirely different according to their character structure. As a matter of fact, much intellectual confusion could be avoided by correct psychological analysis of the meaning of these concepts, since any attempt at a purely logical classification must necessarily fail.

The fact that ideas have an emotional matrix is of the utmost importance because it is the key to the understanding of the spirit of a culture. Different societies or classes within a society have a specific social character, and on its basis different ideas develop and become powerful. Thus, for instance, the idea of work and success as the main aims of life were able to become powerful and appealing to modern man on the basis of his aloneness and doubt; but propaganda for the idea of ceaseless effort and striving for success addressed to the Pueblo Indians or to Mexican peasants would fall completely flat. These people with a different kind of character structure would hardly understand what a person setting forth such aims was talking about even if they understood his language. In the same way, Hitler and that part of the German population which has the same character structure quite sincerely feel that anybody who thinks that wars can be abolished is either a complete fool or a plain liar. On the basis of their social character, to them life without suffering and disaster is as little comprehensible as freedom and equality.

Ideas often are consciously accepted by certain groups, which, on account of the peculiarities of their social character, are not really touched by them; such ideas remain a stock of conscious convictions, but people fail to act according to them in a critical hour. An example of this is shown in the German labor movement at the time of the victory of Nazism. The vast majority of German workers before Hitler's coming into power voted for the Socialist or Communist Parties and believed in the ideas of those parties; that is, the range of these ideas among the working class was extremely wide. The weight of these ideas, however, was in no proportion to their range. The onslaught of Nazism did not meet with political opponents, the majority of whom were ready to fight for their ideas. Many of the adherents of the leftist parties, although they believed in their party programs as long as the parties had authority, were ready to resign when the hour of crisis arrived. A close analysis of the character structure of German workers can show one reason—certainly not the only one—for this phenomenon. A great number of them were of a personality type that has many of the traits of what we have described as the authoritarian character. They had a deep-seated respect and longing for established authority. The emphasis of socialism on individual independence versus authority, on solidarity versus individualistic seclusion, was not what many of these workers really wanted on the basis of their personality structure. One mistake of the radical leaders was to estimate the strength of their parties only on the basis of the range which these ideas had, and to overlook their lack of weight.

In contrast to this picture, our analysis of Protestant and Calvinist doctrines has shown that those ideas were powerful forces within the adherents of the new religion, because they appealed to needs and anxieties that were present in the character structure of the people to whom they were addressed. In other words, *ideas can become powerful forces, but only to the extent to which they are answers to specific human needs prominent in a given social character.*

Not only thinking and feeling are determined by man's character structure but also his actions. It is Freud's achievement to have shown this, even if his theoretical frame of reference is incorrect. The determinations of activity by the dominant trends of a person's character structure are obvious in the case of neurotics. It is easy to understand that the compulsion to count the windows of houses and the number of stones on the pavement is an activity that is rooted in certain drives of the compulsive character. But the actions of a normal person appear to

be determined only by rational considerations and the
necessities of reality. However, with the new tools of
observation that psychoanalysis offers, we can recognize
that so-called rational behavior is largely determined by
the character structure. In our discussion of the meaning
of work for modern man we have dealt with an illustration
of this point. We saw that the intense desire for unceasing
activity was rooted in aloneness and anxiety. This compulsion to work differed from the attitude toward work in
other cultures, where people worked as much as it was
necessary but where they were not driven by additional
forces within their own character structure. Since all
normal persons today have about the same impulse to
work and, furthermore, since this intensity of work is necessary if they want to live at all, one easily overlooks the
irrational component in this trait.

We have now to ask what function character serves for
the individual and for society. As to the former the answer
is not difficult. If an individual's character more or less
closely conforms with the social character, the dominant
drives in his personality lead him to do what is necessary
and desirable under the specific social conditions of his
culture. Thus, for instance, if he has a passionate drive to
save and an abhorrence of spending money for any luxury,
he will be greatly helped by this drive—supposing he is a
small shopkeeper who needs to save and to be thrifty if he
wants to survive. Besides this economic function, character traits have a purely psychological one which is no less
important. The person with whom saving is a desire springing from his personality gains also a profound psychological
satisfaction in being able to act accordingly; that is, he is

not only benefited practically when he saves, but he also feels satisfied psychologically. One can easily convince oneself of this if one observes, for instance, a woman of the lower middle class shopping in the market and being as happy about two cents saved as another person of a different character may be about the enjoyment of some sensuous pleasure. This psychological satisfaction occurs not only if a person acts in accordance with the demands springing from his character structure but also when he reads or listens to ideas that appeal to him for the same reason. For the authoritarian character an ideology that describes nature as the powerful force to which we have to submit, or a speech which indulges in sadistic descriptions of political occurrences, has a profound attraction and the act of reading or listening results in psychological satisfaction. To sum up: the subjective function of character for the normal person is to lead him to act according to what is necessary for him from a practical standpoint and also to give him satisfaction from his activity psychologically.

If we look at social character from the standpoint of its function in the social process, we have to start with the statement that has been made with regard to its function for the individual: that by adapting himself to social conditions man develops those traits that make him desire to act as he has to act. If the character of the majority of people in a given society—that is, the social character—is thus adapted to the objective tasks the individual has to perform in this society, the energies of people are molded in ways that make them into productive forces that are indispensable for the functioning of that society. Let us take up once more the example of work. Our modern industrial system requires that most of our energy be channeled in the direction of work. Were it only that people worked because of external necessities, much friction between what they ought to do and what they would like to do would arise and lessen their efficiency. However, by the dynamic adaptation of character to social requirements, human energy instead of causing friction is shaped into such forms as to become an incentive to act according to the particular economic necessities. Thus modern man, instead of having to be forced to work as hard as he does, is driven by the inner compulsion to work which we have attempted to analyze in its psychological significance. Or, instead of obeying overt authorities, he has built up an inner authority—conscience and duty—which operates more effectively in controlling him than any external authority could ever do. In other words, *the social character internalizes external necessities and thus harnesses human energy for the task of a given economic and social system.*

As we have seen, once certain needs have developed in a character structure, any behavior in line with these needs is at the same time satisfactory psychologically and practical from the standpoint of material success. As long as a society offers the individual those two satisfactions simultaneously, we have a situation where the psychological forces are *cementing* the social structure. Sooner or later, however, a lag arises. The traditional character structure still exists while new economic conditions have arisen, for which the traditional character traits are no longer useful. People tend to act according to their character structure, but either these actions are actual handicaps in their economic pursuits or there is not enough opportunity for them to find positions that allow them to act according to their "nature." An illustration of what we have in mind is the character structure of the old middle classes, particularly in countries with a rigid class stratification like Germany. The old middle class virtues—frugality, thrift, cautiousness, suspiciousness—were of diminishing value in modern business in comparison with new virtues, such as initiative, a readiness to take risks, aggressiveness, and so on. Even inasmuch as these old virtues were still an asset—as with the small shopkeeper—the range of possibilities for such business was so narrowed down that only a minority of the sons of the old middle class could "use" their character traits successfully in their economic pursuits. While by their upbringing they had developed character traits that once were adapted to the social situation of their class, the economic development went faster than the character development. This lag between economic and psychological evolution resulted in a situation in which the psychic needs could no longer be satisfied by the usual economic activities. These needs existed, however, and had to seek for satisfaction in some other way. Narrow egotistical striving for one's own advantage, as it had characterized the lower middle class, was shifted from the individual plane to that of the nation. The sadistic impulses, too, that had been used in the battle of private competition were partly shifted to the social and political scene, and partly intensified by frustration. Then, freed from any restricting factors, they sought satisfaction in acts of political persecution and war. Thus, blended with the resentment caused by the frustrating qualities of the whole situation, the psychological

forces instead of cementing the existing social order became dynamite to be used by groups which wanted to
destroy the traditional political and economic structure of
democratic society.

We have not spoken of the role which the educational
process plays with regard to the formation of the social
character; but in view of the fact that to many psychologists the methods of early childhood training and the educational techniques employed toward the growing child
appear to be the *cause* of character development, some
remarks on this point seem to be warranted. In the first
place we should ask ourselves what we mean by education.
While education can be defined in various ways, the way
to look at it from the angle of the social process seems to
be something like this. The social function of education is
to qualify the individual to function in the role he is to
play later on in society; that is, to mold his character in
such a way that it approximates the social character, that
his desires coincide with the necessities of his social role.
The educational system of any society is determined by
this function; therefore we cannot *explain* the structure of
society or the personality of its members by the educational process; but we have to explain the educational
system by the necessities resulting from the social and
economic structure of a given society. However, the methods of education are extremely important in so far as they
are the mechanisms by which the individual is molded into
the required shape. They can be considered as the means
by which social requirements are transformed into personal
qualities. While educational techniques are not the cause
of a particular kind of social character, they constitute one

of the mechanisms by which character is formed. In this sense, the knowledge and understanding of educational methods is an important part of the total analysis of a functioning society.

What we have just said also holds true for one particular sector of the whole educational process: the *family*. Freud has shown that the early experiences of the child have a decisive influence upon the formation of its character structure. If this is true, how then can we understand that the child, who—at least in our culture—has little contact with the life of society, is molded by it? The answer is not only that the parents—aside from certain individual variations—apply the educational patterns of the society they live in, but also that in their own personalities they represent the social character of their society or class. They transmit to the child what we may call the psychological atmosphere or the spirit of a society just by being as they are—namely representatives of this very spirit. *The family thus may be considered to be the psychological agent of society.*

Having stated that the social character is shaped by the mode of existence of a given society, I want to remind the reader of what has been said in the first chapter on the problem of dynamic adaptation. While it is true that man is molded by the necessities of the economic and social structure of society, he is not infinitely adaptable. Not only are there certain physiological needs that imperatively call for satisfaction, but there are also certain psychological qualities inherent in man that need to be satisfied and that result in certain reactions if they are frustrated. What are these qualities? The most important seems to be the tendency to grow, to develop and realize potentialities which man has developed in the course of history—as, for instance, the faculty of creative and critical thinking and of having differentiated emotional and sensuous experiences. Each of these potentialities has a dynamism of its own. Once they have developed in the process of evolution they tend to be expressed. This tendency can be suppressed and frustrated, but such suppression results in new reactions, particularly in the formation of destructive and symbiotic impulses. It also seems that this general tendency to grow—which is the psychological equivalent of the identical biological tendency—results in such specific tendencies as the desire for freedom and the hatred against oppression, since freedom is the fundamental condition for any growth. Again, the desire for freedom can be repressed, it can disappear from the awareness of the individual; but even then it does not cease to exist as a potentiality, and indicates its existence by the conscious or unconscious hatred by which such suppression is always accompanied.

We have also reason to assume that, as has been said before, the striving for justice and truth is an inherent trend of human nature, although it can be repressed and perverted like the striving for freedom. In this assumption we are on dangerous ground theoretically. It would be easy if we could fall back on religious and philosophical assumptions which explain the existence of such trends by a belief that man is created in God's likeness or by the assumption of a natural law. However, we cannot support our argument with such explanations. The only way in our opinion to account for this striving for justice and truth is by the analysis of the whole history of man, socially and individually. We find then that for everybody who is powerless, justice and truth are the most important weapons in the fight for his freedom and growth. Aside from the fact that the majority of mankind throughout its history has had to defend itself against more powerful groups which could oppress and exploit it, every individual in childhood goes through a period which is characterized by powerlessness. It seems to us that in this state of powerlessness traits like the sense of justice and truth develop and become potentialities common to man as such. We arrive therefore at the fact that, *although character development is shaped by the basic conditions of life and although there is no biologically fixed human nature, human nature has a dynamism of its own that constitutes an active factor in the evolution of the social process.* Even if we are not yet able to state clearly in psychological terms what the exact nature of this human dynamism is, we must recognize its existence. In trying to avoid the errors of biological and metaphysical concepts we must not succumb to an equally grave error, that of a sociological relativism in which man is nothing but a puppet, directed by the strings of social circumstances. Man's inalienable rights of freedom and happiness are founded in inherent human qualities: his striving to live, to expand and to express the potentialities that have developed in him in the process of historical evolution.

At this point we can restate the most important differences between the psychological approach pursued in this book and that of Freud. The first point of difference has been dealt with in a detailed manner in the first chapter, so that it is only necessary to mention it here briefly:

we look upon human nature as essentially historically conditioned, although we do not minimize the significance of biological factors and do not believe that the question can be put correctly in terms of cultural *versus* biological factors. In the second place, Freud's essential principle is to look upon man as an entity, a closed system, endowed by nature with certain physiologically conditioned drives, and to interpret the development of his character as a reaction to satisfactions and frustrations of these drives; whereas, in our opinion, the fundamental approach to human personality is the understanding of man's relation to the world, to others, to nature, and to himself. We believe that man is *primarily* a social being, and not, as Freud assumes, primarily self-sufficient and only secondarily in need of others in order to satisfy his instinctual needs. In this sense, we believe that individual psychology is fundamentally social psychology or, in Sullivan's terms, the psychology of interpersonal relationships; the key problem of psychology is that of the particular kind of relatedness of the individual toward the world, not that of satisfaction or frustration of single instinctual desires. The problem of what happens to man's instinctual desires has to be understood as one part of the total problem of his relationship toward the world and not as *the* problem of human personality. Therefore, in our approach, the needs and desires that center about the individual's relations to others, such as love, hatred, tenderness, symbiosis, are the fundamental psychological phenomena, while with Freud they are only secondary results from frustrations or satisfactions of instinctive needs.

The difference between Freud's biological and our own

social orientation has special significance with regard to the problems of characterology. Freud—and on the basis of his findings, Abraham, Jones, and others—assumed that the child experiences pleasure at so-called erogenous zones (mouth and anus) in connection with the process of feeding and defecation; and that, either by overstimulation, frustration, or constitutionally intensified sensitivity, these erogenous zones retain their libidinous character in later years when in the course of the normal development the genital zone should have become of primary importance. It is assumed that this fixation on the pregenital level leads to sublimations and reaction-formations that become part of the character structure. Thus, for instance, a person may have a drive to save money or other objects, *because* he sublimates the unconscious desire to retain the stool. Or a person may expect to get everything from somebody else and not as a result of his own effort, *because* he is driven by an unconscious wish to be fed which is sublimated into the wish to get help, knowledge, and so forth.

Freud's observations are of great importance, but he gave an erroneous explanation. He saw correctly the passionate and irrational nature of these "oral" and "anal" character traits. He saw also that such desires pervade all spheres of personality, man's sexual, emotional, and intellectual life, and that they color all his activities. But he mistook the causal relation between erogenous zones and character traits for the reverse of what they really are. The desire to receive everything one wants to obtain—love, protection, knowledge, material things—in a passive way from a source outside of oneself, develops in a child's character as a reaction to his experiences with others. If through these experiences the feeling of his own strength is weakened by fear, if his initiative and self-confidence are paralyzed, if hostility develops and is repressed, and if at the same time his father or mother offers affection or care under the condition of surrender, such a constellation leads to an attitude in which active mastery is given up and all his energies are turned in the direction of an outside source from which the fulfillment of all wishes will eventually come. This attitude assumes such a passionate character because it is the only way in which such a person can attempt to realize his wishes. That often these persons have dreams or phantasies of being fed, nursed, and so on, is due to the fact that the mouth more than any other organ lends itself to the expression of this receptive attitude. But the oral sensation is not the cause of this attitude; it is the expression of an attitude toward the world in the language of the body.

The same holds true for the "anal" person, who on the basis of his particular experiences is more withdrawn from others than the "oral" person, seeks security by making himself an autarchic, self-sufficient system, and feels love or any other outgoing attitude as a threat to his security. It is true that in many instances these attitudes first develop in connection with feeding or defecation, which in the early age of the child are his main activities and also the main sphere in which love or oppression on the part of the parents and friendliness or defiance on the part of the child, are expressed. However, overstimulation and frustration in connection with the erogenous zones by themselves do not lead to a fixation of such attitudes in a person's character; although certain pleasurable sensations are experienced by the child in connection with feeding and defecation, these pleasures do not assume importance for the character development, unless they represent—on the physical level—attitudes that are rooted in the whole of the character structure.

For an infant who has confidence in the unconditional love of his mother, the sudden interruption of breast-feeding will not have any grave characterological consequences; the infant who experiences a lack of reliability in the mother's love may acquire "oral" traits even though the feeding process went on without any particular disturbances. The "oral" or "anal" phantasies or physical sensations in later years are not important on account of the physical pleasure they imply, or of any mysterious sublimation of this pleasure, but only on account of the specific kind of relatedness toward the world which is underlying them and which they express.

Only from this point of view can Freud's characterological findings become fruitful for social psychology. As long as we assume, for instance, that the anal character, as it is typical of the European lower middle class, is caused by certain early experiences in connection with defecation, we have hardly any data that lead us to understand why a specific class should have an anal social character. However, if we understand it as one form of relatedness to others, rooted in the character structure and resulting from the experiences with the outside world, we have a key for understanding why the whole mode of life of the lower middle class, its narrowness, isolation, and hostility, made for the development of this kind of character structure.[1]

The third important point of difference is closely linked up with the previous ones. Freud, on the basis of his instinctivistic orientation and also of a profound conviction of the wickedness of human nature, is prone to interpret all "ideal" motives in man as the result of something "mean"; a case in point is his explanation of the sense of justice as the outcome of the original envy a child has for anybody who has more than he. As has been pointed out before, we believe that ideals like truth, justice, freedom, although they are frequently mere phrases or rationalizations, can be genuine strivings, and that any analysis which does not deal with these strivings as dynamic factors is fallacious. These ideals have no metaphysical character but are rooted in the conditions of human life and can be analyzed as such. The fear of falling back into metaphysical or idealistic concepts should not stand in the way of such analysis. It is the task of psychology as an empirical science to study motivation by ideals as well as the moral problems connected with them, and thereby to free our thinking on such matters from the unempirical and metaphysical elements that befog the issues in their traditional treatment.

Finally, one other point of difference should be mentioned. It concerns the differentiation between psycho-

[1] F. Alexander has attempted to restate Freud's characterological findings in terms that are in some ways similar to our own interpretation. (Cf F. Alexander, "The Influence of Psychological Factors upon Gastro-Intestinal Disturbances," *Psychoanalytic Quarterly*, Vol. XV, 1934.) But although his views constitute an advance over Freud's, he has not succeeded in overcoming a fundamentally biological orientation and in fully recognizing interpersonal relationships as the basis and essence of these "pregenital" drives.

logical phenomena of want and those of abundance. The primitive level of human existence is that of want. There are imperative needs which have to be satisfied before anything else. Only when man has time and energy left beyond the satisfaction of the primary needs, can culture develop and with it those strivings that attend the phenomena of abundance. Free (or spontaneous) acts are always phenomena of abundance. Freud's psychology is a psychology of want. He defines pleasure as the satisfaction resulting from the removal of painful tension. Phenomena of abundance, like love or tenderness, actually do not play any role in his system. Not only did he omit such phenomena, but he also had a limited understanding of the phenomenon to which he paid so much attention: sex. According to his whole definition of pleasure Freud saw in sex only the element of physiological compulsion and in sexual satisfaction the relief from painful tension. The sexual drive as a phenomenon of abundance, and sexual pleasure as spontaneous joy—the essence of which is not negative relief from tension—had no place in his psychology.

What is the principle of interpretation that this book has applied to the understanding of the human basis of culture? Before answering this question it may be useful to recall the main trends of interpretation with which our own differs.

1. The "psychologistic" approach which characterizes Freud's thinking, according to which cultural phenomena are rooted in psychological factors that result from instinctual drives which in themselves are influenced by society only through some measure of suppression. Following this

line of interpretation Freudian authors have explained capitalism as the outcome of anal eroticism and the development of early Christianity as the result of the ambivalence toward the father image.[2]

2. The "economistic" approach, as it is presented in the misapplication of Marx's interpretation of history. According to this view, subjective economic interests are the cause of cultural phenomena, such as religion and political ideas. From such a pseudo-Marxian viewpoint,[3] one might try to explain Protestantism as no more than the answer to certain economic needs of the bourgeoisie.

3. Finally there is the "idealistic" position, which is represented by Max Weber's analysis, *The Protestant Ethic and the Spirit of Capitalism*. He holds that new religious ideas are responsible for the development of a new type of economic behavior and a new spirit of culture, although he emphasizes that this behavior is never exclusively determined by religious doctrines.

In contrast to these explanations, we have assumed that ideologies and culture in general are rooted in the social character; that the social character itself is molded by the mode of existence of a given society; and that in their turn

[2] For a fuller discussion of this method cf. E. Fromm, *Zur Entstehung des Christusdogmas*, Psychoanalytischer Verlag, Wien, 1931.

[3] I call this viewpoint pseudo-Marxian because it interprets Marx's theory as meaning that history is determined by economic motives in terms of the striving for material gain, and not as Marx really meant, in terms of objective conditions which can result in different economic attitudes, of which the intense desire for the gain of material wealth is only one. (This was pointed out in Chapter I.) A detailed discussion of this problem can be found in E. Fromm's "Über Methode und Aufgabe einer analytischen Sozialpsychologie," *Zeitschrift für Sozialforschung*, Vol. I, 1932. P. 28 ff. Cf. also the discussion in Robert S. Lynd's *Knowledge for What?*, Princeton University Press, Princeton, 1939. Chap. II.

the dominant character traits become productive forces shaping the social process. With regard to the problem of the spirit of Protestantism and capitalism, I have tried to show that the collapse of medieval society threatened the middle class; that this threat resulted in a feeling of powerless isolation and doubt; that this psychological change was responsible for the appeal of Luther's and Calvin's doctrines; that these doctrines intensified and stabilized the characterological changes; and that the character traits that thus developed then became productive forces in the development of capitalism which in itself resulted from economic and political changes.

With regard to Fascism the same principle of explanation was applied: the lower middle class reacted to certain economic changes, such as the growing power of monopolies and postwar inflation, with an intensification of certain character traits, namely, sadistic and masochistic strivings; the Nazi ideology appealed to and intensified these traits; and the new character traits then became effective forces in supporting the expansion of German imperialism. In both instances we see that when a certain class is threatened by new economic tendencies it reacts to this threat psychologically and ideologically; and that the psychological changes brought about by this reaction further the development of economic forces even if those forces contradict the economic interests of that class. We see that economic, psychological, and ideological forces operate in the social process in this way: that man reacts to changing external situations by changes in himself, and that these psychological factors in their turn help in molding the economic and social process. Economic forces are effective, but they must be understood not as psychological motivations but as objective conditions: psychological forces are effective, but they must be understood as historically conditioned themselves; ideas are effective, but they must be understood as being rooted in the whole of the character structure of members of a social group. In spite of this interdependence of economic, psychological, and ideological forces, however, each of them has also a certain independence. This is particularly true of the economic development which, being dependent on objective factors, such as the natural productive forces, technique, geographical factors, takes place according to its own laws. As to the psychological forces, we have indicated that the same holds true; they are molded by the external conditions of life, but they also have a dynamism of their own; that is, they are the expression of human needs which, although they can be molded, cannot be uprooted. In the ideological sphere we find a similar autonomy rooted in logical laws and in the tradition of the body of knowledge acquired in the course of history.

We can restate the principle in terms of social character: The social character results from the dynamic adaptation of human nature to the structure of society. Changing social conditions result in changes of the social character, that is, in new needs and anxieties. These new needs give rise to new ideas and, as it were, make men susceptible to them; these new ideas in their turn tend to stabilize and intensify the new social character and to determine man's actions. In other words, social conditions influence ideological phenomena through the medium of character;

character, on the other hand, is not the result of passive adaptation to social conditions but of a dynamic adaptation on the basis of elements that either are biologically inherent in human nature or have become inherent as the result of historic evolution.

INDEX

301